# The Pop Festival

# The Pop Festival

## History, Music, Media, Culture

**EDITED BY**
**GEORGE McKAY**

Bloomsbury Academic
An imprint of Bloomsbury Publishing Inc

B L O O M S B U R Y
NEW YORK • LONDON • NEW DELHI • SYDNEY

**Bloomsbury Academic**
An imprint of Bloomsbury Publishing Inc

1385 Broadway
New York
NY 10018
USA

50 Bedford Square
London
WC1B 3DP
UK

**www.bloomsbury.com**

**BLOOMSBURY and the Diana logo are trademarks of Bloomsbury Publishing Plc**

First published 2015



**Library of Congress Cataloging-in-Publication Data**
The pop festival: history, music, media, culture/edited by George McKay.
pages cm
Includes bibliographical references and index.
Summary: "A brilliant collection of essays on popular music festival culture as a whole, from its origins to a wide range of contemporary manifestations"–Provided by publisher.
ISBN 978-1-62356-820-7 (hardback: alk. paper) –
ISBN 978-1-62356-959-4 (pbk.: alk. paper)
1. Music festivals. 2. Popular music–History and criticism.
I. McKay, George, 1960- editor.
ML35.P66 2015
781.64078–dc23
2014045826

ISBN: HB: 978-1-62356-820-7
PB: 978-1-62356-959-4
ePDF: 978-1-62892-196-0
ePub: 978-1-62892-198-4

Typeset by Deanta Global Publishing Services, Chennai, India
Printed and bound in the United States of America

*For Ailsa*

# CONTENTS

# ACKNOWLEDGEMENTS

This book draws on funding and findings from two research projects: HERA/EUFP7 Rhythm Changes: Jazz Cultures and European Identities (in which four contributors were involved: Prof Andrew Dubber, Dr Anne Dvinge, Dr Nick Gebhardt and Prof George McKay; 2010–13), and McKay's Arts and Humanities Research Council (AHRC) Leadership Fellowship for the Connected Communities programme award (2012–15).

The editor would like to thank organizers of and contributors to the following events and projects, which in varying ways fed into the thinking for the book: *Carnivalising Pop* symposium at the University of Salford, 2014; AHRC Creative Economy project, 'Carnivalising the creative economy: jazz festivals research and knowledge exchange', 2014; EFG London Jazz Festival, 2014, 2013; Cheltenham Jazz Festival, 2014; Jazz Messengers conference, University of Aveido, 2013; MSN Festival-goers survey media consultancy, 2013; Lancaster Jazz Festival, 2013; AHRC Connected Communities programme events, 2011–14; AHRC Live Music Exchange project conference, University of Glamorgan, 2012; MA Music Festival Industries validation, Southampton Solent University, 2012; Kendal Calling Professor in Residence, 2011; AHRC Research Network, 'Festival as a state of encounter', Leeds University, 2009–10; ESRC 'Music festivals and free parties: negotiating managed consumption: young people, branding and social identification' project, University of Bath, 2008–10; EUFP6 Society and Lifestyles project, Vytautas Magnus University, 2006–08.

Also, at the University of Salford, thanks to Prof Tony Whyton, Dr Ben Halligan, Dr Michael Goddard, Prof Brian Longhurst, Dr Chris Lee, Dr Deborah Woodman; Amsterdam Conservatory – Prof Walter van de Leur, Loes Rusch; EFG London Jazz Festival – John Cumming, Katrina Duncan, Amy Pearce; Kendal Calling – Ben Robinson; Frukt Marketing and Operations – Chloe Sideris; Cheltenham Festivals – Julia Jenkinson, Tony Dudley-Evans, Ian George, Emily Jones; AHRC/Connected Communities – Prof Keri Facer, Sue Hanshaw, Mark Llewellyn, Gary Grubb, Paul McWhirter and the entire AHRC team really! At home, thanks to Emma McKay and Dora McKay. And thanks also to Mike Weaver, Alan Dearling.

At Bloomsbury – Ally Jane Grossan, for commissioning and then being patient, as well as Carly Bareham, Michelle Chen and Kim Muryani for their assistance. Also from the production side, thanks to Anita Singh.

# PICTURE CREDITS

| | |
|---|---|
| **Figure 35** | Berlin RTS 27 September 1998 street party poster. Free download from Reclaim the Streets online archive http://rts.gn.apc.org/imlib.htm 137 |
| **Figure 36** | Tent City Climate Camp, London, G20 gathering, April 2009. Photograph by Les Hutchins [CC-BY-2.0; http://creativecommons.org/licenses/by/2.0], via Wikimedia Commons 142 |
| **Figure 37** | Nature Lovers Society Solstice Gathering, 21 June 2014. Photo by Bez 23. Dress design by Gemma Carver 151 |
| **Figure 38** | Flyer for the Psychedelic Spring Gathering, 18–21 April 2014. Triplicity in association with Eden, Playground of Life and O.T.G. Artwork by Darren Nailer and George Thompson 153 |
| **Figures 39–42** | Photographs by Alice O'Grady 154, 155, 156, 161 |
| **Figure 43** | Something Different flyer. Artwork by Darren Nailer 161 |
| **Figure 44** | Burning Man, 2012. Photograph by Steve Jirvetson [CC-BY-2.0] via Wikimedia Commons. Black and white, cropped 167 |
| **Figure 45** | The Temple of Burning Man and art car, Burning Man 2012. Photograph by Steve Jirvetson [CC-BY-2.0] via Wikimedia Commons. Black and white 169 |
| **Figure 46** | Dance-Off at Secret Garden Party, 2014. Photograph by Jhitta Gobinder 172 |
| **Figure 47** | Revellers in fancy dress at Secret Garden Party 2014. Photograph by Jenna Foxton 174 |
| **Figure 48** | BoomTown Fair. Photograph by Scott Salt 175 |
| **Figures 49–53** | Photographs by Anne Dvinge, Detroit Jazz Festival, 2009 184, 192, 193, 194 |

Photography in Alan Lodge, photo-essay © Alan Lodge.
http://digitaljournalist.eu

# CONTRIBUTORS

**Chris Anderton** is a senior lecturer in popular music at Southampton Solent University, UK, where he is course leader of BA (Hons) Music Promotion, director of the in-house music organization Solent Music (solentmusic.com) and co-executive producer of SMILEfest (smilefest.co.uk) – a student-managed annual music festival incorporating live music, guest speakers and industry-led workshops. He completed his PhD, entitled *(Re)Constructing Music Festival Places*, at Swansea University in 2007, and is co-author of *Understanding the Music Industries* (Sage, 2013). Chris has also published chapters and articles on music bootlegging, music festivals and progressive rock, and his monograph on British music festivals is forthcoming from Ashgate.

**Gina Arnold** is an adjunct professor of rhetoric and languages at the University of San Francisco. She received her PhD in modern thought and literature at Stanford University and was a teaching fellow in the Centre for Comparative Studies in Race and Ethnicity and subsequently a postdoctoral scholar there as well. Prior to joining the academy, Gina was a rock critic and author and columnist, and has published pieces in *Rolling Stone*, *Spin*, the *New York Times*, the *Village Voice*, *Entertainment Weekly* and a number of other music magazines. She is the author of three books, *Route 666: On the Road To Nirvana* (St. Martin's/Picador, 1993), *Kiss This: Punk in the Present Tense* (St. Martin's/Picador, 1997) and *Exile In Guyville* (Bloomsbury, 2014).

**Joanne Cummings** is a social researcher at the University of Western Sydney, Australia. Her research interests and publications investigate the sociological aspects of music festivals, youth cultures, neo-tribalism and environmental sustainability. Her book chapters include 'The greening of the music festival scene', in Andy Bennett et al., eds., *The Festivalization of Culture* (Ashgate, 2014), and 'Festival spaces, green sensibilities and youth culture', in Gerard Delanty et al., eds., *Festivals and the Cultural Public Sphere* (Routledge, 2011).

**Andrew Dubber** works at both Umeå University, Sweden, where he leads interdisciplinary initiatives and consults within European-funded projects concerning music, creativity, innovation and enterprise, and Birmingham

City University, UK, where he is a professor of music industry innovation. He is also the director of Music Tech Fest – a global festival of music ideas. He is the author of *Radio in the Digital Age* (Polity, 2013) and co-author of *Understanding the Music Industries* (Sage, 2012), and has written and published several independent e-books about music and digital culture. He was a researcher on the HERA/EUFP7 Rhythm Changes: Jazz Cultures and European Identities project (2010–13). His research interests include digital media cultures, media and music innovation, online music enterprise, radio in the digital age, music as a tool for social change and music as culture. He teaches about radio broadcasting, the music industries, music hacking and the online environment. Dubber's background is primarily as a practitioner in the media industries as a radio producer and presenter, label owner and record producer. His website is http://andrewdubber.com.

**Anne Dvinge** holds a PhD in American studies and jazz studies from the University of Copenhagen. Her postdoctoral project on jazz festivals (2009–13) was funded by the Danish Research Council for the Humanities, through her membership of the Rhythm Changes project team. She currently works as a concert arranger and music consultant to cultural institutions in Denmark. She also teaches American studies, cultural studies, music and urban studies at the University of Copenhagen. Her research focuses on music and popular culture in the twentieth and twenty-first century. Anne's articles have appeared in *The Journal for Transnational American Studies*, *African and Black Diaspora: An International Journal*, and *Amerikastudien/American Studies*. Her monograph project, *Festival Junctions: Jazz Festivals and Practices of Community and Cosmopolitanism*, investigates jazz festivals as meeting grounds between local and global understandings of jazz and cultural identity.

**Nicholas Gebhardt** is reader in popular music and media at Birmingham City University, UK, where he leads the jazz research programme. His interests include popular music in the United States, the entertainment industry and jazz history. He co-edits the book series *Transnational Studies in Jazz* for Routledge, and his most recent book, *Music Is Our Business: Popular Music, Vaudeville and Entertainment in American Culture, 1870-1929*, is published by the University of Chicago Press. Nick was also a member of the Rhythm Changes project team. From 1996 to 2002 he worked as a radio producer in Australia, where he was involved in live broadcasts from numerous pop music festivals, and from 2012 to 2014 he was chair of the Board of the Lancaster Jazz Festival, UK.

**Mark Goodall** is a senior lecturer in the Department of Media Design and Technology at the University of Bradford, UK. He is the author of *Sweet and Savage: The World through the Shockumentary Film Lens*

(Headpress, 2006; second edition, 2015) and *Gathering of the Tribe: Music and Heavy Conscious Creation* (Headpress, 2012).

**Jacinta Herborn** is a PhD candidate at the University of Western Sydney, Australia. Her research considers the embodied experiences of youth-oriented live music events.

**Ronald Hitzler** is professor of sociology at the Dortmund University of Technology, Germany. He studied sociology, political science and philosophy at the University of Konstanz and later researched at the Universities of Konstanz, Bamberg, Cologne and Munich. His research specializes in youth scenes, events and the marketing of cities, as well as the sociology of culture and modernization as a 'problem of management'. His books include a co-edited volume with Michaela Pfadenhauer on the techno scene: *Techno-Soziologie: Erkundungen einer Jugendkultur* (Leske + Budrich, 2001) (*Techno Sociology: Investigations of a Youth Culture*) and more recently, the third-revised edition, co-authored with Arne Niederbacher, of *Leben in Szenen: Formen juveniler Vergemeinschaftung heute* (VS-Verlag, 2010) (*Living in Scenes: Current Forms of Juvenile Socialisation*). More information can be found at www.hitzler-soziologie.de.

**Rebekka Kill** is Head of School at The Leeds School of Art, Architecture and Design at Leeds Beckett University. Her research interests include disciplinary constructions of academic identity, practice-based research, festival performance and social media. She is a practicing visual and performance artist, social media enthusiast and also works as a nightclub DJ. Rebekka's DJ gigs have included an underwater disco and a performance work where she played 7-inch records in alphabetical order for 24 hours without stopping. Her TED-style performance 'Facebook is like Disco and Twitter is like Punk' (2012–14), has had worldwide interest online; it can be viewed on her blog at djtheduchess.wordpress.com.

**Alan Lodge** is a photographer who comes from a free festival and traveller background. Living in old buses, trucks and caravans, he drove around the country on 'the circuit' with his family and friends. Since the late 1970s his work has dealt with aspects of 'alternative' lifestyles and subcultures, photographing many free and commercial events, 'free party' events (rave culture), environment protest and land rights campaigning with surrounding social concerns. He has built an archive of images, and supplied photographs to the *Guardian*, *Independent*, *i-D* magazine, *Select*, *Sounds*, *DJ Mag*, *New Statesman & Society*. His work illustrates many articles networked across the Indymedia independent media platform. Alan has also contributed to a number of television films including *May the Force Be with You* and *Spirit of Albion* (Channel four), *An Englishman's Right*, *Trashed*, *Surveillance Society* and *New Age Travellers* (BBC). He contributed still photography and was a consultant for *Operation Solstice*, the 1991 Channel Four documentary about the police action and court trials preventing the 1985 Stonehenge Free Festival. Alan is noted for covering political and environmental actions, such protest frequently involving policing operations, especially in relation to surveillance. His website is http://digitaljournalist.eu.

**George McKay** is professor of media studies at the University of East Anglia, UK, and an AHRC Leadership Fellow for the Connected Communities programme (2012–15). He too was a member of the Rhythm Changes project team. Among his books are *Shakin' All Over: Popular Music and Disability* (University of Michigan Press, 2103), *Radical Gardening: Politics, Idealism and Rebellion in the Garden* (Frances Lincoln, 2011), *Circular Breathing: The Cultural Politics of Jazz in Britain* (Duke University Press, 2005), *Community Music: A Handbook* (co-ed. with Pete Moser, Russell House, 2004), *Glastonbury: A Very English Fair* (Gollancz, 2000), *DiY Culture: Party & Protest in Nineties Britain* (ed., Verso, 1998) and *Senseless Acts of Beauty: Cultures of Resistance since the Sixties* (Verso, 1996). George was founding co-editor in 2002 of *Social Movement Studies: Journal of Social, Cultural & Political Protest* (Routledge). He has been professor in Residence at EFG London Jazz Festival (2014) and Kendal Calling (2011). His website is http://georgemckay.org.

**Sean Nye** is a Provost's Postdoctoral Scholar in the Humanities (2013–15) at the University of Southern California, USA. He received his PhD in Comparative Studies in Discourse and Society from the University of Minnesota in 2013. Sean has been a Fulbright Scholar at the University of Copenhagen, a DAAD fellow at the Humboldt University of Berlin and a fellow of the Berlin Program for Advanced German and European Studies at the Free University of Berlin. His articles, reviews and translations have appeared in, among others, *Dancecult: Journal of Electronic Dance Music Culture, Journal of Popular Music Studies, Echo: A Music-Centered Journal,* and *Cultural Critique*. His research foci include electronic dance music, German studies, cultural musicology and science fiction.

**Alice O'Grady** is associate professor in applied performance at the University of Leeds, UK. Her work is concerned with how participatory forms of performance and modes of play can facilitate change. She is particularly interested in investigating alternative spaces of play and found spaces for performance. Since 2006 she has been exploring the relationship between participation, play and performance in festival settings both in her role as artistic director of ... floorSpace ... and in collaboration with Urban Angels, an aerial circus theatre company based in Leeds. Alice writes about underground club culture and the alternative festival circuit in the UK. She is a member of the editorial team for *Dancecult: Journal of Electronic Dance Music Culture*.

**Roxy Robinson** is a gig promoter and festivals consultant who also lectures at the UK Centre for Events Management, Leeds Beckett University, UK. Her specialist areas of teaching at the Centre include Event Production, Impacts and Risks, and Event Law. Roxy has worked in live events since 2004, starting out as the band booker for a Leeds-based music venue, Carpe Diem. She has worked as the arts programmer for the award-winning Kendal Calling festival and as marketing consultant for Beacons Music and Arts Festival. In 2012, she completed her PhD on the evolution of boutique events and the influence of Nevada's Burning Man on British festivals. This charted the intersections of participatory programming and idealized event production at festivals in the United States and United Kingdom. Roxy continues to provide consultancy services to clients within the events industry, which include marketing strategy, creative programming, theming, and scenographic site design.

**Graham St John** is an Australian anthropologist and cultural historian of electronic dance music movements and their event-cultures with an interest in the complex religious and performative characteristics of transnational event-cultural movements. Graham has been awarded postdoctoral fellowships in Australia, United States, Canada and Switzerland, including a three-year University of Queensland Postdoctoral Research Fellowship in the Centre for Critical and Cultural Studies, and an SSRC Residential Fellowship at the School for Advanced Research, Santa Fe, New Mexico. He is author of *Global Tribe: Technology, Spirituality and Psytrance* (Equinox, 2012), *Technomad: Global Raving Countercultures* (2009), and the edited collections *The Local Scenes and Global Culture of Psytrance* (Routledge, 2010), *Victor Turner and Contemporary Cultural Performance* (Berghahn, 2008), *Rave Culture and Religion* (Routledge 2004) and the free ebook *FreeNRG: Notes from the Edge of the Dance Floor* (Commonground, 2001). Graham is founding executive editor of *Dancecult: Journal of Electronic Dance Music Culture* and an Adjunct Research Fellow in the Griffith Centre for Cultural Research, Griffith University.

# Introduction

*George McKay*

*I'm going on down to Yasgur's farm*
*I'm going to join in a rock 'n' roll band*
*I'm going to camp out on the land*
*I'm going to try and get my soul free.*

JONI MITCHELL, 'WOODSTOCK' (1970)

*Oh is this the way they say the future's meant to feel*
*Or just 20,000 people standing in a field. ...*
*In the middle of the night it feels alright*
*But then tomorrow morning, oh then you come down.*
*What if you never come down?*

PULP, 'SORTED FOR ES AND WHIZZ' (1995)

What is it about, the pop festival? I went to my first as a teenager in England in the late 1970s – Reading Festival three years running, with a group of school friends on the train, half way across the country, carrying tents and sleeping bags, until I realized the music being offered there was becoming less interesting than the music I could see in my local punk club. But, even though I *have* 'come down' (in Jarvis Cocker of Pulp's phraseology), the festival, the impact of that musical mega event, has stayed with me. Those Reading Festivals must have been important, formative events for me – after all, I still have the original programmes, which I have stored and carried around with me from house to house, city to city, for almost forty years, most of my life (Figure 1). And since my first book two decades ago, I have returned regularly to the music festival and carnival as subject (including McKay 1996, 1998, 2000, 2005, 2011). What delights me (I hope, you too) about *this* book, this *collection*, is the range of critical perspectives, political

FIGURE 1 *My back pages: Reading Festival programmes, 1977–79.*

positions, practical experiences (some of our academic authors have also been festival organizers and artists) and international voices it contains. *The Pop Festival* presents a new narrative of popular music festival culture, shifting it back to a pre-1960s decade, focusing on the transatlantic and international dialogues and reworkings of festival practice, considering the role of mediation in the development and contemporary success of the festival, interrogating its politics and play. It does so by employing insights and theories from across disciplinary boundaries. In my view there is a fine set of ideas and readings here, which cumulatively extends knowledge and understanding of the field significantly. And there are pictures – in particular a photoessay by leading British festival activist and photographer, Alan Lodge, but also a generous set of images distributed through the text as a whole as a visual narrative providing example, context, understanding and enhancing the reader's pleasure of this (usually) pleasureful topic.

Popular music festivals are one of the strikingly successful and enduring features of seasonal popular culture consumption for young people and older generations of enthusiasts alike. Indeed, a dramatic rise in the number of music festivals in the United Kingdom and around the world has been evident as festivals become a pivotal economic driver in the popular music industry, are a constituent of urban repertoires of regeneration, are a key feature in the seasonal cultural economy and are a collective ritual event for many groups of young people growing up. According to one recent British report, while 'industry experts ... speculate ... that the UK festival sector has hit saturation point ... the number of UK festivals still appears to be growing' (Brennan and Webster 2010, 25). Today's festivals range from the massive – such as Roskilde or Glastonbury Festival, Notting Hill Carnival or (until recently) Love Parade, Lollapalooza or Big Day Out – to the local, small-scale, community or the recently innovated 'boutique' events. You will recognize already in such a listing a certain definitional openness to the book: we are interested in popular music (including jazz) collective gatherings in a sort of special space-time, in a compressed or heightened experience of multiple performance and playfulness. As Chris Gibson and John Connell put it, 'Most festivals create ... a time and space of celebration, a site of convergence separate from everyday routines, experiences and meanings – ephemeral communities in place and time' (2012, 4). The pop or rock festival as outdoor site taken over for the weekend, with amplified live music on various stages, overnight camping, food and drink and toilet facilities, is the most familiar template (see Figure 2), and one we see several variations of in this collection, but the authors also want to extend and problematize some of that version, as well as explore its meanings.

Should we be surprised that the music festival, from (probably) jazzy origins in (probably) the late 1950s and 1960s, and with a heyday in the late 1960s and 1970s, is not only still with us, but is possibly more popular and prevalent than ever? When much of the rest of the music scenes of those times – a set of snapshots might feature, say, Afghan coats, hippie

**FIGURE 2** *Festival flags catch and signal the open air and lift the vision: WOMAD Festival, Reading, 2003.*

beads, vinyl LPs, 45 rpm singles, gatefold sleeves, groupies, long guitar solos, concept albums, speed psychosis, stylistically delineated subcultures, the rock supergroup, protest songs, gobbing, pogoing, 'hey maan', disco, the university or college gig circuit, headbanging, dancing round handbags – might be seen as quaint, or as at most present through nostalgic discourses of 'vintage' and 'retromania', the festival has not only survived in recognizable form, but also thrives. In *The Festivalization of Culture*, Bennett et al. offer an explanation.

> In a world where notions of culture are becoming increasingly fragmented, the contemporary festival has developed in response to processes of cultural pluralization, mobility and globalization, while also communicating something meaningful about identity, community, locality and belonging. (Bennett et al. 2014, 1)

Popular music festivals have been around for well over half a century: festival communities are no longer exclusively youth oriented. For Bennett the festival can be both an intergenerational music event, young and old coming together, and one for ageing fans to affirm that 'their cultural investment is [still] shared by other members of their generation; it can also offer an opportunity to reengage with particular practices – late-night drinking, dancing, recreational drug use, and so on – which ... assume more cultural resonance when enacted as a collective practice' (2013, 89). The idea of the festival as 'a unique type of event' that is a 'playground for adults' (Stone 2009, 215) is confirmed by several essays here, notably Alice O'Grady's work on deep play and psytrance. Sometimes the 'militantly ludistic carnival rituals' Renate Lachmann writes of in his work on Mikhail Bakhtin and the carnivalesque (1988, 124) have another purpose. Woodstock (1969, USA), Glastonbury (since 1970, UK) and Nimbin (1973, Australia) are early event markers that point us to the utopian desire of the festival, to the way in which that temporary heightened space-time has the fundamental purpose of envisioning and crafting another, better world. Andrew Kerr, dreamer and maker of the legendary early free gathering of Britain's counterculture, the 1971 Glastonbury Fair, sought to explain to local people what he had in mind as an experiment that would take place on their green patch of England that summer:

> It will be a fair in the medieval tradition, embodying the legends of the area, with music, dance, poetry, theatre lights and the opportunity for spontaneous entertainments. There will be no monetary profit – it will be free. ... The aims are ... : the conservation of our natural resources; a respect for nature and life; and a spiritual awakening. (Kerr 2011, 357)

In Australia, a couple of years later, Bill Metcalf was having his own experience of festival as energizing confirmation of possibility: 'By the end of the Aquarius Festival [at Nimbin], we participants had learnt that we were not alone in our dreams and faltering social experimentations . … [Rather,] we were part of a new, utopian social movement' (Metcalf 2000, 3). Festival, for Kerr as for Metcalf, at its most utopian, is a pragmatic and fantastic space in which to dream and to try another world into being. Even the British government was prompted to recognize this for a time, in official actions and reports: a government-owned site (a disused airfield) was formally made available for the 1975 People's Free Festival (see UK Rock Festivals website), while the 1976 Working Group on Pop Festivals report made the case that

> pop festivals – whether commercial or free – are a reasonable and acceptable form of recreation. … Free festivals in particular are developing an interest in a number of activities – for example, theatre, folklore, mime, rural arts and crafts, alternative technology and experimental architecture. … We think that festivals can offer useful experience to young people in living away … from the facilities of modern society. (quoted in McKay 1996, 28)

You will see other versions of utopia in many of our essays – utopia celebrated, critiqued, glimpsed, denied, dreamt, nightmared.

In *The Land Without Music* Andrew Blake charted the post-1960s trajectory of carnivalesque politics, arguing that

> festival can become a site for political activity. In their different ways the 1971 concert for Bangladesh organised by George Harrison, the 1985 Live Aid concert and subsequent phenomena such as the concert for Nelson Mandela, campaigning tours such as Rock Against Racism, the Anglo-Irish Fleadh held annually in North London and the gay, lesbian and bisexual celebration, Pride, all have built on the notion of a popular festival as a way of proposing, trying to create, a truly vital cultural politics. (Blake 1997, 191)

This book contains discussion of a campaigning political practice in festival (most directly in the essays from Graham St John, Andrew Dubber, McKay, as well as in Lodge's photoessay). Of course, social and cultural questions of race are also important (in some historical contexts, central) in discussions of festival and carnival, and in some historical and diasporean contexts – from New Orleans Mardi Gras to Rio Carnival to Notting Hill Carnival – they are central. Essays here by Gina Arnold and Anne Dvinge explore ways in which African American musical and cultural traditions have been at the heart of, as well as excluded from, festival practice. In a digital era the motivation for the social gathering of festival may be in part as compensation for the pervasive atomized and privatized experience of contemporary media and technology. But the mass political-cultural ritual of the carnivalesque protest should not be entirely reduced to being understood as nostalgic or gestural, or simply a safety valve: it has a continuing irruptive energetic potential (McKay 2007). An archetypal 'protestival' (see St John's essay) is evident in the repertoire surrounding the G20 gathering in London in 2009, which included an instantaneous festival-style Climate Camp – activists were urged to 'bring a pop-up tent if you've got one, a sleeping bag', creating a green festival-style temporary landscape in the financial quarter of the city (Reyes 2009). Occupy movement gardens and squatted public city parks and squares of contemporary protest too have often resembled a festival landscape, drawn on festival culture, in celebratory confirmation of the demand for social alternatives.

It is important to acknowledge as well, though, that 'local social tensions may be refracted through festivals, as much as community is engendered' (Gibson and Connell 2011, xvi). Tensions are seen to be stark when local people leave their houses and businesses, even board up shop windows in anticipation of trouble and damage (festival as stormy weather), for the duration of a festival in their community. In the early days, the 1967 Fantasy Fair and Magic Mountain Music Festival in California 'was opposed by the legions of civic "decency"' in the area, according to Jerry Hopkins (quoted in McKay 2000, 31). On the arrival of 20,000 festival-goers for the first Reading Festival in 1971, the local newspaper reported 'signs of an almost hysterical fear building up in the town as the fans stream in', and predicted 'mutual antagonism and resentment that will lead to trouble' (quoted in Murray 1979, 26). In a cost-benefit analysis of festivals, some of the costs include 'detriment to quality of life', 'noise and visual pollution', 'alienation of local residents' and 'potential for intercultural misunderstanding' (Gibson and Connell 2012, 22; see also McKay 2000, 29–47, for a discussion of festival and British law, and Helfrich 2010, for a discussion of community resistance to the organization of Woodstock in 1969). The post-festival clean-up operation can add its own negative legacy, especially since the rhetoric of rural festival in particular is often one of environmentalist idealism and green escape from the urban (see Figure 3). So the detritus-laden fields of, say, Woodstock or Stonehenge Free Festival – despite their back-to-the-land claims – showed that such 'early examples of "green" festivals lacked both the infrastructure and the practical competence to provide an ecologically sustainable environment' (Cummings et al. 2011, 13). Even at that most idealistic of Glastonburys, the 1971 free festival, intended as a celebration of our 'respect for nature', Andrew Kerr remembers soberly that 'the clean-up took a month' (Kerr 2011, 236). Also, festival garbage changes: in 2006 at Reading/Leeds twinned festivals, over 3,000 tents were abandoned by festival-goers, as environmentalism took a hit from disposability (Stone 2009, 221).

Of course, dirt, the body and personal hygiene at the festival form part of its narrative – whether that is Nine Inch Nails performing, caked in festival mud, at Woodstock 1994 or radical rockers, the Manic Street Preachers, importing a private toilet at Glastonbury 1999. More pragmatically, the

**FIGURE 3** *'Environmentalist idealism and green escape'? Glastonbury Festival* 2010.

open-air weekend festival in a location with temporary infrastructure (the fields of a farm, for example) in particular is a case study in the problematic and pragmatic of waste management, including sewage. 'Excrement' is indeed, as Lachmann puts in, following Bakhtin, 'a carnival substance' (1988, 147). Micturation, evacuation and menstruation take on new experiential meaning at festival, as we build up to our regular trip to the smelly, leaky part of the site, where pleasure, play and performance may seem distant, interrupted or postponed: the festival toilets, whether longdrop or portakabin. Here, the corporeality of the Bakhtinian carnivalesque can be powerfully, pungently present. The acceptance of body dirt, of differing levels of personal hygiene at festival, of sweat, of the mosh pit as collective bodily practice, is a cluster of topics discussed in Joanna Cummings and Jacinta Herborn's essay.

How should we think about the place of the live music (usually, and even recorded music is presented 'live', by DJ or sound system), at the music festival?

> 'The line-up is everything,' says pop promoter Vince Power, playing as it does a critical role in determining prospective festival-goers' perceptions of each event, its reputation, and the markets to which it will appeal. ... At a big festival people can 'see' much of their entire record collection in one weekend. (Stone 2009, 211)

Yet other research, as well as festival experience, tells us that the music may in fact be of secondary concern: Bowen and Daniels (2005) ask 'Does the music matter?' to those attending a festival (short answer: not necessarily), while Glastonbury 2015 sold out in less than one hour, when tickets went on sale in late 2014, eight months before the festival and with no confirmed headline acts (see also Gelder and Robinson 2009). In terms of festival culture more generally, music festivals (let alone popular music ones) may not even be the most prevalent type. Gibson and Connell's typology and analysis of Australian festivals in 2007 shows that less than 10 per cent of the almost 3,000 festivals included were music-oriented; agriculture (13 per cent), community (15 per cent) and sports festivals (36 per cent) were each a more common focus of activity (2012, 17). But within music festivals, Chris Stone has constructed a typology of contemporary festival practice in Britain that identifies seventeen varieties of pop festival (2009, 220). Of course, many of the essays in *The Pop Festival* discuss rock music as a popular form privileged at festivals, but several discuss other particular music genres: soul (Arnold), jazz (Dvinge, Goodall), folk (McKay), electronic dance music (St John, O'Grady, and Sean Nye and Ronald Hitzler). It is notable too that essays by Rebekka Kill and Roxy Robinson, and Lodge's photoessay, are about extra- and indeed the non-musical aspects of performance, festival content, alternative living; sometimes the music festival really is not about the music.

The mediated multiplatform nature of much popular music culture today is a given; for Chris Anderton et al., 'the music industries are experiencing a paradigmatic change in the early twenty-first century ... from the electric age to the digital age' (Anderton et al. 2013, 16). But even in contemporary processes of festivalization, the sounds and sites of which are often as compellingly non-digital as folk, acoustic jazz and green fields might suggest,

> we need to recognize and explore the complex uses being made of various new media systems, both by event producers and by audiences, to enhance the audience experience of events. These include, among others, digital multi-channel television, ... large-screen public viewing operations, and video-streaming to fixed and mobile internet platforms. (Roche 2011, 137)

For Yvette Morey et al., the possibilities of digital media mean that festival's potential as 'interactive' space is enhanced and even extended beyond its normative temporality: through social media, the festival experience is anticipated, produced and (re)consumed (Morey et al. 2014). Arguably, the digital turn has had other impacts on festival culture. For instance, in a digital media world of musical practices and technologies like peer-to-peer sharing, downloading and streaming, the live music event has become ever more crucial in the economy of the popular music industry, and the festival is a core component of live music. Also, if we accept the idea of digital atomization or alienation, the desire for the intense experience of face-to-face (musical/cultural) community that a festival can offer makes sense as a compensation for its lack in the everyday life of social media and the computer terminal. Yet let us not lose sight of history in our digital technophilia. While today it may indeed be media sponsorship and multiplatform live broadcast deals, widespread use of social media or the festival app, and side-stage or backdrop screen projections to experience the main bands, we should nonetheless ask whether festivals are more mediated or differently mediated nowadays. In the not so distant past there were daily newssheets produced onsite on Roneo duplicators, message boards as the prime means by which you could meet up with friends and sometimes Restricted Service Licence or pirate radio stations broadcasting over the festival territory. Further, as the essays by Mark Goodall, Nick Gebhardt and Arnold critically testify, films of festivals are at the heart of festival narrativization and mythologizing alike, while Lodge's photography presents a mediated historical moment of radical challenge in and through festival and traveller culture.

Chris Anderton explores in his essay here as well as elsewhere (Anderton 2009, 2011) ways in which contemporary music festivals are increasingly branded events with high levels of commercial involvement and relatively managed and regulated forms of consumption on offer. If this seems more marketplace than carnival, we should remember that the carnival or fair has always been a marketplace too, and indeed historically was often located in the town market square. Where some (older) idealists and researchers might see or seek a continuation of popular music and the festival's existential struggle between 'corporatization and the carnivalesque' (Laing 2004, 16), it appears that the presence of sponsorship and branding is generally accepted by today's festival-goers (Brennan and Webster 2010, 36). The economics of festival are also explored more widely – from the grassroots DIY organization in Dubber's essay to Dvinge's discussion of festival as a key item in the cultural repertoire of regeneration and urban cultural policy.

To conclude, Jonathan Harris challenges the utopian, environmentalist, romantic rhetoric of the 1960s and early 1970s counterculture – the appeal of going 'back to the garden' with Joni on 'Woodstock' – by reminding us that 'the garden was … also already a "garden centre"' (2005, 15), that is, a place of and opportunity for commerce, exchange, transaction. This would make the festival's key figure not the 'child of god', dreaming another world, but The Man, turning a buck. And yet I feel here in the end that I am rather (would rather be) with Barbara Ehrenreich. 'Why not,' insists Ehrenreich in her urgent critical celebration of 'ecstatic ritual', *Dancing in the Streets* – contemporary manifestations of which for her include the 'rock rebellion' of the festival and the 'carnivalization of protest' – 'Why not reclaim our distinctively human heritage as creatures who can generate their own ecstatic pleasures out of music, color, feasting, and dance?' (2007, 260). As I hope the textual and visual contributions in *The Pop Festival* both capture and problematize, there is an 'irrepressible, unsilenceable energy issuing from

**FIGURE 4** *Latitude Festival entrance sign, 2014.*

the carnival's alternative appeal' (Lachmann 1988, 125). After all, if we are lucky, and make it happen – a field, a big top, some sort of stage, or a street, a couple of clubs, some sort of parade vehicle – or can lay our hands on the right tickets, or be someone's + 1 (but we need + 8!), or can breach that stark symbol of the limits of utopia: the festival fence, *then* the festival is upon us, and we are it. Welcome (Figure 4). *Then*, for a while, all together, all together now, 'The sun machine is coming down, and we're gonna have a party. The sun machine is coming down, and we're gonna have a party' (Bowie 1969).

## References

Anderton, Chris. 2009. 'Commercializing the carnivalesque: the V Festival and image/risk management.' *Event Management* 12(1): 39–51.

Anderton, Chris. 2011. 'Music festival sponsorship: between commerce and carnival.' *Arts Marketing* 1(2): 145–58.

Anderton, Chris, Andrew Dubber and Martin James. 2013. *Understanding the Music Industries*. London: Sage.

Bennett, Andy. 2013. *Music, Style and Aging: Growing Old Disgracefully?* Philadelphia: Temple University Press.

Bennett, Andy, Jodie Taylor and Ian Woodward, eds. 2014. *The Festivalization of Culture*. Farnham: Ashgate.

Blake, Andrew. 1997. *The Land without Music: Music, Culture and Society in Twentieth Century Britain*. Manchester: Manchester University Press.

Bowen, Heather E., and Daniels Margaret J. 2005. 'Does the music matter? Motivations for attending a music festival.' *Event Management* 9(3): 155–64.

Bowie, David. 1969. 'Memory of a free festival.' On *David Bowie* (1969), re-issued and re-titled *Space Oddity* (1972). On *Space Oddity* CD. EMI Records.

Brennan, Matt, and Emma Webster. 2010. 'The UK festival market report.' In UK 2010 Festival awards programme, 25–39. http://livemusicexchange.org/wp-content/uploads/Festival-Awards-2010-Report-FINAL.pdf. Accessed 15 October 2014.

Cummings, Joanne, Ian Woodward and Andy Bennett. 2011. 'Festival spaces, green sensibilities and youth culture.' In Giorgi, Liana, Monica Sassatelli and Gerard Delanty, eds. *Festivals and the Cultural Public Sphere*. London: Routledge, 142–55.

Ehrenreich, Barbara. 2007. *Dancing in the Streets: A History of Collective Joy*. London: Granta.

Gelder, Gemma, and Peter Robinson. 2009. 'Motivations for attending music festivals: a case study of Glastonbury and V Festivals.' *Event Management* 13(3): 181–96.

Gibson, Chris, and John Connell, eds. 2011. *Festival Places: Revitalising Rural Australia*. Bristol: Channel View Publications.

Gibson, Chris, and John Connell. 2012. *Music Festivals and Regional Development in Australia*. Farnham: Ashgate.

Harris, Jonathan. 2005. 'Abstraction and empathy: psychedelic distortion and the meanings of the 1960s.' In Christop Grunenberg, and Jonathan Harris, eds. *Summer of Love: Psychedelic Art, Social Crisis and the Counterculture in the 1960s*. Liverpool: Liverpool University Press, 9–17.

Helfrich, Ronald. 2010. '"What can a hippie contribute to our community?" Culture wars, moral panics, and the Woodstock Festival.' *New York History* 91(3): 221–44.

Kerr, Andrew. 2011. *Intolerably Hip: The Memoirs of Andrew Kerr*. Kirstead, Norfolk: Frontier Publishing.

Lachmann, Renate. 1988. 'Bakhtin and carnival: culture as counter-culture.' Trans. Raoul Eshelman, and Marc Davis. *Cultural Critique* 11 (Winter 1988–89): 115–52.

Laing, Dave. 2004. 'The three Woodstocks and the live music scene.' In Andy Bennett, ed. *Remembering Woodstock*. Aldershot: Ashgate, 1–17.

McKay, George. 1996. *Senseless Acts of Beauty: Cultures of Resistance since the Sixties*. London: Verso.

McKay, George, ed. 1998. *DiY Culture: Party & Protest in Nineties Britain*. London: Verso.

McKay, George. 2000. *Glastonbury: A Very English Fair*. London: Gollancz.

McKay, George. 2005. *Circular Breathing: The Cultural Politics of Jazz in Britain*. Durham, NC: Duke University Press.

McKay, George. 2007. '"A soundtrack to the insurrection": street music, marching bands and popular protest.' *Parallax* 13(1): 20–31.

McKay, George. 2011. *Radical Gardening: Politics, Idealism & Rebellion in the Garden*. London: Frances Lincoln.

Metcalf, Bill. 2000. 'Alternative and communal Australia? Or, The education of young Bill.' In Alan Dearling, and Brendan Hanley, eds. *Alternative Australia: Celebrating Cultural Diversity*. Lyme Regis: Enabler, 2–6.

Mitchell, Joni. 1970. 'Woodstock'. On *Ladies of the Canyon* CD. Reprise Records.

Morey, Yvette, Andrew Bengry-Howell, Christine Griffin, Isabelle Szmigin and Sarah Riley. 2014. 'Festivals 2.0: consuming, producing and participating in the extended festival experience.' In Andy Bennett, Jodie Taylor and Ian Woodward, eds. *The Festivalization of Culture*. Farnham: Ashgate, 251–68.

Murray, Dave. 1979. 'Eight years of rock history.' Reading Rock '79 official programme, 26.

Pulp. 1995. 'Sorted for Es and whizz.' On *Different Class* CD. Island Records.

Reyes, Oscar. 2009. 'We're having a climate camp in the city.' *Red Pepper* (March). http://www.redpepper.org.uk/We-re-having-a-climate-camp-in-the/. Accessed 15 October 2014.

Roche, Maurice. 2011. 'Festivalization, cosmopolitanism and European culture: on the sociological significance of mega-events.' In Giorgi, Liana, Monica Sassatelli and Gerard Delanty, eds. *Festivals and the Cultural Public Sphere*. London: Routledge, 124–39.

Stone, Chris. 2009. 'The British pop music festival phenomenon.' In Jane Ali-Knight, Martin Roberston, Alan Fyall and Adele Ladkin, eds. 2009. *International Perspectives of Festivals and Events: Paradigms of Analysis*. London: Elsevier, 205–24.

UK Rock Festivals website. 'The Watchfield Free Festival, 23-31 August 1975.' http://www.ukrockfestivals.com/watchfieldfestival-menu.html. Accessed 29 October 2014.

# CHAPTER ONE

# 'The pose ... is a stance': Popular music and the cultural politics of festival in 1950s Britain

*George McKay*

*the pose held is a stance...*

THOM GUNN, 'ELVIS PRESLEY' (1957)

The aim of this chapter is to contribute to our understanding of the relation between popular music, festival and activism by focusing on a neglected but important area in festival history in Britain, what can arguably be seen as its originary decade, the 1950s. So I chart and interrogate the 1950s in Britain from the perspective of the rise of sociocultural experimentation in the contexts of youth, some of the 'new ... old' (Morgan 1998, 123) sonic landscapes of popular music, social practice and political engagement. I foreground the shifting cultures of the street, of public space, of this extraordinary period, when urgent and compelling questions of youth, race, colonialism and independence, migration, affluence were being posed to the accompaniment of new soundtracks, and to the new forms of dress and dance. Some of the more important popular culture events where these features manifested, performed and celebrated themselves produced what I see as a significant phenomenon: the youthful gathering of the festival, the surprising splash and clash of street culture (McKay 2007).

The chapter offers another narrative to contest or complement the national gesture of celebration, post-war reconstruction and post-imperial positioning (though the empire itself was 'the place that was barely represented' in the Festival: Conekin 2003, 5) that was the 1951 Festival of Britain (see Figure 5), but I acknowledge that presenting the 1950s as a decade of festival – rather than simply one of, say, post-war austerity – is an argument considerably aided by the 1951 opening event. After all, its purpose over 'five summer months' in London and nationwide was to present

> Exhibitions, Arts Festivals, conferences, pageantry, championship sporting events, simple village celebrations – the living record of a nation at work and at play. Never before has anything been planned quite like the Festival of Britain. Its outward manifestations will be gay and arresting. Its serious purpose will be to demonstrate the continuing vitality of the

**FIGURE 5** *1951 Festival of Britain advance publicity leaflet: 'Never before has anything been planned quite like the Festival of Britain'.*

> British people in the Arts, Sciences and Industry, and their ability and determination to play their full part, now as in the past, in the peaceful progress of mankind. (Festival of Britain 1950)

Becky Conekin argues for a complex understanding of the Festival of Britain. It presented '*competing* versions of Britain and "Britishness" ... [it] was a government strategy to increase foreign tourism ... [it] was a Labour extravaganza, with a social democratic agenda' (2003, 27; emphasis added). Yet I also acknowledge that questions of post-imperial positioning as well as of the shifting consensus on the construction of national identity are inscribed problematically within the cultural praxis of many of the festivals I go on to look at, too, from, for instance, a peer of the British realm embracing *American* jazz as the soundtrack of modernity to Caribbean migrants in London releasing calypso records in celebration of Ghanaian independence in 1957, to the foundation of the Campaign for Nuclear Disarmament (hereafter, CND) in 1958 as a British project 'to seize the moral leadership of the world' (Veldman 1994, 118). For post-imperial positioning and shifting national identity were among the compelling questions of the day in official and alternative political discourse and cultural praxis alike. Also, like the Festival of Britain, these festivals in Britain were among the kinds of event innovations that 'announced the end of scarcity and the arrival of post-war affluence' (Mort 2007, 44).

The significant festival events that interest me in both city and country from the 1950s are:

| | |
|---|---|
| 1955 | first Soho Fair, London |
| 1955 | first Sidmouth Folk Festival, Devon |
| 1956 | first Beaulieu Jazz Festival, Hampshire |
| 1958 | first Aldermaston CND march, Berkshire |
| 1959 | first Trinidadian carnival at St Pancras, London. |

There is a cluster of issues including social change, youth, popular music, race, national identity, carnivalesque irruption and political engagement – within and frequently breaking out of the special boundaried space and practice of festival – that requires closer attention. My first argument, then, is that the new formations of social and cultural gathering in 1950s festivals reflected and generated developments in modes of political identity, that the crowds observing and participating exploited these group opportunities for solidarity, that the new public spaces carved out, even if temporarily, were often understood or claimed as expressions of cultural creativity and social innovation at the same time. I present this argument via a critical mapping of the significant festival events of the decade, their significance delineated by their cultural and political imperatives. It includes the necessary (historical) process of narrativization, since not all of the stories themselves are familiar to cultural studies. I am interested and always intrigued by what might be characterized as the cultural marginalia of the new (if such it was) politicking of the period. What attracts me here as elsewhere are strands of the zeitgeist of cultural innovation, the often elusive or discarded cultural traces that really do or did melt into the air (and I am hearing music in particular now). But there are some persistent difficulties with such critical terrain. Tracing the influence or impact of some cultural forms at the time under discussion is problematic because of their elusive, emotive or transitory nature, and the festival as a carnivalesque combination of pop and protest is emblematic in this context. As Neil Nehring (echoing Raymond Williams) has both helpfully and unhelpfully noted in *Flowers in the Dustbin*, a study of 'cultural anarchism' which includes analysis of the 1950s literary-cultural arena and its relation to activism and social change:

> The linkages here ... are not meant to suggest a direct correspondence between imaginative activities and economic and political pressures, but a deeper, not always conscious connection. Directly or indirectly, various creative efforts responded to the structure of feeling or ideological tone. ... (Nehring 1993, 179)

Also, such cultural forms and practices have not always been treated well over the course of time – some have been discarded, or forgotten, or remembered without prestige.

During the 1950s the politics of culture and indeed of attitudinality – central to subculture theory and cultural politics – were beginning to be articulated and interrogated: not simply the claim that 'the pose ... *is* a stance', but also asking (posing) the question, what is the relation between stylistic or musical pose and political stance? And in what felt like the rarefied new space-time of the festal, this question could seem one of compelling experimentality and urgency. Of course, it remains necessary to qualify the extent of social, cultural and political innovation on the part of the new carnivalizers of the 1950s by acknowledging the existing connections between street culture, a pleasureful proto-carnival and political mobilization in Britain (see also McKay 2003). Mick Wallis has traced ways in which the British left exploited 'the potential of historical pageant-making ... [as a means of] taking history on to the streets' during the 1930s (1998, 54). According to Lawrence Black, in the early 1960s, the Young Socialists organization 'still undertook traditional socialist youth activities, *familiar to its League of Youth predecessor*: speakers' contests, camps and rambles – the Aldermaston marches were not such a novel departure' (2003, 62; emphasis added). Nonetheless, the 1950s, as we will see, begin to offer glimpses of alternate formations of carnival which would confirm its capacity to 'invert ... the everyday, workaday world of rules, regulations and laws, challenging the hierarchies of normality in a counterhegemonic, satirical, and sartorial parody of power' (Kershaw 1992, 72).

## The development of popular music, its festivals and politics, in 1950s Britain: Soho ... Sidmouth ... Beaulieu ... Aldermaston ...

During the 1950s both jazz and folk musics rode waves of popularity and visibility, demonstrated by the 'trad boom' of New Orleans–style jazz in the popular music charts, and the second folk revival (see also Frith et al. 2013 for wider developments in live music during this decade). Each of these musics' enthusiasts claimed a decentred authenticity for their form, manifested in the perception of their music being one rooted within a sense of struggle and history (race and class respectively), possessing an anti-commercial ethos, predicated on a grassroots organization, produced by amateurs. On the other hand, folk largely claimed a white indigenous Britishness, while jazz was understood in the context of its transatlantic blackness. But this opposition is too simple also: folk had its transatlantic impetus through the influence of the likes of music archivist Alan Lomax, while nearly all 'trad' and revivalist jazz in Britain was played by white musicians. What is intriguing is the relationship with the export cultures of the United States within the leftist political areas of Britain's 'affluent society' since, as Black argues, 'affluence chafed with socialism. Socialists were hostile to hire-purchase, consumerism, commercial TV, advertising and American mass culture' (2003, 13; see also McKay 2005, introduction). Nonetheless, as noted, the politics of jazz and folk alike sprang from a common grassroots aesthetic and practice. Debatably the two musics came together within the burgeoning youth culture to form skiffle, which was itself a short-lived but important DIY popular music practice, centred originally on the Soho area of London (McDevitt 1997; Brocken 2003 ch. 5; McKay 1998). According to Frank Mort,

> Soho was London's cosmopolitan quarter consisting of a square mile of densely-packed streets and narrow cross routes sited south of Oxford Street, east of Regent Street, and west of Charing Cross Road. The district's heavily gendered and sexually specific forms of cultural production and consumption had long distinguished Soho as an exotic space, not just in terms of the organization of the West End's pleasure economy but also in the national imagination. ... Soho's reputation for cultural exceptionalism was both historically sedimented and extremely diverse. (Mort 2007, 30–1)

Soho Fair was an annual summer event established in July 1955, which ran until at least 1961 (see Figure 6). It was designed as a commercial and cultural celebration of that cosmopolitan, musical (and also to an extent underworld) area of central London, held over a week, and featuring street processions, *ad hoc* outdoor performances, popular music competitions, which drew

**FIGURE 6** *Omega Brass Band play at Soho Fair, c. 1955 : 'it was in the first Soho Fair that the real spirit of Aldermaston was born' – Jeff Nuttall,* Bomb Culture.

crowds of the young, the curious, the partying. As a contemporary marker of the cachet of the event, pop guitarist Bert Weedon released a single in 1957 entitled 'Soho Fair' – a late effort to catch some of the market of the brief skiffle craze then sweeping Britain, which was centred on the new sociocultural spaces for young people that were the coffee bars of Soho. Chris Welch describes the musical and social 'change [that] was in the air':

> In July 1956, during the annual Soho Fair, Wally Whyton, leader of The Vipers Skiffle Group, popped into the 2Is [coffee bar] and asked if his band could play in the basement. ... The cellar bar was only 25 feet long and 16 feet wide, but soon it was packed with fans. It wasn't long before teenagers were queuing round the block to get in. (2002, 18)

As an austerity-era event organized in a context of consumerism, it was unusual in that Soho Fair was effectively a trade fair which also had an occasional unexpected political resonance – or could be interpreted as having such by some attending: the 1956 Soho Fair, for instance, was 'held to coincide with Bastille Day', noted skiffle musician McDevitt (1997, 113). Jeff Nuttall, critically nostalgizing in *Bomb Culture* only a decade or so later, recalled that, during the 1950s,

> Soho was alive with cellar coffee-bars, where skiffle and jazz could be played and heard informally and where the rich odour of marihuana became, for the first time, a familiar part of the London atmosphere. ... It became obvious that parental control was going to stop at about the

> age of fifteen for a large number of young people. Teenage wages were going up and so were student grants. ... *The Soho Fair ... was a festival of the ravers*. Bands and guitars and cossack hats and sheepskin waistcoats flooded out of the cellars and into the streets. It was so good that it had to be stopped, so good that *it was in the first Soho Fair that the real spirit of Aldermaston was born.* (1968, 40; emphasis added)

Nuttall here connects carnivalesque cultural celebration (the transformed and transgressive urban space of Soho Fair), political energy (CND and its annual Aldermaston marches) and generational division (parents losing control of increasingly financially independent teenage children) – a point also made at the time, interestingly enough, in the right-wing newspaper the *Daily Telegraph*, even if its motivation differed. Its report of the 'motley' crowd of protestors on the first Aldermaston march of 1958, who 'laughed, talked and "*skiffled*" their way along' on the first leg from Trafalgar Square to the Albert Memorial, may have been intended as a dismissive evaluation of youth politics through juvenile pop, but it was also an astute recognition of the fact that the youthful marchers themselves were stepping newly and rhythmically, in a corporeal display and confirmation of the link between music and mobilization (quoted in McDevitt 1997, 34; emphasis added). According to McDevitt, the skiffle repertoire confirmed political sympathies: 'most skiffle groups, whether consciously or not, favoured the politics of the left and songs like "Union maid", "The miner's lifeguard", "We shall not be moved" and "Joe Hill" were great favourites' (1997, 134). John Hasted, organizer of the Soho-based 44 Skiffle and Folk Song Club, who helped launch the radical folk magazine *Sing* in 1954 and contributed to the writing of what became the CND anthem 'Don't you hear the H-bomb's thunder', was to observe in his *Alternative Memoirs* that 'very seldom was there any complaint that our folk revival was part of a communist plot, despite the strong political convictions of many of the prominent singers' (quoted in McDevitt 1997, 133). There are other important connections. Revivalist New Orleans–style jazz musicians Ken Colyer and Sonny Morris formed the Omega Brass Band, the first formal and uniformed jazz parade band in Britain, for the inaugural Soho Fair (see McKay 2003); the Omega went on to lead many political demonstrations, most notably the Aldermaston marches. Writing in 1958, David Boulton – himself a jazz historian *and* CND activist – speculated on the cultural and political potential of the 'British marching style' of the parade band, of this jazz in the streets: 'If we were to bring jazz out into the streets of our towns and cities, reviving the functions and parades which characterised old New Orleans, then jazz might once again develop *a music of the people*, moving perhaps from jazz as we know it to a new and self-contained urban folk-music' (Boulton 1958, 137; emphasis added).

Innovations in folk and jazz music *festivals* during the mid-1950s contributed directly and indirectly to political developments. We can see this by looking at the experiences of the Sidmouth Folk Festival (founded in 1955, and remaining a significant annual event in the British folk calendar – though see Morgan 2007 for ways in which the organization of the event has changed over the years) and the Beaulieu Jazz Festival (1956–61). The fact that important festivals such as these were being established at the time is further evidence of the popularity of both musics, but also of a desire on the part of young people to participate in the relatively liberatory practice of festival-going – 24-hour peer company; life outside the domestic everyday; alcohol, drugs and sex (or the promise of them); dancing under the summer stars or clouds; the green escape to nature at the beach or in the countryside;[1] sometimes camping in tented communities; the now familiar, and today tirelessly marketed, festival template of excessive possibility of the carnival first being set …

Although I am emphasizing connections between these two new festivals, established within a year of each other, there are important differences that should not be ignored. Primary in the context of practical ideology and political engagement are their contrasting origins and motivations:

**FIGURE 7** *Folk-dancing in the streets by the English seaside: Sidmouth Folk Festival 1956.*

Sidmouth came about in part through enthusiasts for indigenous song and dance gathering at an English seaside town (see Figure 7), Beaulieu as a commercial transatlantic enterprise by the scandalous young peer of the realm Lord Montagu at his stately home. (Montagu's bisexuality and his public trial and imprisonment on homosexuality charges in 1954, prior to establishing the festival, signal an intriguing potential perspective of the queer origins of pop festival.) Yet, such obvious differences notwithstanding, at these coastal or rural gatherings young people enthused over what they considered new music, in a largely new form of participatory social behaviour, where politics formed a topic of debate, and the very culture of festival itself would be employed in contemporary protest. This last point refers in particular to the carnivalesque social and political weekend that was the annual Aldermaston march.

Georgina Boyes has noted that, while 'jazz bands provided much of the music for the marches organized by the Campaign for Nuclear Disarmament, it was folksong which became synonymous with protest' (1993, 214). Dave Harker has traced some of the concrete connections, arguing that 'the intervention of the Communist Party and its fraternal organizations was absolutely crucial in the second folksong revival, and to a lesser extent in the blues revival which was to follow' (1980, 151). The folk magazine *Sing* printed folk songs from the national and international repertoire, but also contained articles on the political issues of the day – the first edition alone featuring 'material entitled "Talking Rearmament", "The Atom Bomb and the Hydrogen!" and "Kenyatta"' (Brocken 2003, 44). Even in recent years, the latest version of Sidmouth Folk Festival has maintained a kind of political edge: the homepage of the Sidmouth Folk Week 2010 website featured among a very small number of linking logos that for the campaign 'Folk Against Fascism', which was established to challenge the British National Party's then cultural strategy of appropriating folk music and seeking to construct it as an indigenous, white and exclusive traditional form (Sidmouth Folk Week website).

Yet, while folk music and the left were closely associated, the febrile sounds and bodies of jazz, and its clashing forms and clashing groups of enthusiasts, would, in fact, throw up the most carnivalesquely irruptive moment of early British festival culture. The so-called 'Battle of Beaulieu' on the Saturday night of the summer 1960 festival (Figure 8) saw a small battle between rival groups of trad and modern jazz fans, the event filmed and partially broadcast on BBC Television's live outdoor broadcast coverage of the festival (see McKay 2004). This moment of subcultural contestation and negotiation, with its mediated display of minor violence and damage, remains framed and effectively obscured by (scholarship on) more spectacular or notorious subcultural innovations: the 'race riots' or 'white riots' of teddy boys of one or two years earlier, the seaside confrontations between mods and rockers of a year or two later. Yet the Battle of Beaulieu, the 'beatnik beat-up' of one newspaper's

**FIGURE 8** *Poster for 1960 Beaulieu Jazz Festival, at which 'the beatnik beat-up' occurred.*

gleeful coverage (quoted in McKay 2005, 76), is a compelling early example in festival history of the capacity of carnival to challenge or invert social norm.

According to Colin MacInnes, in a 1962 article on anarchism,

> Suddenly, from 1956 onwards, there came a crack in the social-political situation that released old allegiances and left conventional parties frozen into postures that ignored these changes. There came Poland, Hungary, Suez, death of Stalin, rise of Africa, the New Left, the teenage phenomenon, the race riots, the teacher strikes, Osborne and the new wave writers, and, *for what it is worth*, CND. … (quoted in Gould 1983, 123; emphasis added)

MacInnes's casual dismissal of CND, only four years old at the time of his writing, is harsh. The annual CND Aldermaston Easter marches from 1958 on stand as the most politicized carnivalesque development of the period. Here, each year, not simply was there a political-cultural-social gathering that formed an influential constituency, but, because it extended over several days and nights (marchers sleeping in town halls and churches *en route*), *a community of activists* was constructed and refreshed annually. From its beginnings just prior to the Aldermaston Nuclear Weapons Research Centre marches from 1958 on, we can see in CND what would become recognizable as a youth or lifestyle protest movement. David Widgery memorably described the Aldermaston march as 'a student movement before its time, mobile sit-in or marching pop festival; in its midst could be found the first embers of the hashish underground and premature members of the Love Generation as well as cadres of forthcoming revolutionary parties' (1976, 104). Aldermaston did not spring from nowhere, nor did it spring only from an earlier tradition of leftist public mobilizations: my point is that the new combined practice of music, politics and *festival* occurring from the mid-1950s on contributed significantly to the Aldermaston generation's innovation.

The cultural countermodernism of nuclear disarmament found its most visible expressions *not* in the city but in the countryside. For some, the rural English landscape was experienced to the soundtrack of early jazz marching bands, folk and dance, and the easy participatory pleasures of skiffle. The political strategy employed in this landscape and culture embrace was that 'the English past could be and was used to criticize and challenge the nuclear present' (Veldman 1994, 203). The eccentric tribal gathering in the deep green ancient New Forest that began to characterize the Beaulieu Jazz Festivals, as with the collective spring-time excursion through the English Home Counties countryside that was the Aldermaston march, and too the seaside jaunt of folksong and dance that happened annually on the streets of Sidmouth – each sought to satisfy 'a hungering ... for the pastoral' (Nuttall 1968, 41–2). The concurrence of the first Aldermaston CND march of 1958 with the first large-scale jazz festival at Beaulieu is important: New Orleans–style bands playing for the camping marchers, packed with youth, through green Berkshire at Easter 1958, New Orleans–style bands playing for new audiences, packed with youth, in the ancient New Forest of green Hampshire a few summer months later. Lord Montagu of Beaulieu has himself acknowledged that the 'Aldermaston March and the Beaulieu Jazz Festival were foremost among the high days of the alternative society' (Montagu 2000, 273), even if this statement seems to wear its importance as a historical revision extremely lightly: for most, 'the high days of the alternative society' would be around 1968, not 1958. The Beaulieu-CND subcultural conjunction was more widely reported as well: the *Glasgow Herald* wrote of 'all the usual *Aldermaston-cum-Jazz-Festival* uniforms – tight jeans, baggy sweaters painted with the

CND symbol, bowler hats, long hair for all sexes', for instance (31 July 1961; emphasis added).

## Notting Hill Carnival (1959–present)

Overall then, the festivals and fairs that popularized the participatory musics of skiffle and the wider folk and jazz movements were recognized at the time as contributing directly and indirectly to the developing political consciousness and cultural practice of the New Left (see Figure 9), especially through Aldermaston. (Jazz and folk musicians would also become active in the Anti-Apartheid Movement of 1959 and 1960, of course, but there is not the same level of festival input with this campaign. What there *was* within the AAM was a clear recognition of the legitimacy of culture in political discourse and practice, the radical priest and key organizer Trevor Huddleston having called for a cultural boycott of South Africa as early as 1955: Denselow 1990, 49.) There is one further essential carnivalesque moment from the period that I want to introduce though, because it widens the political scope of campaign and understanding to include questions of race and post-colonialism, and it speaks still compellingly to contemporary Britain. This is, or this became, the Notting Hill Carnival. According to Paul Gilroy,

> The entry of blacks into national life was itself a powerful factor contributing to the circumstances in which the formation of both cultural studies and New Left politics became possible. It indexes the profound transformations of British social and cultural life in the 1950s. (Gilroy 1993, 10)

**FIGURE 9** *Omega Brass Band marching at a political demonstration, late 1950s: 'FREE OUR HEALTH SERVICE'.*

Both the Windrush generation of 1948 (its name taken from the first ship carrying migrants from the Caribbean to Britain as part of post-war mass migration: see Phillips and Phillips 1998) and other migrants soon following strengthened the Caribbean culture of London and some provincial cities significantly. Included on board the Windrush's original passengers were a number of important Trinidadian calypsonians who would make their mark in London and internationally. According to Richard Noblett,

> In London they joined a milieu of fine band musicians familiar with Caribbean musical forms, and already represented on numerous recordings crucial to the development of British swing and jazz music. Travelling with their own core audience, the Trinidadian calypsonians brought with them the vocal music of Carnival. ... During [the 1950s], certainly, it was the enthralling soundtrack of Black Britain. (2002, no pagination)

The diaspora sounded in other ways too: Trinidadian calypsonian Mighty Terror migrated to Britain in 1953 and the following year recorded and released 'No carnival in Britain' (at a time when, of course, there *was* no carnival in London). In Noblett's view, this song 'gathered poignancy when Terror won the [prize] Crown at the concerts – a prelude to the world-famous Notting Hill Carnival – organized by [communist and black activist] Claudia Jones after attacks on the West London Black community' in 1958 (Noblett 2002; see Figure 10). Intriguingly, the recording's actual chorus as sung by Mighty Terror is 'No mas here in Great Britain'; presumably it was translated on the record label from 'No mas[querade]' to the less idiomatic 'No carnival' (Mighty Terror 1954).

Others were not so keen on some aspects of a changing Britain. Teddy boys were the one highly visible youth culture of the 1950s which the left had difficulty in viewing sympathetically, let alone recruiting. Debates about the place of youth within the affluent society stumbled at what was perceived as the cultural inarticulacy and social violence of this subculture. The teddy boy not only interrogated but also seemed actually to embody the limits of youth subcultural innovation and attitude for the left. Clustering whiteness, working-class masculinity, the threat of violence and the brash commercial American soundtrack of rock 'n' roll, teds were an intimidating and unpleasant presence. According to Brocken, there were clear class-based expressions of cultural value around the new popular musics. For instance, 'skiffle was welcome at the BBC and with the left, in youth clubs and coffee bars, because it was politically correct, safe and jolly – unlike rock "n" roll' (2003, 74). Colin MacInnes articulated the left's anxiety in terms of racial politics, in a piece of writing published before what he called the 'nigger-hunting expedition' of the summer of 1958 in West London, which led to what he subsequently termed, in a notable nuance, the '"race riot", not a race riot' around Notting Hill (quoted in Gould 1983, 132, 134). MacInnes

**FIGURE 10** *Notting Hill Carnival 2004, articulating and processing the ideals: UNITY RESPECT PEACE LOVE.*

wrote of the teddy boys that one could see, 'in their teenage neutralism and indifference to politics, and self-sufficiency, and instinct for enjoyment – in short, in their kind of happy mindlessness – the raw material for crypto-fascisms of the worst kind' (quoted in Gould 1983, 128). Actually, fascist organizations like the White Defence League and the Union Movement *did* rapidly attempt to exploit the situation in London (Gould 1983, 133) – 'KBW' had been a familiar graffito in the area for some time ('KEEP BRITAIN WHITE': Olende 2008). Though critical of the 'aimless frenzy of their leisure life', Stuart Hall did perceive in teddy boys the possibility of political energy and social change, imagining their alienation as a step towards a radical critique (quoted in Black 2003, 75).

While 'youth served as an index of social anxiety at the same time [as] it was a metaphor for social change' (Nehring 1993, 187), music and carnival played a part here too. There is a neglected musical and social campaign organization directly addressing race and racism in Britain, which was formed in response to the disturbances during the summer of 1958 in Nottingham and London. Although short-lived, it is just about possible to see the Stars' Campaign for Inter-Racial Friendship as a precursor to a more successful organization such as the heavily carnival-inflected Rock Against Racism of the late 1970s. At its peak in 1978, RAR's 'politics of polycultural solidarity' were displayed in a series of five major carnivals combining popular music and anti-racist politics (Dawson 2005, 11; see also Widgery 1986), while thirty years later an anniversary carnival was organized (Figure 11). The purpose of SCIF two decades earlier was to articulate through the combined presence of popular music and popular culture, *and* left activists and writers, a cultural politics of racial inclusion and social solidarity at a time of crisis. Colin MacInnes was a founding member of SCIF, and others active or willing to lend their name included Britain's highest profile multi-racial jazz couple Cleo Laine and John Dankworth; jazz musicians Ken Colyer, Humphrey Lyttelton, Chris Barber; from the skiffle and pop world, Lonnie Donegan, Tommy Steele, Frankie Vaughan; and left-wing music critics like Max Jones and 'Francis Newton' (Eric Hobsbawm's pseudonym when writing about jazz). An eight-page free newssheet entitled 'What the Stars Say' was produced by SCIF and distributed to houses in the riot area of London – though the contents were apparently 'mostly showbiz stuff about Sammy Davis Junior' (quoted in Gould 1983, 137). Another SCIF activity in 1958 was a televised 'inter-racial' children's Christmas party in North Kensington. In her 1960 book *Newcomers: The West Indians in London*, Ruth Glass observed that

**FIGURE 11** *Carnival as cultural expression and celebration of the 'politics of polycultural solidarity'.*

SCIF had 'a rather energetic, "newsworthy" start ... [but] since then it has been rather quiet' (quoted in Gould 1983, 138). Other activists though made what would come to be seen as less gestural and altogether longer lasting responses to the worsening racial context of youthful England. Following the 1958 disturbances in Nottingham and London, and the racial murder of a young Caribbean migrant, a group of activists and cultural workers drew on Caribbean socio-musical traditions to present a new kind of festival for London.

> The first carnival – a Caribbean 'fayre' staged in St Pancras town hall in 1959 – was ... an attempt to galvanise London's black community. Arranged by the Trinidadian communist Claudia Jones, founder of the West Indian Gazette, the fayre embodied Jones' recognition of the political force of culture. With something of the Harlem Renaissance emphasis on folk tradition (Jones grew up in Harlem), the early fayre drew on Trinidadian traditions of costume and the scurrilous political commentary of Calypso. (Melville 2002)

This early effort at Trinidadian carnival would be relaunched within a few years, when strands of the urban white counterculture of the mid-1960s worked closely with black British community groups campaigning around housing issues to establish the Notting Hill Carnival (see McKay 2000, 7–11).

## Conclusion

From the Festival of Britain in 1951 to Aldermaston or Beaulieu or St Pancras in the latter 1950s constitutes a decade span containing a series of considerable experiments on the possibilities and limits of festival, organized from above (Festival of Britain), or below (Aldermaston, St Pancras/Notting Hill), or commercially, when the event could be adapted (Soho Fair) or subverted (the Battle of Beaulieu) by its participants. These regular festival events, whether as urban carnivals or rural gatherings, have rung the ethnic, stylistic, attitudinal and sonic changes of the times. Such changes resonated socially and politically, as well as culturally, as the carnival embraces spectators, second liners (Figure 12). Many of them have become the characteristic cultural-political-social spaces of the left, new or otherwise, as accessible, high-profile, and public or media events. Across the decades they have struggled and thrived, all the while energetically adapting themselves to shifts in cultural taste and political context alike. In 1959, E. P. Thompson could write of the labour movement with controlling confidence that 'the bureaucracy will hold the machine; but the New Left will hold the passes between it and the younger generation' (quoted in Sedgwick 1964, 131).

**FIGURE 12** *Notting Hill Carnival, 2006: Spectators as participants.*

Yet, when we begin to examine the carnivalesque moments of the period itself we can see that, in fact, spaces *without* passes, for raging or singing or dancing *against* the machine, were already being built up, torn down, and all in between.

## Notes

1 I do not think I am claiming 'green' as environmental consciousness in these early festivals; in fact, even in *later* rural-based festivals a green consciousness can be elusive. Researchers have found for example that 'almost all (94 per cent) of attendees of the Sidmouth Folk Festival use cars to get there, whereas larger urban events such as ... an open air concert by "The Who" in Hyde Park were more likely to be patronised by users of public transport' (see Laing and Frost 2010, 263).

## References

Black, Lawrence. 2003. *The Political Culture of the Left in Affluent Britain, 1951-64.* Basingstoke: Palgrave Macmillan.

Blake, Andrew. 1997. *The Land without Music: Music, Culture and Society in Twentieth Century Britain.* Manchester: Manchester University Press.

Boulton, David. 1958. *Jazz in Britain.* London: W. H. Allen.

Boyes, Georgina. 1993. *The Imagined Village: Culture, Ideology and the English Folk Revival.* Manchester: Manchester University Press.

Brocken, Michael. 2003. *The British Folk Revival, 1944-2002.* Aldershot: Ashgate.

Casado-Diaz, M., S. Everett and J. Wilson, eds. 2007. *Social and Cultural Change: Making Space(s) for Leisure and Tourism.* Eastbourne: Leisure Studies Association.

Chun, Lin. 1993. *The British New Left*. Edinburgh: Edinburgh University Press.
Conekin, Becky. 2003. *The Autobiography of a Nation: The 1951 Festival of Britain*. Manchester: Manchester University Press.
Dawson, Ashley. 2005. '"Love Music, Hate Racism": the cultural politics of the Rock Against Racism campaign, 1976-1981.' *Postmodern Culture* 16(1). http://jefferson.village.virginia.edu/pmc/text-only/issue.905/16.1dawson.txt. Accessed 19 March 2013.
Denselow, Robin. 1990. *When the Music's Over: The Story of Political Pop*. London: Faber. Rev. edn.
Festival of Britain. 1950. *Festival of Britain May 3 – September 30 1951: Britain at Home to the World*. Advance publicity booklet. London: HMSO.
Frith, Simon, Matt Brennan, Martin Cloonan and Emma Webster. 2013. *The History of Live Music in Britain, Volume 1: 1950-1967*. Farnham: Ashgate.
*Glasgow Herald*. 31 July 1961. Beaulieu Jazz Festival press cuttings files, Beaulieu Motor Museum Archive, Hampshire.
Gilroy, Paul. 1993. *The Black Atlantic: Modernity and Double Consciousness*. London: Verso.
Gould, Tony. 1983. *Inside Outsider: The Life and Times of Colin MacInnes*. London: The Hogarth Press.
Gunn, Thom. 1957. 'Elvis Presley.' In *The Sense of Movement*. London: Faber, 31.
Harker, Dave. 1980. *One for the Money: Politics and Popular Song*. London: Hutchinson.
Kenny, Michael. 1995. *The First New Left: British Intellectuals after Stalin*. London: Lawrence and Wishart.
Kershaw, Baz. 1992. *The Politics of Performance: Radical Theatre as Cultural Intervention*. London: Routledge.
Laing, Jennifer, and Warwick Frost. 2010. 'How green was my festival? Exploring challenges and opportunities associated with staging green events'. *International Journal of Hospitality Management* 29(2) (June 2010): 261–67.
McDevitt, Chas. 1997. *Skiffle: The Definitive Inside Story*. London: Robson Books.
McKay, George, ed. 1998. *DiY Culture: Party & Protest in Nineties Britain*. London: Verso.
—. 2000. *Glastonbury: A Very English Fair*. London: Gollancz.
—. 2003. 'Just a closer walk with thee: new Orleans-style jazz and the Campaign for Nuclear Disarmament in 1950s Britain.' *Popular Music* 22(3) (Autumn): 261–81.
—. 2004, '"Unsafe things like youth and jazz": Beaulieu Jazz Festivals (1956-61) and the origins of pop festival culture in Britain.' In Andy Bennett (ed.), *Remembering Woodstock*. Aldershot: Ashgate, 90–110.
—. 2005. *Circular Breathing: The Cultural Politics of Jazz in Britain*. Durham, NC: Duke University Press.
—. 2007. '"A soundtrack to the insurrection": street music, marching bands and popular protest.' *Parallax* 13(1) (January 2007): 20–31.
Melville, Caspar. 2002. 'A carnival history.' *Open Democracy* (4 September 2002). www.opendemocracy.net/arts-festival/article_548.jsp. Accessed 1 December 2013.
Mighty Terror. 1954. 'No carnival in Britain'. Melodisc Records. Available on *London is the Place for Me: Trinidadian Calypso in London, 1950-56*. Honest Jon's Records: HJRCD2 (2002).

Montagu, Edward. 2000. *Wheels Within Wheels: An Unconventional Life*. London: Weidenfeld and Nicolson.
Morgan, Kevin. 1998. 'King Street blues: jazz and the left in Britain in the 1930s-1940s.' In Andy Croft, ed. *A Weapon in the Struggle: The Cultural History of the Communist Party in Britain*. London: Pluto Press, 123–41.
Morgan, Michael. 2007. 'Festival spaces and the visitor experience.' In M. Casado-Diaz, S. Everett and J. Wilson, eds. *Social and Cultural Change: Making Space(s) for Leisure and Tourism*. Eastbourne: Leisure Studies Association, 113–30. http://eprints.bournemouth.ac.uk/4821/1/99__Morgan.pdf. Accessed 26 November 2013.
Mort, Frank. 2007. 'Striptease: the erotic female body and live sexual entertainment in mid-twentieth-century London.' *Social History* 32(1) (February 2007): 27–53.
Nehring, Neil. 1993. *Flowers in the Dustbin: Culture, Anarchy, and Postwar England*. Ann Arbor: University of Michigan Press.
Noblett, Richard. 2002. Liner notes to CD. *London is the Place for Me: Trinidadian Calypso in London, 1950-56*. Honest Jon's Records: HJRCD2.
Nuttall, Jeff. 1968. *Bomb Culture*. London: Paladin, 1970.
Olende, Ken. 2008. 'The Notting Hill riot and a carnival of defiance.' *Socialist Worker* online, issue 2115 (23 August 2008). www.socialistworker.co.uk/art.php?id=15764. Accessed 19 May 2014.
Phillips, Mike, and Trevor Phillips (1998), *Windrush: The Irresistible Rise of Multi-racial Britain*. London: HarperCollins.
Sedgwick, Peter. 1964. 'The two New Lefts.' In David Widgery, ed. 1976. *The Left in Britain, 1956-68*. Harmondsworth: Penguin, 131–53.
Sidmouth Folk Week. 2010. www.sidmouthfolkweek.co.uk/index.html. Accessed 19 November 2013.
St John, Graham. 2008. 'Protestival: global days of action and carnivalised politics in the present.' *Social Movement Studies: Journal of Social, Cultural and Political Protest* 7(2) (September): 167–90.
Veldman, Meredith. 1994. *Fantasy, the Bomb, and the Greening of Britain: Romantic Protest, 1945-1980*. Cambridge: Cambridge University Press.
Wallis, Mick. 1998. 'Heirs to the pageant: mass spectacle and the Popular Front.' In Andy Croft, ed. *A Weapon in the Struggle: The Cultural History of the Communist Party in Britain*. London: Pluto Press, 48–67.
Welch, Chris. 2002. *Peter Grant: The Man who Led Zeppelin*. London: Omnibus.
Widgery, David. 1986. *Beating Time: Riot 'n' Race 'n' Rock 'n' Roll*. London: Chatto & Windus.

# CHAPTER TWO

# Out of sight: The mediation of the music festival

*Mark Goodall*

*The children danced night and day.*

ERIC BURDON AND THE ANIMALS, 'MONTEREY' (1967)

The pop festival grows from nothing; it rises up from an empty space into an audio-visual spectacle, captivating the thousands of individuals who have made the pilgrimage to witness it. Over the years these musical stage events, with a strong visual dimension, have attracted media producers, especially film-makers. This chapter explores how the pop festival has been mediated over time, from the early pioneering films of music festivals to the modern festival. I wish to discuss how the pop festival was mediated, with an examination of the techniques and methods used by media producers. I focus on film, the most 'remediated' form of media. Bolter and Grusin (2000) argue that, through the imperatives of hypermediacy and immediacy, new media achieve their cultural significance by paying homage to, rivalling and refashioning such earlier media as painting, photography, film and television. But I want to discuss this in relation to the actual music offered at these festivals. Much analysis of the pop music festival concentrates, perhaps understandably, on the sociopolitical function of the festival. This is important, but neglects to address the principal reason people flock to these festivals and later consume mediated versions of these festivals, namely, their passion for modern popular musical forms.

The story of the mediation of the pop festival appears to have followed this somewhat familiar trajectory:

1 Life (the birth of the festival film)
2 Death (the trauma of the mediated festival)
3 Rebirth (a new form of mediation/remediation)

Socially and culturally speaking, the relationship between the mass media and festivals centres on reportage of the events. For the big festivals of the 1960s and 1970s media provided coverage of festivals as news dwelling especially on local fears and apprehensions about the influx of hippies, freaks and undesirables (as seen in the interviews opening the 1970 *Woodstock* film: Wadleigh 1970). The predictable reactionary and inconsistent messages were sent out by the mass media in regard to festivals. For example, the newspaper coverage of the Woodstock festival 'flipped' from 16 August 1969, when the *New York Times* described the festival as 'an outrageous episode' (and in the UK, *The Times* asked 'what kind of culture is it that can produce so colossal a mess?'), to the day after when the *New York Times* suddenly viewed Woodstock as 'essentially a phenomenon of innocence' and even as 'a declaration of independence' (Peterson 1973, 110–11; see also Warner 2004). In one prescient interview with a participant at the 1970 Isle of Wight Festival the (female) interviewee said that the festival as a whole was a 'bummer' but one that 'would look better in the movie' (quoted in Peterson 1973, 111). As Peterson notes, 'the media did not act as a neutral mirror but played an active role in shaping everyone's view of reality' (Peterson 1973, 116). This is what we see suggested in the above Isle of Wight quotation. Festivals, live music, their promise of authenticity and community are the ultimate realization of 'the Bowie theory': the performance of music becoming the 'only unique situation that's going to be left' (Kreuger, quoted in Frith 2007, 6).

It is clear that the mediation of the music festival enhances the already spectacular nature of the event (Figure 13). Writing in the early days of festival, Richard Peterson defined music festivals as 'multi-day gatherings of diverse people drawn together to participate in a particular form of music and share a communal spirit in which the world was momentarily remade in the image celebrated in the music' (1973, 99). This dimension of the music festival has been much discussed: these so-called 'Gatherings of the Tribe' and the way in which these large-scale collective events, at least in the late 1960s and early 1970s, seemed to shape the times they existed in (see Hoffman 1969; Spitz 1979; Braunstein and Doyle 2002, for instance). The actual Gathering of the Tribes festival, otherwise known as the Human Be-In, held in Golden Gate Park, San Francisco, in 1967, was said to be 'the prototype of all 1960s counter culture celebrations' (Magic Bus website). Those fortunate enough to have been to these festivals have a particular

**FIGURE 13** *Photographing the Arctic Monkeys, Roskilde Festival 2014.*

story to tell (and increasingly tell it: see the very low quality but extensive packaging and promotional materials documenting the Bickershaw Festival in England in 1972, for example: Hewitt and Hewitt 2007).

Since the 1960s, audio-visual media have played an increasingly important role in the understanding of the rock festival. It seems as if only the audio-visual spectacle of the feature film, the vibrancy of the film image mixed with a high-impact soundtrack, was capable of capturing what Richard Barsam defines as the 'state of mind' of these seismic events (Barsam 1992, 332). Julie Lobalzo Wright shows how the connection between performer and audience is developed in films such as *Woodstock* (where there is a sense of unity) and *Gimme Shelter* (where there is a sense of alienation). Either way, the 'communal gaze' and 'disconnecting gaze' inform a cinematic audience of the power of contemporary rock music (Wright 2013, 73). Arnold argues that the importance of the *Woodstock* film as a 'mainstay of the rock business's sense of cultural relevance ... cannot be understated' (Arnold 2014, 129). The film's lavish visual style and rich presentation of a range of musical styles continues to resonate into the twenty-first century. Those left behind, or too young to have been there, experience the festival via the festival film, or the live broadcast of the event, increasingly being beamed to cinema spaces in theatres or city centres. For example, comparing the way in which the Glastonbury Festival has been mediated over the decades, we can see a classic cinematic representation of the festival in 1971 (Nicholas Roeg and Peter Neal's *Glastonbury Fayre*), carefully and skilfully structured after the event, based on materials collected at the time, with the BBC's live streaming of the festival, across multiple media platforms, which has become a ubiquitous contemporary aspect both of the festival itself and of the BBC's summer scheduling. Both are fragmentary (and necessarily so, given that a complete film/broadcast of the festival would require around three *continuous* days of broadcast/cinematic time), but in different ways.

The skills and the produced text of a post-event edit process and a live television mix differ widely. As with the approach to the visualization of music in other festival films of the time (such as Wadleigh's *Woodstock*), 'these were essentially musical events: the cameras engaged in reportage, the musicians primarily engaged in the live delivery of their music' (Edgar et al. 2013, 3). In the 'TV Glastonbury', in place of the anonymous voices of the MC heard on older films, excitable professional presenters shape our experience (often not for the better). There is also a point here to be made about the hierarchy of media production: for D. A. Pennebaker, the director of the classic 1968 festival film *Monterey Pop*, television would 'demean any subject like this' (Pennebaker 2006).

But how did the mediated form of music festival come about? In order to understand the now common filmic representation of the pop festival, we must look at the mediation of an event that was not even really 'pop': the Newport Jazz Festival of 1958.

## *Jazz on a Summer's Day*: A taxonomy of the festival film

The Newport Jazz Festival, held in the small US state of Rhode Island, was established in 1954 by socialites Elaine and Louis Lorillard. Despite periodic crises, it still runs every summer, even if, according to the 2014 website, it is 'presented by Natixis Global Asset Management', and thus has arguably lost some of its hip credentials. In truth, the festival was always a magnet for an elite East Coast crowd of hipsters, providing entertainment for the yachting crowds gathering during the holiday season. For the 1958 festival a young fashion photographer named Bert Stern was assigned the task of recording the festival on colour film. Stern worked with director Aram Avakian who also edited the film. Stern's production utilized five cameras simultaneously. As a photographer, Stern knew to make use of high-quality handheld cameras with telephoto lenses and made exceptional use of 35 mm Kodak fast positive-reversal colour film. Stern remarked on reflection that his images 'just jumped off the screen'. Stern also noted that, in the cultural tradition of the time, 'jazz films are all black and white ... kind of depressing and in little downstairs nightclubs. This brought jazz out into the sun. It was different' (quoted in Kurtz 2010).

*Jazz on a Summer's Day* (first public screening in 1959) is a visually remarkable film, and the politics of its representations have been widely discussed. Thomas F. Cohen, for example, carefully argues that Stern's representation of black performers on the film is flawed and reactionary (Cohen 2012). The film poorly documents the emerging radical jazz performers and the politics of new black consciousness (evidence of this for Cohen is that Thelonious Monk's performance is truncated and broken up by endless cut-aways).[1] Nonetheless, Stern unwittingly created a blueprint for all subsequent representations of pop festival films, and it is this that I think is worth discussing further. Because of Stern's training as a photographer he emphasized image rather than sound (the 'glaring omissions' of the film in terms of the performing artists actually excluded are listed with the jazz critic's zeal in Kurtz 2010). Therefore, what Cohen sees as faulty with the way in which Stern cuts away from the performers to external elements of the festival (birds, water, yachts) is actually one of *Jazz on a Summer's Day*'s most exciting dimensions. In particular, Sterns's restless lens captured fragments of the festival experience that would very quickly become standard within the repertoire of visualization of the festival in film. Here are some of those key features from *Jazz on a Summer's Day.*

## The face in the crowd

At various points in the film, Stern trains his camera on the audience members. My own perception as a viewer is that the audience for the Newport Jazz Festival is given as much screen time as the music acts are. Concentration and focus on capturing the subjects of the festival was paramount. This was the first film to locate the beautiful people of the festival crowd. At various points, Stern picks out attractive young women, both black and white (something that Cohen argues is problematic), but also shown are men in button-down shirts and pork pie hats. A particularly striking image is that of a young woman in a red sweater wearing a straw hat with a matching red trim (see Figure 14). The colour of the Kodak process picks out these hues in rich and vibrant measure. During the edit process Avakian argued

**FIGURE 14** Jazz on a Summer's Day. *The woman in the red sweater.*

that there should be cross-cutting between the red-sweater woman and the performers, but Stern insisted that the single long shot of the woman be retained, a clear indication that his style was impressionistic rather than dynamic (now the standard form of editing for pop festival media) (Stern 2001). This improvised style raises questions for music fans of 'authenticity'. Cohen (2012), for example, is critical of Bert Stern's cutting to shots of racing yachts during the performers' key solos. These small details are what make the film so fascinating.

## *The face of God*

Stern's filming of jazz performers, for all its apparent flaws, captures the mystical dimension of the performing artist. By scrutinizing in close-up the faces of performers in action, *Jazz on a Summer's Day* invites the audience of the film to gaze in awe at their technical prowess and ability to captivate a crowd. The 'bad positioning' common to the early festival films, where there was no concession made to where the film camera could operate, forced film-makers to improvise and adapt and make good use of their lenses and of the cramped and claustrophobic locations. This film was the first cinematic work to invite us to take the popular music performer seriously as an artist and to appreciate the skill involved in making such music. Associations can be made between the performer and the audience. This happens most notably where during a solo by saxophonist Sonny Stitt, the contours of his instrument are matched with those of the figure of a young woman in the audience. Thus the era of performers as 'demigods' (Gordon 1970, 41) is launched.

## *The face of the filmmaker*

Stern creates several sequences in the film that stage reality. These include a group of festival-goers enjoying a party in one of the houses they have rented; a sequence of the jazz group Eli's Chosen Six riding along the road in an old jalopy, and a record of Chic Hamilton's group rehearsing in another rented property. Another memorable moment occurs when Stern shows, via a candid camera position, Anita O'Day picking something off the sole of her shoe before stepping on stage. These sections break up the illusion of reality easily created by sequences of performers on stage. Stern was not afraid to reveal that this record of the Newport Jazz Festival was a cinematic and photographic creation. The subsequent authentic approach of the Direct Cinema directors was not yet fully evident.

In my view, the enduring creative innovation of *Jazz on a Summer's Day* was the profound linking of bodies with music and sound. The film was structured not only in the shooting but also in its editing, so as to connect the sounds being made by the musicians with the movement of the performers and also the audience, creating a kind of symbiosis. As Cohen points out, when discussing the performance of Sonny Stitt, in this film there is an audio-visually induced 'analogy between horn and woman' (Cohen 2012, 31). This device, the drawing together of bodies in movement (both audience and performer) and the properties of musical sound, would continue well into the further development of the pop festival film, becoming a ritual aspect of the festival film.

## Festival films and the mediation of the counterculture

The media projected Woodstock.

George Paul Csicsery (quoted in Eisen 1970, 234)

If one were asked to name a good example of the pop festival film, two particular examples would immediately spring to mind. The first is *Monterey Pop* (1968), directed by D. A. Pennbaker, the second *Woodstock* (1970) directed by Michael Wadleigh. The reasons these films became and have remained archetypes of the pop festival film are less to do with the fact they occurred within the over-garlanded 'golden era' of rock and pop music (which loosely begins with the breakthrough of The Beatles and ends with the arrival in 1976 of punk rock) and more to do with the vivid power of the cinematic art form. *Woodstock* and *Monterey Pop* are defined as documentary records of these festivals but are rendered according to a particular form of documentary film: Direct Cinema. D. A. Pennebaker, the director of *Monterey Pop*, was in fact, along with Robert Drew, one of the pioneers of this form of raw and intuitive form of cinema. The pioneering film-makers of direct cinema believed in the 'spontaneous, uncontrolled and cinematic recording of important events, issues and personalities' (Barsam 1992, 305) and combined the traditional documentary film with journalism to create this exciting new form. The direct cinema mode is characterized aesthetically by 'indirect address, the use of long takes and synchronous sound ... spatiotemporal continuity rather than montage' all designed to evoke a strong feeling of being in the 'present tense' (Renov 2004, 174). The most striking elements of these pop festival films were developed in earlier documentary films such as *Primary* (1960), *Salesman* (1969) and Pennebaker's *Don't Look Back* (1967), a record of Bob Dylan's 1965 UK tour. The aesthetics were defined by new lightweight film cameras and portable sound equipment and a desire to represent 'reality', with as little manipulation as was possible. The point of Direct Cinema, to capture the moment via a handheld camera aesthetic, was developed in such films and, even when matched with devices such as triple-screen effects, produced a definitely rewarding experience ('even when it's boring ... it's not boring', Mark Sinker said of *Woodstock*; 1994, 55). Another reason that this form of cinema has continued to resonate is that it draws on literary models in combining documentary realism with a strong sense of drama (Truman Capote's infamous *In Cold Blood*, an evocative retelling of a set of gruesome and senseless murders in Kansas in 1959, is a good example of the kinds of texts the Direct Cinema producers were trying to emulate). Also critical is a continuation of the 'cinematic' techniques developed by Stern in *Jazz on a Summer's Day,* such as extensive use of split-screen, freeze-frame and extreme long-shot focus. Like Antonioni's influential *Blow Up* (1966), all these films make protracted use of running frames so slowly that they become still images. In particular, the authenticity of the direct nature of the documentary festival films seemed to stand in opposition to the existing manufactured films of the rock 'n' roll and pop era (Cliff Richard's films or The Beatles's 1964 film *A Hard Day's Night,* for example). Woodstock, and its ilk, were then a 'product of the mass media' (Loss 1998, 134).

It is useful to remember when discussing pop festival films that they are audio-visual art forms. While it is tempting to dwell on the visual dimension of the films we must acknowledge the importance of 'cinema sound' to the overall effect. After all, these films are about music as much as visual aesthetics and cultural politics. It is clear that successful festival films have not let the images 'get in the way' of the music but have instead offered a *symbiosis* of sound and image. Think of the astonishing early footage of Richie Havens in *Woodstock* where the driving beat of his percussive guitar and the accompanying conga drums is accentuated with extreme almost abstract close-up shots of this feet and hands. We can also detect a more or less *synaesthetic* experience in the sequence of Otis Redding, in *Monterey Pop*, particularly in his rendition of the song 'I've been loving you too long', where at one point the coloured stage lighting floods the camera (which is shooting *into* the light), overpowering the figure of Redding, who is glimpsed in silhouette (see Figure 15). At this moment we lose the image of the star singer, but the music and sound is arguably enhanced by the abstraction and fragmentation of the image. In the same film there is the spectacle of Hendrix playing 'Wild thing', one of his most famous songs. Cohen describes this performance as 'carnivalesque' (2012, 40) and its power derives from the coming together of visually striking images and, in sound terms, a disturbing wall of noise.

The sacramental nature of the pop festival was indicated in *Glastonbury Fayre*, the film of the 1971 free festival at Glastonbury. In this film it is not only the music of the stage performers that is foregrounded but also that of the crowd. The participation of the audience in the festival film is again critical. A memorable sequence of the film seeks to reinforce the mystical nature of the communion between music and some kind of higher or other power, unsurprisingly given that the choice of festival location in the first

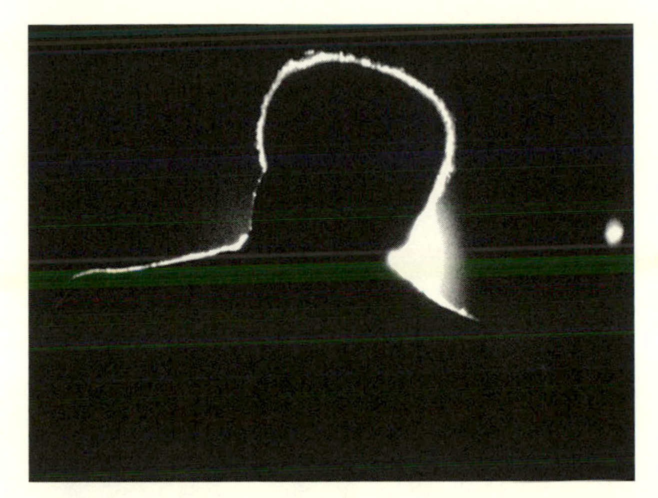

**FIGURE 15** *Otis Redding in* Monterey Pop*: 'we lose the image of the star but the music is enhanced'.*

place was concerned with 'tapp[ing] into the emerging zeitgeist of Aquarian and later New Age ideals' (McKay 2000, 59). This is the performance of Arthur Brown's Kingdom Come which has placed a series of burning crosses at the front of the stage, and the set begins with explosions of fireworks. The footage of Brown in action is preceded by images of a group of festival-goers climbing Glastonbury Tor to St Michael's tower in search of a good position to watch the sunrise. Suddenly, we see a shot of the moon, wreathed in clouds. Then cut in is a brief interview with Bill Harkin, the designer of the famous Pyramid stage. 'I could see the audience dematerialise in front of me', he observes (see Figure 16). Any sense of temporal continuity here is abandoned (Arthur Brown's performance is clearly unfolding at night) in favour of a recreation of a sacred musical happening.

What these moments in countercultural films like *Monterey Pop* and *Glastonbury Fayre* seek to attain is an element of the transcendental (see Goodall 2013), the audience moving beyond simply observing the festival unfold but becoming immersed in the revolutionary or spiritual nature of the epoch, through the audio-visual experience. The *vérité* nature of the countercultural pop festival film and Direct Cinema is revelatory. The fragmentary shots (e.g. the reduction of the image to single, crawling freeze-frames) are not the spectacular images expected of today's mediated festival experience (which seem to confirm what Peterson predicted in 1973 as a trend to 'gigantism') (Peterson, 1973, 102). They are removed from the curse of the director's cut, or from something like the gimmicky facility for DVD viewers to be able to re-mix the festival film to suit their own tastes offered in Julien Temple's 2006 documentary about Glastonbury (Temple 2006). The music as delivered in festival films may lack any clear narrative or any sense of the 'motives' (Cohen 2012, 10) of the characters involved (and in

**FIGURE 16** *Bill Harkin building the Pyramid stage for the 1971 Glastonbury Fayre.*

any case Direct Cinema founder Robert Drew once claimed that 'narration is what you do when you fail': Drew 1996, 273). Instead, these festival films ultimately leave a strong impression because of the 'transformative power of the cinematic vision' (Rust 2011, 51).

Gordon (1970) argues there were two tendencies in the 1960s American festivals, which we can see reflected in the media reportage of these events. The first is the revival of the May or spring festivals where renewed fertility of nature is celebrated. Gordon relates this particularly to *Woodstock*, with its 'back to the garden' sensibility (as Crosby, Stills, Nash and Young sang of in their version of Joni Mitchell's 'Woodstock'), a 'return to the pastoral' (Gordon 1970, 44), and we can also see it re-enacted in near-contemporaneous films such as *Glastonbury Fayre*. The second tendency is the simulation of the Lord of Misrule where sacrilegious rites are performed in order to disrupt the social order and to mock authority. Such drives are a 'sanctioned release for anarchic and satanic impulses' (Gordon 1970, 32). We can trace the change that took place, in part, by comparing the appearances by Jimi Hendrix in *Monterey Pop* (where his notorious 'spectacular' performance incorporated simulated sexual intercourse with his guitar and employed pyrotechnics – setting his guitar on fire – and destruction – the smashing of his guitar) with that in *Woodstock*, where a flat, low-key, mournful set (featuring his improvised rendition of 'The star-spangled banner') is captured by Wadleigh himself in a single, four-minute abstract take. It is tempting to deduce from this that the end of the film *Woodstock* captured the end of the 1960s dream. Yet, for Gordon, writing in 1970 and touched by the lament of the moment, the decade anyway 'was coming to a close' becoming a 'paradise lost' (Gordon 1970, 70).

The most obvious cinematic example of this second tendency is *Gimme Shelter* (1970), a film by Albert and David Maysles and Charlotte Zwerin, chronicling the last weeks of The Rolling Stones' 1969 US tour which culminated in the disastrous free concert given by the group in northern California. At this event, officially titled The Altamont Speedway Free Festival, Hell's Angels were invited to act as the security, and a festival-goer was murdered in front of the stage as the band played. Grainy footage captured the death on film. Whereas the Aquarian Age of the Woodstock generation appears to have been captured by the film camera in the way it focuses on the ideology of free love and peace, with frequent interviews with the crowd and organizers (as Tim Lucas notes, the real stars of Woodstock are the audience: 'at least they're searching': 2009, 88), *Gimme Shelter* focuses on the business of The Rolling Stones and the ultimate tragedy of a rock group playing with satanic impulses in order to shock and to sell records and merchandise (what Stephen Mamber calls 'the continuing exploitation ... of *cinema vérité* for the purpose of making publicity films about rock stars': 1973, 15). The form of Direct Cinema, unmediated and raw, ideally rendered the disturbing aspects unfolding at Altamont and projected the dark side of the 1960s. In this way a simple documentary film was able to conjure up the spirit of the end of the 1960s dream, an atmosphere described by Joan Didion as typified by a 'demented and seductive vortical tension' (Didion 2009, 41–2).

Powerful media representations of festivals combine the aesthetics of new technologies with another critical element: the role of (spectacular) performance. Performance here of course refers to the performance of bands on stage (as captured by the camera), but also to the performative nature of film itself – something Direct Cinema directors thrived on. A well-known example of this occurs in the opening of *Gimme Shelter* where Rolling Stones drummer Charlie Watts is filmed sitting at the Steenbeck edit machine listening to the audio of the chaos of the Altamont concert (see Figure 17). Later in the film Mick Jagger is also shown viewing the footage, notably the sequence capturing the murder of Meredith Hunter. Rust focuses on the way in which direct cinema techniques (especially the freeze-frame and slow motion) in this film reflect back to the audience the 'artificiality' of the film process thus combining, paradoxically, 'spontaneity' (a live event) with 'contingency' (the reconstruction of that event in the studio) (Rust 2011, 49). As Taylor argues, 'film-makers and audiences alike have a contiguous relationship with the space that is represented on screen, and an existential bond with the social actors who exist in the same world as they do' (Taylor 2011, 47). Frith discussed the live performance aspect of festivals as an 'abstract ideal'. We can ask though how this plays out with the older films? In *Jazz on a Summer's Day* and *Woodstock*, for example, the performative dimension to the films is of course mediated and constructed in the edit suite, and abstract. Yet this is often of most thrilling dimensions of the film experience. The effect of 'being there' cannot be

**FIGURE 17** Gimme Shelter. *Charlie Watts listens.*

fully re-created despite recent attempts (see below); it is audio-visual spectacle that is key, and therefore this complex relationship between the original performers, film directors and audiences (both for the festival and the media representation) is of critical importance in making the festival film successful as a work of art.

Some critics, for example, Kael (1970) and Peterson (1973), have argued that the tone and mood of *Gimme Shelter* was shaped by the film crew and The Rolling Stones colluding together. At Altamont, The Rolling Stones allegedly waited until it was dark to create a dramatic and dangerous mood so that the film crew could get good lighting, 'bright colours and deep shadows' (Peterson 1973, 109). Thus the media spectacle of the film *Gimme Shelter* had a key role in creating the horror. Peterson claims that 'the confrontation scene at Altamont was created and fed at each stage by the pressure to produce a film in spite of everything'. Amos Vogel, writing in general about death on screen, paid particular attention to the frames of *Gimme Shelter*: 'It is your unconscious perception of the gap between actuality and invention that gives the accidentally filmed knife murder of the black spectator in … *Gimme Shelter* such tremendous power.' We, audience of spectators and would-be festival-goers, are 'caught in the sweet and deadly trap of the voyeur' (Vogel 1974, 263).

Ultimately, the claims of the countercultural festival film are exaggerated. Peter Buckley argues that 'pop festivals may be the dinosaurs of the Age of Aquarius, and they may have eaten or drugged themselves into extinction, but Altamont was not the be-all and end-all of the youth culture' (Buckley 1971, 37). Other writers have argued that false mediated representations festivals destroyed their power. Festivals were 'rapidly overexposed … perhaps killed by overexposure' (Gordon 1970, 44).

## The contemporary mediated festival

While it is arguable that festival media (in the form of the subsequent films and records of live performances) have always been about making money – whether as a further profit stream or as a late effort to cover losses – the grandest of the modern festivals have become about expansion of economies of scale across the board, on the basis of the crowd size (even in 2007 the audience at Glastonbury Festival numbered 175,000). Simon Frith defines the modern festival as 'a key asset in the portfolios of the international corporations now dominating concert promotion' (Frith 2007, 4). Exclusive media deals and extensive television coverage helps this, as does the recent popularization of cinema screenings of live performances.

The editing of films like *Woodstock* (by Thelma Schoonmaker and Martin Scorsese) and *Monterey Pop* did not aim simply record the events but, according to Tim Lucas, even sought to explore 'the consciousness of its audience and times' (Lucas 2009, 88). But while some aspects of the 'classic' festival film endure (the presentation of the crowd as the star and the spectacle of the stage), the contemporary festival film differs in important ways from the earlier examples. In place of the impressionism of *Jazz on a Summer's Day*, and the abstraction of *Woodstock* and *Monterey Pop*, the pace of cuts in modern films is now dictated by the editorial practice developed from the music video from the 1980s on and reveals, if you like, the MTV aesthetic. Further, while this partly reflects changes in musical forms (the long improvisations common in jazz and the experimental fugues of psychedelic rock encouraging a more languid and reflective series of editing choices in the earlier films), it is also dictated by production shifts in television and the internet (now the primary media for the consumption of the festival film). At the same time, critics have argued that the post-cinematic mediation of the pop festival has not improved on the so-called artificiality of film. Keith Negus, for example, writes of the way in which performers, musicians and composers saw television as a 'natural lens, rather than a transformative medium that can redefine, or develop, innovative types of musical performance' (Negus 2006, 314).

That said, consumers of the festival film still want to get lost in music. The modern jazz audiences in *Jazz on a Summer's Day*, and the rock and folk fans in *Woodstock,* find their echo in the modern rave film, where still the intent is to allow the audio-visual experience to return them to, or immerse them in, the total festival experience. But I wonder whether documentaries about new festivals are effectively extended promotion and marketing tools. The claim for an Electronic Dance Music (EDM) film such as *Under the Electric Sky* (Cutforth and Lipsitz 2014) is that 'the fans are the headliners', while in the similar *Electric Daisy Carnival Experience* (2011) parallels are articulated with earlier festivals: the event 'was really mystical', says one attendee onscreen; for another it was 'a *Woodstock* moment ... something changed' (Kerslake 2011). Yet serious critical reception of EDM festival films has been muted. Even the special 3D presentation of *Under the Electric Sky*, like the 'vapid' (Harvey 2014) music it extolled, was seemingly bereft of any genuine countercultural depth. According to the *Variety* review following its screening at Sundance Film Festival in 2014, the film

> provides lots of sexy, neon-hued eye-candy but not many images of deeper resonance. Bookended by flat sequences (before and after the festival), the 3D format surprisingly isn't exploited all that effectively in Reed Smoot's otherwise accomplished lensing. Other tech/design contributions are top-shelf, and of course the sound mix is ace. Still, if ever a movie begged for revival of butt-rumbling 1970s theater gimmick Sensurround, it's *Under the Electric Sky* with its incessant audio orgasms of thumping bass. (Harvey 2014)

The DJ, even a superstar DJ, is visually less interesting on film than the pop or rock performer who, with their dynamic movement and freedom to roam the performance space, always 'brings the body back into the line of sight' (Cohen 2012, 21).

The festival films discussed above illustrate the complexities of the representations being formed both in the production of these films and in the reception of the films, upon immediate release, and with hindsight many years later. Gina Arnold has argued that there is a 'paradox' at the core of films like *Woodstock* and *Gimme Shelter* and that such films want to be a conventional documentary about the workings of rock music, and at the same time a rejection of traditional aesthetic, political and social values (Arnold 2014, 134). She argues that our understanding of these countercultures is 'entirely imaginary' (Arnold 2014, 136) and it is clear that these filmic representations play a part in that myth-making fantasy. Films such as *Woodstock* and *Gimme Shelter* offer the viewer a 'reshaped idea of the commodity as something not necessarily material ... an aura, a feeling' (Arnold 2014, 137). Perhaps that is their appeal? However, I wish to conclude that despite the potential faults of these festival films, they still inspire a sense for the viewer of the potential revolutionary aspects of rock festivals, rock music and the media representations of this explosive combination. It is wrong to simply argue, as Frith has done (1981, 164), that the music is not an important part of the rock festival; that the sociology of the festival is its sole purpose. Live music was the reason audiences flocked to festivals in the past and why audiences continue to flock to festivals today. It is the effectiveness of truly creative music, the sound and the affect, that ultimately inspires successful documentary films, films that people continue, in the twenty-first century, to want to watch.

## Notes

1 Intriguingly, in the context of an argument that festival is mediated and re-represented via the film of the event, there are other examples of the festival film *getting it wrong*, or *mis*representing the event. This was a criticism of Murray Lerner's 1967 film *Festival!,* when David Pirie accused the film-makers of 'complete indifference' to Bob Dylan's infamous electric performance (Pirie 1971, 141).

## References

Arnold, Gina. 2014. 'Nobody's army.' In Sheila Whiteley, and Jediah Sklower, eds. *Countercultures and Popular Music*. Farnham: Ashgate, 123–40.

Barsam, Richard M. 1992. *Non-fiction Film: A Critical History*. Bloomington: Indiana University Press.

Bolter, Jay David, and Richard Grusin. 2000. *Remediation: Understanding New Media*. Cambridge, MA: MIT Press.

Braunstein, Peter, and Doyle, Michael William, eds. 2002. *Imagine Nation: The American Counterculture of the 1960s and '1970s*. New York: Routledge.

Buckley, Peter. 1971. 'Why are we fighting? A closer look at *Gimme Shelter*'. *Films and Filming* 17(11): 33–7.

Burdon, Eric, and The Animals. 1967. 'Monterey.' Available on *The Very Best of The Animals*. 1998. Spectrum Audio. CD.

Cohen, Thomas F. 2012. *Playing To The Camera: Musicians and Musical Performance in Documentary Cinema*. London: Wallflower Press.

Cutforth, Dan, and Lipsitz, Jane. 2014. *Under the Electric Sky*. DVD. Directed by Dan Cutforth and Jane Lipsitz. Universal.

Didion, Joan. 2009. *The White Album*. New York: Farrar, Strauss and Giroux.

Drew, Robert. 1996. 'Narration can be a killer.' In Kevin Macdonald, and Mark Cousins, eds. *Imagining Reality: The Faber Book of Documentary*. London: Faber and Faber, 271–3.

Eisen, Jonathan. ed. 1970. *Altamont: Death of Innocence in the Woodstock Generation*. New York: Avon Books.

Edgar, Robert, Kirsty Fairclough-Isaacs and Ben Halligan, eds. 2013. *The Music Documentary: Acid Rock to Electropop*. London: Routledge.

Frith, Simon. 1981. 'The magic that can set you free': the ideology of folk and the myth of rock.' *Popular Music* 1: 159–68.

Frith, Simon. 2007. 'Live music matters.' *Scottish Music Review* 1(1): 1–17.

Goodall, Mark. 2013. *Gathering of the Tribe: Music and Heavy Conscious Creation*. London: Headpress.

Gordon, Andy. 1970. 'Satan and the angels: Paradise loused.' In Jonathan Eisen, ed. *Altamont*. New York: Avon Books, 30–71.

Harvey, Dennis. 2014. 'Sundance Film Festival review: *Under the Electric Sky*.' *Variety* (22 January). http://variety.com/2014/film/reviews/sundance-film-review-under-the-electric-sky-2-1201066543/. Accessed 7 July 2014.

Hewitt, Tom, and Chris Hewitt. 2007. *The Bickershaw Festival*. DVD. Directed by Tom and Chris Hewitt. Ozit.
Hoffman, Abbie. 1969. *Woodstock Nation*. New York: Vintage.
Kael, Pauline. 1970. 'The current cinema: beyond Pirandello.' *New Yorker* (19 December): 112.
Kerslake, Kevin. 2011. *Electric Daisy Carnival Experience*. DVD. Directed by Kevin Kerslake. Manifest.
Kurtz, Alan. 2010. 'The Dozens: *Jazz On A Summer's Day*.' Jazz.com. http://www.jazz.com/dozens/the-dozens-jazz-on-a-summers-day. Accessed 3 July 2014.
Loss, Archie. 1998. *Pop Dreams: Music, Movies, and the Media in the American 1960s*. Belmont: Wadsworth.
Lucas, Tim. 2009. 'Back to the garden.' *Sight and Sound* 19(9): 88.
*Magic Bus* website. http://magicbussf.com/january-14-1967-the-human-be-in-aka-gathering-of-the-tribes-golden-gate-park/. Accessed 4 October 2014.
Mamber, Stephen. 1973. 'Cinéma vérité and social concerns.' *Film Comment* 9(6): 9–15.
McKay, George. 2000. *Glastonbury: A Very English Fair*. London: Gollancz.
Negus, Keith. 2006. 'Musicians on television: visible, audible and ignored.' *Journal of the Royal Musical Association* 131(2): 310–30.
Pennebaker, D. A. 2006. Interview with Lou Adler. *Monterey Pop*. DVD, Directed by D. A. Pennebaker, 1968. Criterion, 2006.
Peterson, Richard A. 1973. 'The unnatural history of rock festivals: an instance of media facilitation.' *Popular Music and Society* 2(2): 97–123.
Pirie, David. 1971. '*Festival!*' (review). *Monthly Film Bulletin* 38(450): 41.
Renov, Michael. 2004. *The Subject of Documentary*. Minneapolis: University of Minnesota Press.
Roeg, Nicholas and Neal, Peter. 1972. *Glastonbury Fayre*. DVD. Directed by Nicholas Roeg and Peter Neal. 2009, Odeon.
Rust, Amy. 2011. 'Hitting the "vérité jackpot": the ecstatic profits of freeze-framed violence.' *Cinema Journal* 50(5): 48–72.
Sinker, Mark. 1994. '*Woodstock: 3 Days of Peace and Music: the Director's Cut*' (review). *Sight and Sound* (September), 4(9): 55.
Spitz, Robert Stephen. 1979. *Barefoot in Babylon: The Creation of the Woodstock Music Festival, 1969*. New York: Viking Press.
Stern, Bert. 2001. (Director's Commentary). *Jazz on a Summer's Day*. DVD. Directed by Bert Stern, 1959. Charly.
Taylor, Aaron. 2011. 'Angels, Stones, Hunters: murder, celebrity and direct cinema.' *Studies in Documentary Film* 5(1): 45–60.
Temple, Julien. 2006. *Glastonbury*. DVD. Directed by Julien Temple. 20th Century Fox.
Vogel, Amos. 1974. *Film as a Subversive Art*. New York: Random House.
Wadleigh, Michael. 1970. *Woodstock*. DVD. Directed by Michael Wadleigh. Warner.
Warner, Simon. 2004. 'Reporting Woodstock: some contemporary press reflections on the festival.' In Andy Bennett, ed. *Remembering Woodstock*. Aldershot: Ashgate, 55–74.
Wright, Julie Lobalzo. 2013. 'The Good and Bad and the Ugly 60s: the Opposing Gazes of *Woodstock* and *Gimme Shelter*.' In Edgar, Robert, Fairclough-Isaacs, Kirsty and Halligan, Benjamin, eds. *The Music Documentary: Acid Rock to Electropop*. London: Routledge, 71–86.

# CHAPTER THREE

# 'Let there be rock!' Myth and ideology in the rock festivals of the transatlantic counterculture

*Nicholas Gebhardt*

> *I want you all to know that right now, you are witnessing my dream! I want to thank you from the bottom of my heart for having me and my band tonight. I always wanted to be a rock star, and tonight, we are all rock stars. I want you to forget about your worries, forget about your troubles. I want you to get lost in this music tonight. I want to make beautiful memories and be free tonight.*
>
> BEYONCÉ KNOWLES (LIVE ON BBC GLASTONBURY, 2011)

From her riff on the Arabic mode in the opening bars of her 2003 hit song, 'Crazy in love', to her demand that the audience lose themselves in her music, Knowles's performance on the famous Pyramid stage at the 2011 Glastonbury Festival refigured the meaning of rock 'n' roll for a contemporary global audience, while relying on its most powerful and enduring myths in order to legitimize her appearance as the first female headline act in over twenty-five years of the festival.[1] In this chapter, I want to explore the ideological significance of these myths in the context of the most influential and iconic rock festivals of the late 1960s and early 1970s. In the United States, these were the Monterey Pop Festival in 1967, the Woodstock Music and Art Fair in 1969 and the Altamont Free Concert in 1969; while in the United Kingdom, the key events were Isle of Wight Festival in 1968–70 (Figure 18) and Glastonbury Fair in 1971.[2] I want to focus primarily on the position that these festivals have within the broader narrative of rock history, and, in particular, on the countercultural claims that were (and continue to be) made about them (McKay 2000).

How did these festivals contribute to the widespread belief in rock music as a genre that was based on a permanent cycle of youth rebellion? In what ways did these events involve participants in new ideas about collective consciousness and cultural practice? And to what extent was the music – its forms, lyrical contents and sonic properties – essential to the claims that were made about these events? These questions highlight the problem of explaining the historical significance of rock festivals and especially their relevance to issues of cultural continuity and change in popular culture (Ethen 2014; Grossberg 1983–84; Schowalter 2000). If we treat the great countercultural rock festivals of the late 1960s and early 1970s as responses to a more general collective crisis in modern, Western bourgeois societies, especially the United States, Canada, Australia and many European nations, then one surprising fact about them is that they appear to be as relevant to as many people today as they were for an earlier generation of hippies, dropouts, protestors, cultural radicals, anti-war protestors and student activists (Bindas and Houston 1989). This invariably raises a further critical question: Has the meaning of rock festivals changed since the 1960s?

One of the first attempts to explore these issues was a 1973 essay by sociologist Richard Peterson, in which he tracks the 'unnatural' (early) history of rock festivals in the United States and compares them to other

**FIGURE 18** *Isle of Wight Festival, 1970.*

large-scale collective movements such as the race riots and the resurgence of the Ku Klux Klan in the 1920s, the labour strikes in the 1940s and the ghetto riots and student uprisings of the 1960s. He argues that the central premise in each of these events was that they promised or threatened to alter society in some fundamental way, and as such, their 'energy' was derived from, and was responding to, much larger and more complex changes taking place in American culture (Peterson 1973, 97). Moreover, in Peterson's view, the period in which rock festivals made a significant cultural impact was relatively brief, lasting only from 1967 to 1971. He claims that subsequent festivals lacked the potential to challenge society, to speak to and for the social demands of a universal audience of young people. Instead, as their organizers came up against a worldwide coalition of city officials, moral leaders, legal experts, corporate executives, community groups and politicians, the movement fragmented around particular musical genres and became focused primarily on celebrating the values and practices of specific sub-cultures or returning to older values and practices (Peterson 1973, 117).[3]

Why does Peterson make such a claim? Arguing for a broadly structural approach to understanding the emergence of rock festivals, he suggests that the social conditions that made it possible to successfully organize a 'high-energy cultural revolution celebration' were quickly closed off by those individuals and social groups opposed to countercultural events (1973, 117). As with race riots or union strikes, Peterson claims that the festival movement raised some fundamental questions about the basic tenets of liberal-capitalist societies such as the United States or Germany or Great Britain, particularly around issues of reason and passion, art and life, individualism and social hierarchy, and ownership and property. Festivals were thus identified with much larger, and increasingly complicated, social conflicts in these societies, in which people's core beliefs about the forms of human social and political organization were undergoing intensive, and in many instances collective, revision. My interest in such contemporary accounts as Peterson's is meant to highlight the extent to which our understanding of rock festivals is inseparable from what we take those conflicts to be about.

At the beginning of Chris Hegadus and D. A. Pennebaker's film, *Monterey Pop*, the film-makers interview a young woman waiting to enter the stadium. When they ask her what she thinks it's going to be like, she replies, 'I think it's gonna be like Easter and Christmas and New Year's and your birthday all together, you know, hearing all the different bands, you know. Like I've heard a lot of them. ... All at the same time, it's just going to be too much. I mean the vibrations are just going to be flowing everywhere' (Hegadus and Pennebaker 2002). This idea of 'vibrations ... flowing everywhere' is a central theme in what Peter Wicke describes as the ideology of rock. 'One of the myths about rock music', he writes, 'is that it arises spontaneously out of the common experience of musicians and fans' (Wicke 1990, 91). For Wicke, the ideology of rock depends above all on a set of claims about the individuality of the artist's sound, the immediacy of the musical experience and the highly personalized relationship between artist and audience (1990, 94–5). Although it was created within an organized system of musical production, and so dependent on the collective enterprise of promoters, producers, agents, bankers, lawyers, accountants, technicians, designers, suppliers, sales persons and others, in order to reach a global audience, rock was consistently defined as an authentic and, perhaps even more paradoxically, an unmediated expression of the individuality and personality of the performer (Wicke 1990, 99). This is evident in the following comment by the critic and producer, Jon Landau: '[w]ithin the confines of the media, these musicians articulated attitudes, styles and feelings that were genuine reflections of their own experience and of the social situation which had helped to produce that situation' (Landau 1972, 130).

Such views relied on mobilizing some long-standing myths about the music as both a return to a more authentic mode of cultural expression and a radical break with existing traditions and values. According to Bernard Gendron, these myths involve two major founding claims: first, rock introduced real sexuality and the authentic blackness of rhythm and blues into mainstream popular music in the 1950s; secondly, it revealed to its young audience the superficiality of the songs produced on Tin Pan Alley, and more importantly, the inherent conservatism of the culture that had produced them (2004, 298). To demonstrate the effect these myths have on our understanding of the music, Gendron focuses on the recordings and performances of Jerry Lee Lewis, whose demonic stage persona and evocation of uncontrollable sexual desire remain prime examples for rock critics and historians of the music's transformative powers and its profound radicalism. He cites a passage from Robert Palmer's biography of the singer as an example of what he means by this. 'Jerry Lee Lewis and his allies are the real revolutionaries', writes Palmer. 'Rocking out, really rocking out the way Jerry Lee Lewis did in "Whole lotta shakin' goin' on" ... is the most profoundly revolutionary statement an artist can make in the rock and roll idiom' (Palmer, quoted in Gendron 2004, 298). For Gendron, the widespread tendency to conceive of rock solely in terms of its revolutionary potential for social change obscures, rather than clarifies, the important continuities it had with the songs produced by composers such as George Gershwin or Cole Porter, as well as other equally significant popular music genres and the cultural practices and values associated with them. Moreover, the tendency in many accounts of rock is to reduce a complex story of musical change to a simple narrative of revolt.

The point of summarizing Gendron's discussion here is to highlight the extent to which these myths have formed the basis for most historical and theoretical studies of rock, as well as the presuppositions of popular music journalism and critical commentary about rock culture (see Durant 1985, 97–8). From Bill Haley's cover of 'Rock around the clock' to the mobilizing of the Woodstock Nation, to the current resurgence of new, and the revitalization of existing, rock festivals around the world, attempts to explain the music's meaning focus, for the most part, on its authentic modes of expression and appeal, above all, to a specific kind of collective identity derived from a shared passion for the music. As Greil Marcus suggests: 'We fight our way through the massed and levelled collective taste of the Top forty, just looking for a little something we can call our own. But when we find it and jam the radio to hear it again it isn't ours – it is a link to thousands of others who are sharing it with us. As a matter of a single song this might mean very little; as culture, as a way of life, you can't beat it' (Marcus 1977, 115).

There are two important points to make here about Marcus's claims. First, when understood against the background of wider cultural conflicts of the 1960s, his identification of rock with 'a way of life' connects the emergence of the music with the development among its audience of something like a collective consciousness. There is no clear consensus about what this consciousness consisted of, but in most accounts it involves a radical break with the past, producing a (kind of) coherent and politically meaningful vision of the world that appeared in dramatic contrast to the dominant values of the 1950s. Some saw this new collective consciousness negatively; for Daniel Bell, in his influential study of post-industrial societies, '[b]y the end of the 1960s, the new sensibility had been given a name (the counter-culture) and an ideology to go with it. The main tendency of this ideology – though it appeared in the guise of an attack on the "technocratic society" – was an attack on reason itself' (1976, 143). Members of the counterculture thus turned to rock as their primary means of expression precisely because it appeared to speak directly to (and through) them and to give an aesthetic form to this broader, in Bell's view, 'anti-rational' vision of the world. An alternative account of this new consciousness forms the basis for Theodore Roszak's 1968 path-breaking study of the counterculture. 'We have no serviceable language in our culture', he claims, 'to talk about the level of the personality at which this underlying vision of reality resides. But it seems indisputable that it exerts its influence at a point that lies deeper than our intellectual consciousness. ... When I say that the counter culture delves into the non-intellective aspects of the personality, it is with respect to its interest at this level – at the level of vision – that I believe its project is significant' (Roszak 1968, 80–1). In both cases, rock music appears to relate in some fundamental ways to deeper issues of personal commitment and the structures of belief in modern societies.

Second, the distinction Marcus makes between music 'we can call our own' and 'the massed and levelled collective taste of the Top 40' is a recurrent theme in rock criticism and forms the basis for one of the central claims of rock ideology. As Gendron explains in another essay exploring the critical reception of rock, the music's 'appearance at a particular juncture of class, generational, and cultural struggle has given it a preeminent role among mass cultural artifacts as an instrument of opposition and liberation'

(Gendron 1986, 19). According to Gendron, most critics adhere to the *auteur* theory of rock, which places a great premium on the agency of the artists who produce it and the youth audiences who consume it, in order to make a series of claims about the rock's authenticity (1986, 34). What is missing from such accounts is any reference to the complex series of mediations that make it possible for rock musicians to reach their vast global audiences. As long as we think of rock as primarily about the music and its fans, it is difficult to conceptualize the convoluted system that contributes to the creation of meaning in rock (Gendron 1986, 34). What all this suggests is that the countercultural festivals were critical to the process by which the ideology of rock became an essential element to the wider social conflicts of the 1960s and thus were integral to consolidating the primacy of rock (and its various sub-genres, such as metal, punk, grunge, 'indie' and so on) as *the* dominant form of countercultural (and so oppositional) music for a worldwide audience of young people (Grossberg 1983–84).

As noted above, rock's ideological appeal was based on the claim that the music had emerged spontaneously from the everyday experiences of performers and audiences, and that it was primarily a medium of expression for disaffected young people (Bennett 2001, 7–23; Wicke 1990). Moreover, the particular social space opened up by these countercultural festivals both intensified, and then fundamentally reconfigured, the music's meaning within a broader set of themes relating to freedom, escape, passion, revitalization and renewal (Curtis 1987, 221–34). If we are to understand how this happened, then we have to recognize the extent to which these events were also connected to, and in many ways, continuous with, other post-Second World War social and artistic movements that celebrated spontaneous happenings, sit-ins, improvisation and performance art, as a means to achieving new and more holistic forms of individual and collective consciousness. The way in which the series of countercultural festivals unfolded across the United States, Britain and Europe was thus connected to a more general questioning of the consequences of modernity and modernization that was evident in the art, poetry, literature, art music and theatre of the period, from Pop Art to Minimalism (Pippin 1999, 160–79).

What I want to focus on for the remainder of this chapter is the process by which rock and its festivals became identified as the primary expressive medium of countercultural expression, and highlight some of ways in which critics made sense of that process. As Peterson makes clear, the first event to explicitly incorporate rock into a broader statement of countercultural consciousness was held in June 1967, on Mt. Tamalpais, outside of San Francisco. The Fantasy Fair and Magic Mountain Music Festival (Figure 19) was organized by local music fans; it featured arts and crafts, and most of the people involved donated their services. The bands appearing were Jefferson Airplane, The Doors, The Byrds, Country Joe, Dionne Warwick and Smokey Robinson, all of whom performed for nominal fees and became key figures in the bigger festival movement. Tickets were $2, and any profits

**FIGURE 19** *Last-minute stage construction at the Fantasy Fair and Magic Mountain Festival, California, June 1967.*

were donated to an African American ghetto charity. More importantly, however, the audience for this event was primarily made up of hippies, beats and other countercultural groups from the San Francisco Bay area. As Peterson also notes, however, the event was promoted in the San Francisco *Oracle*, an underground magazine, as an extension of the 1967 Human Be-In festival in Golden Gate Park in San Francisco (Peterson 1973: 120 n. 20), which aimed to unite the counterculture with the anti-war, civil rights and student movements through broad principles of 'love and activism' (Perry 1970, 55–60).

The belief that rock somehow embodied the essence of the counterculture, and that it was primarily a medium for imagining and expressing the alternative realities, began to take shape in the critical commentaries that surrounded these festivals, especially among journalists (Jones 2002, 19–40). As several key studies have noted, however, it was at the Monterey festival in the same year that the relationship between countercultural consciousness and rock music was most firmly established for a global audience, and largely as a result of the media coverage of the event (Bennett 2009, 474–89; Bennett 2004; Hill 2006, 28–40; Miller 1999). Lou Adler, who founded the event, understood how important this element was to the event's historic significance as a cultural happening. 'The media coverage was worldwide', Adler says, 'and that had never happened before. You can send out all the press releases you want, and if it's not in the media's psyche, then forget it. We had Derek Taylor, the Beatles's publicist, doing press, and we knew we had a lot of requests for media credentials, but it was still a shock, on the morning of the festival, to wake up and see all these TV crews from all over the world' (quoted in Arnold 2001, 14–20). The iconic images of major rock performers in Pennebaker's film of the event shifts our frame of reference dramatically, as well as redefining our understanding of what the festival was about. Although rock was not the sole genre featured, it was through the sounds and gestures of performers such as The Who, Janis Joplin, Jefferson Airplane, the Jimi Hendrix Experience and so on that the music became identified as the foremost medium for registering social dissent, expressing individual and social liberation and forging a new collective consciousness. Moreover, the media coverage of the festival ensured that rock achieved this new cultural significance on a global scale; and this, in turn, set a precedent for subsequent films and television coverage of countercultural festivals (Bennett 2004; Kitts 2009).

Once set in motion, however, rock's anti-establishment and liberationist ideology became the basis for its worldwide commercial success, and by 1970 the major rock festivals across the United States and throughout Britain and Europe had come to embody in many ways the most overt, and most collective, of those representations of the counterculture (Peterson 1973, 113). This extended from the sonic properties of the music to the assertion that rock was a music uniquely grounded in the individuality and independence of artists and audiences alike (Frith 1981). As Bill Graham, the promoter and owner of the Fillmore East and West rock venues, suggested in an interview in 1971, '[t]he young people used rock 'n' roll to say to the world, "We can be independent. This is our way of life. We're revolutionaries"' (quoted in Jones 1980, 135). A pamphlet produced by the Eagles Liberation Front, a group of high school students in Seattle, Washington, confirms just how prevalent this understanding of the music was during this period:

> Rock music began as an alternative community, our community. Rock expresses the ethos of our community, its force is filled by our struggle. But over the years the established entertainment industry – promoters, agents, record companies, media, and every name group – has gradually transformed our music into an increasingly expensive commodity. (quoted in Denisoff 1975, 354)

What stands out in this statement is the distinction the students draw between rock as an alternative community, produced by and for its participants, and rock as a commodity, owned and controlled by the industry, and therefore separated from its listeners by its increasingly unaffordable price tag. In Simon Frith's view, the major countercultural festivals had come to exemplify by the end of the 1960s this image of the rock community. They revealed the music's inherent contradictions, precisely because of the way in which festivals seemed to mediate the claims and values of the counterculture within the popular imagination (and the shared memories that structured that social imaginary), as well as appearing to resolve those same contradictions. 'Unlike the traditional pop package show', he argues, 'put together *for* the fans out there, the rock festival – in its length, its size, its setting, its reference to a folk tradition – was an attempt to provide materially the experience of community that the music expressed symbolically' (Frith 1984, 66). And it was out of this particular experience of directness, in which artist and audience were identified with each other, one acting as the mirror of the other through the unmediated medium of the music (exemplified most powerfully in Michael Wadleigh's film *Woodstock*: Wadleigh 1999), that this claim for the rock festival as an alternative social space took shape (Bennett 2004; Kitts 2009).

We see the same point being made repeatedly about each of the main countercultural festivals of the late 1960s and early 1970s, from Woodstock to the Isle of Wight. In his study of the popular recording industry, for example, Serge Denisoff argues that the 'importance of Woodstock in any examination of popular music cannot be overestimated since, as *Time* [magazine] correctly observed, "The spontaneous community of youth that was created at Bethel was the stuff of which legends are made; the substance of the event contains both revelation and a sobering lesson." Woodstock generated an ethos, a mythology, which lent support to the most ardent proponents of the dawning of a new community' (Denisoff 1975, 343). Likewise, Christopher Small describes the process by which, at the Isle of Wight Festival, there 'came into a least partial existence the potential society which lies otherwise beyond our grasp; young people released from the stresses and restrictions of their everyday life were engaging in the celebration of a common myth, a common life-style. ... [M]usic became the centre of a communal ritual' (Small 1977, 171). More recently, for Arthur Marwick, '[r]ock music (and the idolatry it inspired), nature, love, drugs, and mass togetherness – where they all joined hands was in the open-air music festival, the greatest of all the types of spectacle invented in the sixties' (1998, 497). According to such claims, rock festivals refigured the social spaces of social activism, collective consciousness and individual subjectivity, by calling on and reproducing within the structures and sound of the music itself – from new techniques of amplification to practices of distortion and overlay – the countercultural demand for a new transnational community of free individuals (Moore 2004, 80–3).

Such interpretations raise immediately the basic problems we encountered in Gendron's analysis of rock ideology in that they share in the notion that the most influential countercultural rock festivals – and especially those that have come to be seen as definitive – Monterey, Woodstock, Altamont, Isle of Wight, Glastonbury – reveal in one way or another something essential about the nature of rock music *as* counterculture, and that because of this history, those pivotal events have come to exemplify the emergence of a transatlantic (and in many respects, global) movement of young people defined by their anti-hierarchical, anti-establishment, dissatisfaction with an 'old consciousness' (as Charles Reich referred to it). Moreover, as mythic countercultural spaces, rock festivals continue to hold out the possibility of the emergence of a 'new consciousness' (Reich 1972, 241–48). Hence the frequent references to, and the widespread belief in, the potential for rock festivals to alter our experience of the world, however much we are aware of the commercial imperatives that make them possible in the first place and which invariably seem to compromise or distort their utopian claims. It is precisely this history of the rock festival as *the* expression of the counterculture which continues to open up a social space for a pop star like Beyoncé to speak of dreaming of becoming a rock star, but also for her to conceive of inviting her audience to do the same.

## Notes

1 According to the BBC press office, the television audience for Knowles's performance peaked at 2.6 million viewers: http://www.bbc.co.uk/pressoffice/pressreleases/stories/2011/06_june/30/glastonbury.shtml. Accessed 10 July 2014

2 It is also critical to recognize the influence of less iconic (but no less important) events, such as Die Internationalen Essener Songtage, which was held in 1968 in Essen, Germany, so as to further highlight the historic conjuncture in the late 1960s of rock music and the formation of a transnational counterculture that was identified with new forms of collective consciousness.

3 For example, in 1971, when the major countercultural rock festivals were in decline, there were seventy-nine bluegrass festivals held in the United States alone (Peterson, 117).

## References

Arnold, Gina. 2011. 'Perfect pop.' *Metro* (June 14–20).
www.metroactive.com/papers/metro/06.14.01/montereypop-0124.html. Accessed 1 August 2014.

BBC Glastonbury. 2011. http://www.bbc.co.uk/events/eg49mb/acts/a358q9#p00j280x. Accessed 1 June 2014.

Bell, Daniel. 1976. *The Cultural Contradictions of Capitalism*. London: Heinemann.

Bennett, Andy. 2009. '"Heritage rock:" rock music, representation and heritage discourse.' *Poetics* 37(5–6): 474–89.

Bennett, Andy. 2001. *Cultures of Popular Music*. Buckingham: Open University Press.

Bennett, Andy, ed. 2004. *Remembering Woodstock*. Aldershot: Ashgate.

Bindas, Kenneth, and Craig Houston. 1989. '"Takin' care of business": rock music, Vietnam, and the protest myth.' *Historian* 52: 1–23.

Curtis, Jim. 1987. *Rock Eras: Interpretations of Music and Society, 1954-1984*. Bowling Green: Bowling Green State University Popular Press.

Denisoff, Serge. 1975. *Solid Gold: The Popular Recordings Industry*. New Brunswick: Transaction Publishers.

Durant, Alan. 1985. 'Rock revolution or time-no-changes: visions of change and continuity in rock music.' *Popular Music* 5: 97–121.

Ethen, Michael. 2014. 'The festival is dead, long live the festival.' *Journal of Popular Music Studies* 26: 251–67.
Frith, Simon, 1981. '"The magic that can set you free": the ideology of folk and the myth of the rock community.' *Popular Music* 1: 159–68.
Frith, Simon. 1984. 'Rock and the politics of memory.' *Social Text* 9(10): 59–69.
Gendron, Bernard. 1986. 'Theodor Adorno meets the Cadillacs.' In Tania Modleski, ed. *Studies in Entertainment*. Bloomington: Indiana University Press, 18–36.
Gendron, Bernard. 2004. 'Rock and roll mythology: race and sex in "Whole lotta shakin' going on."' In Simon Frith, ed. *Popular Music: Critical Concepts in Media and Cultural Studies*, vol. 2. London: Routledge, 297–310.
Grossberg, Lawrence. 1983–84. 'The politics of youth culture: some observations on rock and roll in American culture.' *Social Text* 8: 104–26.
Hegadus, Chris, and D. A. Pennebaker. 2002. *Monterey Pop*. Criterion DVD.
Hill, Sarah. 2006. 'When deep soul met the love crowd. Otis Redding: Monterey Pop Festival, June 1967.' In Ian Inglis, ed. *Performance and Popular Music: History, Place and Time*. Aldershot: Ashgate, 28–40.
Jones, Landon Y. 1980. *Great Expectations: America and the Baby Boom Generation*. New York: Ballantine.
Jones, Steve, ed. 2002. *Pop Music and the Press*. Philadelphia: Temple University Press.
Kitts, Thomas M. 2009. 'Documenting, creating, and interpreting moments of definition: *Monterey Pop*, *Woodstock* and *Gimme Shelter*.' *Journal of Popular Culture* 42: 715–32.
Landau, Jon. 1972. *It's Too Late To Stop Now: A Rock 'n' Roll Journal*. San Francisco: Straight Arrow.
Marcus, Greil. 1977. *Mystery Train: Images of America in Rock 'n' Roll Music*. London: Omnibus.
Marwick, Arthur. 1998. *The Sixties: Cultural Revolution in Britain, France, Italy, and the United States, c. 1958-c.1974*. Oxford: Oxford University Press.
McKay, George. 2000. *Glastonbury: A Very English Fair*. London: Victor Gollanz.
Miller, James. 1999. *Flowers in the Dustbin: The Rise of Rock and Roll, 1947-1977*. New York: Simon & Schuster.
Moore, Allan F. 2004. 'The contradictory aesthetics of Woodstock.' In Andy Bennett, ed. *Remembering Woodstock*. Aldershot: Ashgate, 74–89.
Perry, Helen. 1970. *The Human Be-In*. London: Allen Lane.
Peterson, Richard A. 1973. 'The unnatural history of rock festivals: an instance of media facilitation.' *Popular Music and Society* 2: 97–123.
Pippin, Robert B. 1999. *Modernism as Philosophical Problem*. Oxford: Blackwell.
Reich, Charles. 1972. *The Greening of America*. Harmondsworth: Penguin.
Roszak, Theodore. 1968. *The Making of A Counterculture: Reflections on the Technocratic Society and Its Youthful Opposition*. Reprint 1995. Berkeley: University of California Press.
Schowalter, Daniel. 2000. 'Remembering the dangers of rock and roll: toward a historical narrative of the rock festival.' *Critical Studies in Media Communication* 17: 86–102.
Small, Christopher. 1977. *Music-Society-Education*. London: John Calder.
Wadleigh, Michael. dir. 1999 *Woodstock: The Director's Cut*. Warner DVD.
Wicke, Peter. 1990. *Rock Music: Culture, Aesthetics and Sociology*. Cambridge: Cambridge University Press.

# CHAPTER FOUR

# 'As real as real can get': Race, representation and rhetoric at Wattstax, 1972

*Gina Arnold*

One weekend in the middle of the last century, an outdoor concert for 25,000 people was held in a small Catskills community within an easy driving distance from Manhattan. The concert was sponsored by radical leftists and featured wildly popular artists, some of them African American, whose music drew on traditional American folk vernaculars. The concert caused some consternation among locals, who pledged to boycott its perceived commie sympathizing platform of artists and to drive off those who dared to attend.

No, it was not Woodstock, and nor did it end up as a giant love letter to the counterculture, although the foregoing description mirrors in almost every particular the rhetoric that preceded the events at Bethel in 1969. Moreover, in direct contrast with Woodstock, this concert – held in Peekskill, New York, in the September of 1949, 20 years previous to Woodstock – ended in a bloody riot with injury to over 50 people and enormous amounts of property damage. State police called in to quell the violence were seen to beat concert-goers as they left, and even local residents who condoned the concert were driven afterwards to sell up and leave the area (Balaji 2007, 275). Headliner Paul Robeson later called the concert a landmark event in the Cold War, and one, he added, that went 'to the root of the whole struggle for freedom of speech and freedom of assembly, but they especially concern the struggle of we Negro people' (quoted in Balaji 2007, 288.)

Robeson would no doubt have been surprised by the different reception given to Jimi Hendrix, headlining a far larger concert in the same locale 20 years later. Though by then the civil strife that was visibly transforming social values far outweighed the unrest that undergirded Cold War politics of the late 1940s, Hendrix, the highest-paid performer at Woodstock, was given license to strip 'The star spangled banner' of its dignity, shredding the very fabric of the song in a performance which was hailed by many as the sonic equivalent of the political *zeitgeist* (Gilroy, 1991); indeed, Greil Marcus recently called it 'the greatest and most unstable protest song there is' (2014, 226.) Few moments better illustrate the cultural shift that had occurred since Robeson's performance at Peekskill. And yet, the shift may not have been so much in the cultural values of people in the Catskills, who in 1969, according to a local inn owner and memoirist Elliot Tiber, were as bigoted and rightwing as ever, but in the presentation and dissemination of these new, contentious values through a medium – the rock festival – that allowed audiences ways of processing contested ideas about society in ways that are very different than earlier outdoor musical events (see Tiber and Monte 2007).

The events at Peekskill emphasize this change. In 1949, an overtly communist sympathizing event sponsored by Artists International resulted in a serious riot. Twenty years later, in a similarly politicized era and equally polarized location, audiences (and locals) at Woodstock were able to peaceably reconcile their deeply negative feelings about America and its Cold War mission with their own values and beliefs. Woodstock was (and is) always and forever deemed a success because of its ability to do this, and because of its pervasive iconography: 40 years on, the culture of Woodstock and its cultural values are invoked with reverence, and Woodstock-like festivals, in a more commodified form, have proliferated across the globe with varying degrees of success. Festival organizers are now able to use the model to promote sometimes contentious ideas – about ecology (Live Earth), social justice (Live Aid) and the legalization (and valorization) of drug use – only now they pin their ideological discourses not on the politically radical content of the artists (as we saw with Robeson or Hendrix) but on the representational dominance of festival ideology itself. Because of Woodstock, rock festivals are consistently represented to the public as utopian spaces of multiculturalism, freedom and peace. But the Woodstock model for a discursively powerful rock festival is successful only under certain conditions, namely, when 'culture' is configured as something normed to the white middle classes. It becomes a more fragile model when it is interrogated alongside ideologies of difference, such as race, class and gender.

The role of African Americans, and African American culture at large, in the outdoor rock festivals is particularly problematic, in part because African American music is so central to rock music, and also because, speaking generally, African Americans themselves are often neither included in nor persuaded by commercial festival rhetorics. By studying the role of race at these types of rock festivals, we can see the limitation of the rock festival as a vehicle for social change. This chapter argues that the failure of African Americans and other marginalized groups to embrace the rock festival as a meaningful site of social justice is symptomatic of Woodstock rhetoric's reliance on a monolithic vision of American culture which is normed to a middle-class white population.

The crux of this study is based on the following observation. Although there are many smaller scale festivals and concerts that *do* draw black audiences, a free, outdoor festival of Woodstock-like proportions attended by a largely black audience has yet to have occurred in America. The closest equivalent was Wattstax, a festival held at the Los Angeles Coliseum in 1972. Wattstax (its name a deliberate echo of Woodstock, of course) is a useful discursive tool with which to compare Woodstock because it too was filmed, although the movie of it had a rather different reception than did *Woodstock: 3 days of Peace and Music.* A discussion of the way race played into these alternative discourses may suggest a different question altogether: not why African Americans *don't* attend large rock festivals in vast numbers, but rather, why so many events featuring black artists and audiences do not *count* as Woodstock-like 'festivals', with Woodstock-like properties of transcendence and reconciliation, in the American imagination. It is, however, not my intention to entirely undermine the idea of the rock festival. Ideally, I believe that a great music festival serves the important societal function of creating a space where audiences can reconcile conflicting ideologies and, as Pierre Nora puts it, 'participate emotionally' in history (Nora 1974, 234). Such a space could be crucial for reconciling racial conflicts in America, but, as this chapter argues, so far, this has not occurred.

The differing life experiences of whites and blacks in America may help to explain the often ignored schism between black and white audiences at live performances of music. The schism has two sides to it, one geographic, and one aesthetic. Festivals like Woodstock (and more contemporarily, the recurring festival Bonnaroo) occur in hard to get to rural locations, but the majority of African Americans in America are urban dwellers with less access to cars. They also have less interest in nature than your average white suburbanite. Though today's rock festivals feature intensely multi-racial bills and often have prominent African American headliners (OutKast, Dr. Dre, Jay Z, Kanye West and the Black Eyed Peas, for instance, have all served as major draws in recent years), audiences at such festivals are predominantly white. In one self-reported poll on the festival's official website, Coachella-goers reported themselves as being 4 per cent African American, or one-third of the proportionate demographic in the United States on the whole (Ethnic Demographics, 2013). A survey at the New Orleans Jazzfest made by Anthropologist Shana Walton reported that the audience was less than 5 per cent African American (although New Orleans itself is around 60 per cent African American, and Jazzfest explicitly celebrates African

American heritage music). And Boots Riley of the Coup has called the audience for his radical hip hop 'the Cotton Club', a reference to black clubs catering to white patrons in 1920s Harlem (see Kitwana 2005).

The second schism is artistic in nature. The schism was pronounced even in the 1960s and 1970s, when popular black music – soul, jazz, r & b and pop – tended to celebrate rather than castigate the black experience in America. But since the popularization of hip hop, a genre which sees its mission as chronicling the black experience in polemicized ways, rock and pop music audiences have become even more stratified, particularly in live settings. Even within the black community there is severe disconnect between the fans of older pop traditions – soul, r & b, blues – and younger ones, like hip hop. With its undoubted emphasis on poverty, gangs, gun violence and misogyny, hip hop has also served to increase already-extant anxieties in the white community about the nature of black culture.[1] Certainly a festival like Wattstax – the one extremely large festival with an almost all-black audience that has ever been held on American soil – could not exist in a post-hip-hop world.

Wattstax demonstrates some of the liminal aspects of the rock festival, and not only because it is one of the only concerts of its kind, but also because it shows the ways in which many of the rhetorics and assumptions about rock festivals *can* work when they are de-coupled from some of the white middle-class norms and are reanimated with other ones. Thus, whereas Woodstock worked to encourage sceptical youth audiences to extol the pleasures of a free-market society without assuming the guilt that more overt displays would have shown, Wattstax exhibits to its audience a differently nuanced facet of capitalism: the idea that black culture was (and is) saleable and that black-owned businesses could succeed in America. Despite the overt difference in locations – Wattstax took place in the most urban of settings, while Woodstock celebrated rural America – Wattstax clarifies the notion that the Woodstock model can also be applied to an African American audience, allowing them the pleasure of reconciliation to and resolution of unhappy historical residue.

In this case, the conflict to be resolved was not the Cold War, it was the success of civil rights, narrowly interpreted through race relations in Watts, but the festival's rhetoric still allows its audience to process and accept the status quo idea of blacks as successful entrepreneurs disseminating their own culture, despite some evidence to the contrary. That Wattstax allowed for this resolution is probably why, despite contemporary evidence to the contrary, it is now considered one of the finest examples of post-Woodstock festival. Unlike the Harlem Cultural Festival (sometimes called 'The Black Woodstock', though the first in the series was held a year before Woodstock), Wattstax was filmed and widely distributed. This explains why it is better remembered than the Harlem event, which certainly hews more closely to the utopian ideals of free festivals, and which deserves more attention than can be given here.[2]

Wattstax was a benefit concert and celebration of the seventh anniversary of the Watts riots that featured performances by many of the most famous artists on the Memphis-based record label Stax. It was held at the Los Angeles County Stadium on 9 August 1972; tickets cost $1, and it was sold out to a largely local, African American crowd. Writer and historian Nelson George calls Wattstax 'a symbol of black self-sufficiency', although Brian Ward points out that it was largely underwritten by white corporations, including Columbia Pictures, which bought the film rights, and Schlitz beer, which rented the Coliseum and which was attempting to diffuse a proposed boycott of their product by the black community at the time. (In pre-publicity, the LA *Sentinel* is careful to call it 'the Schlitz-sponsored festival' as a warning to potential patrons.) Still, Ward adds, 'on a number of levels the politics, economics, iconography and almost sacramental ritualism of [Wattstax] vividly illustrated the relationship between rhythm and blues, black consciousness, corporate commerce and the freedom struggle in the heart of the black power era' (Ward 1998, 222.) The festival raised about $100,000, which was divided between African American civil rights activist Jesse Jackson's then new campaign organization PUSH (People United to Save Humanity), the Watts Summer Festival fund, the MLK Jr. Hospital Fund and the Sickle Cell Anemia Foundation (Berry 1972).

Wattstax differs from the white rock festivals like Woodstock onwards in several crucial ways, most importantly because it was held in a stadium. Stadiums have their own acoustics, crowd dynamics and even theorists: Elias Canetti, for example, makes a distinction between what he calls open crowds and closed crowds. The open crowd, which one observes at festivals like Woodstock and Altamont, where fencing is either nonexistent or far enough from the music to seem nonexistent, is one which at least gives the appearance of growing indefinitely. The open crowd, say Canetti and Stewart, wants to consist of more people; it wants to 'seize everyone within reach; anything shaped like a human being can join it' (Canetti and Stewart 1984, 16). In contrast, the closed crowd – like the one at Wattstax – is bounded, as by the walls of arenas, and the boundary not only prevents the crowd from increasing – and postpones its dissolution – but more importantly, creates a kind of bond between those on the inside versus those on the outside. Thus, argue Canetti and Stewart:

> Outside, facing the city, the arena displays a lifeless wall; inside is a wall of people. The spectators turn their backs to the city. They have been lifted out of its structure of walls and streets and, for the duration of their time in the arena, they do not care about anything which happens there; they have left behind all their associations, rules and habits. ... There is no break in the crowd which sits like this, exhibiting itself to itself. ... It embraces and contains everything which happens below; no one relaxes his grip on this; no one tries to get away. Any gap in the ring

> might remind him of disintegration and subsequent dispersal. But there is no gap; this crowd is double closed, to the world outside and in itself. (1984, 28)

By closing out the world, the stadium creates an 'us' and 'them' dynamic, much like the 'us and them' dynamic created by segregation, only in this case, reversed. More importantly, however, unlike Yasgur's farm, Altamont Speedway, the Glen Ellen Regional Park or other sites of famous festivals, a stadium is an implicitly political location, an architectural reminder of the repressive nature of power. From images of Roman emperors watching their captured slaves battle to the death to stadiums crowded with political rallies in Nuremburg and political prisoners in Argentina, to refugees from Hurricane Katrina, stadiums echo not only with bygone cheers but also with the silent memory of oppression. They are cement reminders of suffering and surveillance and architectural structures of discipline. It is not surprising, perhaps, that the largest rock festival catering exclusively to a black audience took place in a stadium located in a poorer part of Los Angeles. Yet, here, blacks gathered in safety and in comfort, entirely estranged from nature. That the stadium is an essentially urban apparatus is a fact that the film-makers of *Wattstax* never forget, beginning the film with a montage of shots of Watts, circa 1972: storefronts, sidewalks, parking lots and cement 'playgrounds' peopled with African American city dwellers (see Figure 20). The gritty urban nature of the opening reminds us immediately that the film works as a response to *Woodstock: 3 Days of Peace & Music*, then less than 2 years old and still wildly successful.

*Wattstax* was directed by Mel Stuart, a white director best known for directing *Willie Wonka and the Chocolate Factory* around the same time. In direct contrast to *Woodstock*'s back to the land-opening shots with their pastoral, sunshine-laden sequence, *Wattstax* begins with a montage of urban scenarios. After a brief look at the Watts Towers, we see the streets, cars,

**FIGURE 20** *'A montage of urban scenarios' in a festival film:* Wattstax.

housing developments, wire, fences, welfare lines, nurses, misshapen elderly people, ragged children, drunks ... and riots. In the background, the song 'Whatcha see is what you get', by the Dramatics, plays: 'Cos what you see/is what you get/because I'm as real/as real can get/and real ... is the best thing yet.' Here, the film-makers declare, is the opposite of the utopian dream of 'the garden': here is what Louis Althusser would call 'the real conditions of our existence' (Althusser 1972, 109). In the terms of this film, the real conditions of existence are 'the best thing yet'. (The song, performed in a tuneful r & b style, presages the soon-to-be invented world of rap, where utopian notions about the value of realness will be used to re-frame how inhabitants perceive the burnt-out areas of the Bronx and Compton.)

This visual comment on the disjunction between Woodstock and Wattstax continues with the next shot, which shows the stage being built at the Coliseum. In *Woodstock,* the erection of the stage was depicted as a barn-raising, done by bare-chested blonde youths, in a holy spirit of communion. At Wattstax, the stage is erected by burly white union guys. In this universe – the universe where 'the real' is as 'real can get' – work is not depicted as religious, but as labour. Even when it's done by whites, work is work.

As this sequence indicates, *Wattstax* differs in every particular from *Woodstock*, from the national anthem, sung respectfully by Kim Weston (in opposition to Jimi Hendrix's famous shattered version), to its final dystopian vision of America: a helicopter shot of the LA Coliseum which pulls slowly away to show the urban wasteland that is south central LA. As a film, it feels far more cobbled together than *Woodstock*, combining concert sequences with crowd shots intercut with scenes of a Richard Pryor monologue and with interviews with local Watts residence that are clearly shot elsewhere (in Pryor's case, on a darkened soundstage). The constant cutting away from the concert footage is a distraction, and the ending of the film is particularly contested, as there are two: the original, which featured a faked sequence with Isaac Hayes playing 'Coming down the mountain' on a soundstage, and the anniversary release, which features the concert's real ending, with Hayes entering the stadium with a police escort in a gold-painted station wagon and bursting onto the stage to sing 'Shaft'. The second ending makes the film into a powerful statement, but it was only added to the DVD release in 2004. *Woodstock*, by contrast, ended with a lingering shot of a pristine forest, linking nature, music, peace and humanity.

These filmic differences are striking and intentional and underscore the many ways that the audience at Wattstax the concert differs from the one we witnessed, on film, at Woodstock. For example, at Wattstax, we periodically see the entirely black audience of 92,000 on its feet, dancing respectfully, even decorously, in the stands and on the field. This is a very different vision from the naked hippie chicks and stoned young men who make up Woodstock's cast of characters. Unfortunately, the decorum exhibited by the audience at Wattstax underscores not Woodstock's anarchic pleasures and societal defiance, but the fact that such behaviour is a privilege unavailable to the African American community. Woodstock's defining moment happened when hippies broke down the fences so they could attend for free. At Wattstax, when the crowd bursts onto the field to dance to Rufus Thomas's 'Funky chicken', we hear Thomas enjoin them all back to their seats: 'More power to the folks going back to the stands. More power to the folks going back to the stands.' The crowd files amicably back to the stands, leaving one exuberant dancer with a broken umbrella on the field. 'That's a Brother all right', says Thomas to a delighted crowd, 'but I be damned if he *my* Brother'. This is not a sentiment you will hear at Woodstock, which spent an inordinate amount of time emphasizing brotherhood.

But if Woodstock implied a hippie utopia, Wattstax acknowledges a past that is truly dystopian. The final sequence of the remade version – that is, the film of what *really* happened at the end of the concert – shows Isaac Hayes, at the time one of Stax's biggest stars, arriving on stage in a black and red cape, his bald head and reflective sunglasses shining ominously in the lights, as the 92,000 crowd leaps to its feet, and the score board flashes the words BLACK MOSES. As the rhythm section roils up the opening riffs of 'Shaft' – that unforgettable, irreplaceable sequence of bass notes that are now one of pop's most iconic riffs – Hayes steps up to the microphone, throws off his cape and intones the opening line: 'Who's the private dick who's a sex machine to all the chicks?'

He is dressed entirely in golden chains (Figure 21). Today, this image of Hayes seems to encapsulate some nostalgic notion that the concert is allowing its attendants to reclaim black history by rewriting it in a more triumphant key. This belief may be what gives *Wattstax* such power. Yet the written record of Wattstax, the concert, gives a far more conflicted version of events. The article in the *Los Angeles Times* describing the concert itself, for example, was downright negative, and the review of the movie,

**FIGURE 21** *Isaac Hayes in 'golden chains' at Wattstax.*

released six months later, is if anything worse, taking Hayes himself to task for a performance it calls 'overblown'. The film itself was characterized by critic Dennis Hunt (who is himself African American) as 'fragmented and skittery' (1973, 10). In his review it is chaotic and tedious, 'full of long stretches of boredom that occur when an interviewee lapses into rhetoric or a singer lumbers through a number'. Hunt also calls most of the musical performances 'inept'. Yet, in 2004, the film was re-released and broadcast on PBS, to ecstatically positive press (*Wattstax* 2004). Indeed, it is now generally spoken of with reverence.

One reason for the change in tone may be that the re-release has a different ending: in it, Hayes is shown performing 'Shaft' live. In the original release, it was the song's licensing arrangements that prevented this sequence from being shown. But although 'Coming down the mountain' certainly is a far less powerful finish in the earlier version, it cannot quite account for the vastly different tone surrounding the film today than originally. That *Los Angeles Times* review, for instance, complained that the concert suffered from poor staging, poor acoustics, too many acts. Writer Lance Williams grudgingly admitted there was 'a mood of camaraderie' in the crowd but also claimed it was 'bored' much of the time and that it seldom got to its feet to dance. He also took Hayes to task, saying his act was a repeat of a recent performance at the Hollywood Bowl, giving it a sense of 'colossal déjà vu'. Hayes, he adds, did two takes of 'Shaft' for the cameras (Williams 1972).

That the *Los Angeles Times* was sceptical of this endeavour is not surprising. But the *Sentinel,* LA's largest black newspaper, took a similar tone. Soon after the event the paper ran an editorial by Emily F. Gibson, in which the writer calls Wattstax 'a diversionary tactic' because the festival 'help[ed] to silence dissent in the ghetto by keeping the summer cool'. She continues, in a charged critique of the event that constructs festival as a profoundly anti-liberatory zone and happening:

> What is there to celebrate? Are the conditions which gave rise to an unparalleled unleashing of tempers then any different than they are now? ... Have (the Watts Summer Festivals) been instrumental in bringing about black unity for the purpose of strategising the liberation? ... The opportunists and demagogues who perpetuate the idea of the Watts Festival are as guilty of the crimes committed against black and poor as the most vicious racists, money hungry merchants, blood thirsty police, and panhandling politicians. (Gibson 1972)

Between the *Los Angeles Times*' tepid coverage and the *Sentinel*'s open hostility, one gains the impression that Wattstax was far from the success it seems in retrospect. In fact, it was better received from afar. The concert received a rave review from syndicated columnist Bob Considine, for example – although he did not actually attend it. In an October issue of the Wisconsin *Pharos-Tribune*, he announces the occurrence of the then month-old concert.

> There was little press coverage, and no TV coverage at all to record a truly historic event. In my opinion, the media ignored the event because there were no fights, no riots, no one was injured and no one killed. ... But if one bottle had been thrown, if one placement had clubbed one teenager, Wattstax'72 would have been all over the front pages and received sensational coverage from TV. (Considine 1972, 4)

By 1973, the impression that Wattstax was a significant event was already in play (thanks no doubt to the power of Columbia Studios). Marilyn Beck's syndicated column devotes quite a bit of space to the film's late January premiere, including concerns that it will receive an R rating (for language), thus preventing 'an audience of young people from seeing it who would benefit from the portrait of the black experience' (Beck 1972). A few weeks later, Sandra Haggerty of the Tucson *Citizen* chimes in, calling it a 'moving documentary of the black experience in America' (Haggerty 1973, 19). Once opened, the film received many rave reviews, including ones in *Newsweek* ('1,000,000 flamboyant foxes and dapper dudes enjoying themselves in a hip-stomping, hip shaking celebration': Cooper 1973) and the *Saturday Review* ('A film of incredible vitality, pertinence and humor!': Knight 1973). Wattstax is also known for being the occasion of Jesse Jackson's resounding 'I *am* somebody' speech. Jackson was at the time head of the campaign organization PUSH and clearly using the concert as an overt political platform for his own ambitions.[3] It's notable that he is not shoved off the stage, like yippie activist Abbie Hoffman had been at Woodstock. Instead, Jackson's speech – like Weston's performance of the black national anthem – is taken by the crowd at face value, as 'a soulful expression of the black experience', to quote Richard Pryor in the film.

*Wattstax* ought by rights to have been an apotheosis, rather than a unique event, for despite its contemporary critics, looked at as a semiotic device, it was everything subsequent rock festivals purport to be: authentic, transgressive, utopian, even (almost) free. But whereas white audiences have interpreted the ideal of freeness as a monetary value *music* should be *free* – black audiences have interpreted it as a form of liberty – freedom as a quality of life. This is the essential difference between *Wattstax* and *Woodstock*. *Woodstock* (and the US festival more generally) displayed a free market. *Wattstax* tells an alternative history of America, very different from the ideologically fantastic one on display at Woodstock. Where Woodstock heightened the idyllic aspects of the American spirit, its natural beauty, its independence and its reliance on individuality, *Wattstax* speakers remind the audience of African American history: of slavery, segregation and, ultimately, the fight for civil rights. The experiences of the Watts residents who are interviewed throughout the film speak of an American experience very far from the one alluded to in Woodstock, and as they do so, they help illustrate the way that culture is intimately bound up with community. But by so doing, it reveals the absence of this connection at the heart of Woodstock and other festivals. The community depicted in Woodstock was a fictitious construct, set to dissipate come Monday morning. The community at the heart of Wattstax – Compton, standing in for countless other urban black neighbourhoods in the United States – is, as the film promised, 'as real as real can get'.

## Conclusion

Despite its contested roots, *Wattstax* is now celebrated as one of the finest concerts and concert films of an era. Forty years later, no other vast rock festival featuring all-black acts has called to an all-black audience in the same way. Black acts like Public Enemy, Kanye West and 50 cent have all launched grand tours of indoor arenas, but these acts play to largely white audiences, and their earning capacity pales in comparison to white rock giants like U2, Bruce Springsteen, the Eagles and the Grateful Dead. And while individual acts like Snoop Dogg, West, Black Eyed Peas and Jay Z have all been served up as headlining acts at large outdoor festivals like Glastonbury, Bonnaroo and Coachella, none of these festivals have called to largely (or even somewhat) black audiences. All that remains is an event that allegorically invokes multiculturalism, allowing black acts a space to perform a white-managed vision of cultural diversity. Indeed, so complete is the African American audience estranged from its own heritage that its absence is even noticeable at festivals featuring popular African musicians. Writing in the *New York Times*, historian Michael Veal (2001) notes that the absence of African American audiences at African music concerts in America has 'less to do with Africa than they do with America's charged racial dynamic', and argues that African music's popularity in the United States reflects two divergent problems, one, the legacy of black cultural nationalism, which emphasized traditional forms and cultural arts like drumming and dance, and the other, its countercultural presence, epitomized by the marijuana smoking and religious exoticism of Bob Marley.

Although Veal's diagnosis is doubtless correct, it points towards another problematic. Black-attended events are not simply whitewashed, they are erased. If anything, they are doubly erased: once from the public record, when blackcentric festivals like the Harlem Cultural Festival do not get mainstream coverage, and a second time, because gatherings with a black heritage mission – like, say, the New Orleans Jazz & Heritage Festival (see Regis and Walton 2008) – no longer count as rock festivals in the same way that Woodstock and Wattstax do. Moreover, this erasure has some social repercussions, since it means that black audiences have lost that space for reconciliation which white audiences take for granted.

This chapter has sought to prove that African Americans' and other marginalized groups' failure or reluctance to embrace the rock festival as a meaningful form of cultural memory is symptomatic of the Woodstock rhetoric's reliance on a monolithic vision of American culture which is normed to white audiences. This norming shows the limits of festival rhetoric to make its points. Any marked, alienated, group that cannot fully embrace the appeal of these rhetorics – not just African Americans, but women, Asians, Hispanics, the elderly and the poor – will not be hailed by this rhetoric in the same way. Moreover, this chapter has argued that the loss of this space of reconciliation is particularly damaging to African Americans, whose musical culture and heritage of course underpins so much of festival rhetoric.

But this does not mean that the festival space cannot, under certain circumstances, work as the utopian, multicultural ideal that it claims for itself. Indeed, it can, particularly if it removes the mechanisms which keep non-white crowds from easily attending them. A close analysis of Wattstax and its filmed representation shows that discourses of the music festival, when presented without rhetorics aimed solely at white males, *can* cut across all age groups and all social classes; it also shows that the rhetoric of difference which it invoked is a particularly powerful one. The lesson we need to take away from that is not that rock festivals are, like so many other things, wholly the province of the white middle class; merely that as long as festivals are not for everyone (even and especially when they say that they *are*), they will have very serious limitations.

## Notes

1 Quite a bit of hip-hop music does not celebrate violence, violence against women and crime. But sadly, this is the less popular branch of the form.

2 The Harlem Cultural Festival is also an omnibus name for six different concerts, all held at Edwards Park between 1968 and 1969. The fluctuations in attendance and different artists makes it difficult to fit into the Woodstock model or narrative.

3 According to Ward (1998), he also had a recording contract with Stax Records.

## References

Althusser, Louis. 1972. 'Ideology and ideological state apparatuses.' *Lenin and Philosophy, and Other Essays*. New York: Monthly Review. No pagination.

Balaji, Murali. 2007. *The Professor and the Pupil: The Politics of W.E.B. Du Bois and Paul Robeson*. New York: Nation.

Beck, Marilyn. 1972. 'Hollywood Hotline.' *Pasadena Star News* (4 December).

Berry, William Earl. 1972. 'How Watts festival renews black unity.' *Jet* (14 September).
Canetti, Elias, and Carol Stewart. 1984. *Crowds and Power*. New York: Farrar Straus Giroux.
Cooper, Arthur. 1973. 'Watts happening.' *Newsweek* (26 February): 88.
Considine, Bob. 1972. 'There's good news today.' *The Pharos Tribune and Press* (15 October): 4.
'Ethnic Demographics 2013.' Coachella.com/forums. http://www.coachella.com/forum/showthread.php?63620-Coachella-Ethnic-Demographics-for-2013. Accessed 28 August 2014.
Gibson, Emily F. 1972. 'Annual Watts summer festival has come and gone.' Los Angeles *Sentinel* (31 August). Page A7.
Gilroy, Paul. 1991. 'Sounds authentic: black music, ethnicity, and the challenge of a "changing" same.' *Black Music Research Journal* 11(2): 111–36.
Haggerty, Sandra. 1973. 'Black tragedy becomes celebration.' *Tucson Daily Citizen* (18 January): 19.
Hunt, Dennis. 1973. 'Pryor highlight of "Wattstax" collage.' *Los Angeles Times* (21 February): Part IV, 10.
Kitwana, Bakari. 2005. 'The Cotton Club.' *Village Voice*, 21 June. http://www.villagevoice.com/2005-06-21/music/the-cotton-club/.
Knight, Arthur. 1973. 'Facing Reality.' *Saturday Review* (10 March): 71.
Marcus, Greil. 2014. *The History of Rock 'n' Roll In Ten Songs*. New Haven, CT: Yale University Press.
Nora, Pierre. 1974. 'Le Retour De L'Evenement.' *Faire De L'histoire*. Paris: Gallimard, 217–37.
Regis, Helen A., and Shana Walton. 2008. 'Producing the folk at the New Orleans Jazz and Heritage Festival.' *Journal of American Folklore* 121(482): 400–40.
The Dramatics. 1971. 'What you see is what you get.' *Soul Hits of the Seventies*. CD.
Tiber, Elliot, and Tom Monte. 2007. *Taking Woodstock*. Garden City Park, NY: Square One.
Veal, Michael. 2001. 'African music and African American audiences.' *New York Times* (8 July).
Ward, Brian. 1998. *Just My Soul Responding: Rhythm and Blues, Black Consciousness, and Race Relations*. Berkeley, CA: University of California.
*Wattstax*. 1973. Dir. Mel Stuart. Prod. Mel Stuart and Larry Shaw. By John A. Alonzo, David E. Blewitt, Robert K. Lambert, Richard Pryor, Isaac Hayes, Albert King, Milton Little, and Mavis Staples. Columbia Pictures, 1973.
*Wattstax*, 30th Anniversary Special Edition. 2004. Dir. Mel Stuart. Prod. Mel Stuart and Larry Shaw. By John A. Alonzo, David E. Blewitt, Robert K. Lambert, Richard Pryor, Isaac Hayes, Albert King, Milton Little, and Mavis Staples. Warner Home Video.
Williams, Lance. 1972. 'Wattstax: giving something back to the community.' *Los Angeles Times* (20 August).
*Woodstock, 3 Days of Peace & Music*. 1970. Dir. Michael Wadleigh and Martin Scorsese. By Michael Wadleigh, Michael Wadleigh, Martin Scorsese, Richie Havens, Arlo Guthrie, Janis Joplin, Jimi Hendrix, and Joe Cocker. Prod. Bob Maurice. Warner Bros., 1994.

# CHAPTER FIVE

# The artist at the music festival: Art, performance and hybridity

*Rebekka Kill*

This chapter explores the way that artists show their work at music festivals. Specifically, I am interested in the way that programming non-music artworks in a music festival context may affect the art and performance that is being created and shown. I want to understand the degree to which the music festival site is generative of new work, propagating new forms or new modes of art practice. Through case studies of the contemporary British festival Latitude and the Impossible Lecture event at Beacons Festival and in the United Kingdom, I will examine the type of work that is being programmed and the various processes by which this programming come about. Is art work simply being re-staged, or curated, into the festival space with little effect of the work itself, or is a process of creative innovation occurring in the special, different and temporary place of the festival site? In terms of how we might consider commissioned or site-specific work at music festivals a key issue may be methodologies for making work and potentially new forms of expression.

Much of the work that is shown by artists at music festivals is relational, immersive or interactive; it can be considered relational art. Nicolas Bourriaud defines relational art as 'art as a state of encounter' (Bourriaud 2002, 18). He states that this is 'art taking as its theoretical horizon the realm of human interactions and its social context, rather than the assertion of an independent and private symbolic space' (Bourriaud 2002, 14). Relational art can be found in traditional spaces such as galleries, museums and theatres but it may also be located in 'meetings, encounters, events, various types of collaboration between people, games, festivals, and places of conviviality'

(2002, 28). Through a series of events and a practice as research project, Alice O'Grady and I worked towards a definition of relational performance:

> Relational performance is live performance often encountered in and emanating from unexpected places; in a dancing crowd, on a corner, in the campsite. Relational performance may occur on a stage but does not necessarily conform to conventions associated with the fictive space of the theatrical stage. Whilst it may occur without prior knowledge, warning or agreement from the audience, it requires dialogue, interaction or audience intervention to make it work. (O'Grady and Kill 2013, 278)

Our work explored ideas of encounter and of interaction in festival performance; however, the focus of this new research is the effect that the festival site has on the practice itself. Do festivals generate new, novel or innovative modes of creative practice?

Rock festivals became very popular in the later 1960s and early 1970s, and they have proliferated internationally in the decades since; in Britain there were around 240 festivals in 2006 and 530 events in 2008 (Mintel 2006, 2008). These outdoor, three- or four-day events have been described as kinds of carnivalesque sites where people indulge in 'fattening food, intoxicating drink, sexual promiscuity, altered ego-identity, the inverse and the heteroglot' (Stallybrass and White 1986, 189). This has led to scholars (Hewison 1986; Blake 1997; McKay 2000; Hetherington 2001) characterizing these events as a locus for a kind of contemporary carnivalesque. In the carnivalesque we exist in a different space and time and are 'temporarily liberated from the prevailing truth and from the established order' (Bakhtin 1984, 10). In this space we can escape our everyday existence, behave in a transgressive way, and social norms are turned on their heads. However, more recently, as Chris Anderton notes, the carnivalesque experience that many festival-goers have desired or imagined is becoming increasingly sanitized, packaged and commercialized.

> Festivals become part of that postmodern consumerist identity formation, and while there may be countercultural influences, typified in the 'legal highs' sold at festivals in the mid-2000s, or the penchant for luxury yurt accommodation and so on, we can recognize these consumption activities as offering a commercialized form of the countercultural carnivalesque. (Anderton 2011, 154)

As festivals proliferate, aspects of what have become known as audience segmentation and brand differentiation have become more important. Some festivals have long had a broader range of programming across many art platforms. For example, Lollapalooza in Chicago is a huge festival that, although its focus is on rock music (it was originally established by Jane"s Addiction singer Perry Farrell in 1991) also has a comedy stage, significant amounts of dance programming as well as providing a platform for political and not-for-profit organizations. Other festivals have significantly invested in child-friendly or family elements, experience design, immersive environments and an extensive range of food and drink options. Examples of these, in the United Kingdom, might be Camp Bestival, catering for retired club kids and their toddlers, Green Man Festival, described by the *Guardian* newspaper as 'the indie pagan's nirvana' and Secret Garden Party, a much more adult-oriented playground with a keen attention to detail. In Australia, note Chris Gibson and John Connell, 'gourmet food, wine and music' have offered a combined regional attraction at some festivals; one festival 'simply describes itself as promoting "liquid geography" where the music is almost an afterthought' (2012, 29, 31).

Many festivals with rock, pop and dance music as the main element of their programming are increasing the amount of visual art, performance art, comedy, cabaret and film that they programme (see Figure 22). Indeed McKay notes that

> at their best, music festivals aren't really about music, are they? Its centrality is undercut by the sheer range and wealth of other entertainment on offer. ... [Arguably i]t was the free festival movement that really widened out the cultural ambition of festival culture (though the ambition was there at Woodstock in 1969, called the Music *and Art* Fair). ... Performance art commissioned for the [Glastonbury] festival covers a wide range. ... Ritual ceremonies ... [around] summer solstice [and other] things neo-pagan. Then there are the street performers distributing weirdness around the crowds. ... (McKay 2000, 150–51; emphasis original)

**FIGURE 22** *Banksy artwork at Glastonbury Festival, 2008: ice cream van/police riot van.*

We might also think of the combined Leeds and Reading Festival (UK). Reading Festival first took place in 1971, with its sister festival starting in 1999. This paired festival has the same line-up alternating at each location over a three-day end-of-summer national holiday weekend in late August. The majority of the programming is music based with high-profile rock headliners such as, in recent years, the Arctic Monkeys, the Cure, Green Day and Muse. However, there has also been significant expansion on the non-music Alternative Stage, from one day of programming to a full programme for the three days of the festival, of comedians, performance art and late-night film screenings.

It is clear from developments such as these that festival programmers and festival-goers alike see value in this kind of programming running in parallel with live music. In these examples the artists who are booked are touring a particular show, and the directors or curators of the festival select shows that might be appropriate for that particular context. Festivals are also increasingly working with visual artists, film-makers and performers to make site-specific work for the festival.

## Site-specific art at festivals

Many boutique and music festival programmes and commissions are site-specific work. Latitude Festival began in 2006; it attracts an audience of over 30,000 annually to its site near the Suffolk coast and includes a broad range of arts practices. Indeed, this festival provides opportunities for a number of Arts Council-funded National Portfolio Organisations, the kinds of arts groups that receive regular and sustained state support. According to Arts Council England:

> Highlights from the programme on offer include a series of spectacular outdoor performances from The Lyric Hammersmith, Latitude, Greenwich + Docklands International Festival and Watford Palace Theatre. With performances taking place across the festival site throughout the weekend, the organisations will collaborate with the likes of RashDash, Nabokov and Les Enfants Terribles. Battersea Arts Centre will also present a trio of shows: a sell-out production The Paper Cinema's Odyssey – a visually beautiful puppet show told through cinema projection and cunning tricks; spoken word artist Kate Tempest's Brand New Ancients which will premiere at the theatre in September; and showcasing event Freshly Scratched which gives festival-goers the chance to take the stage. (ACE website 2014)

The festival's website states that 'Latitude is proud to offer its guests a spectacular choice of distinguished shows, star acts and innovative site-specific commissioned pieces' (Latitude Festival website). According to culture website Run Riot, 'Latitude was the pioneer of making art essential to music festivals, and now boasts a programme so rich its Arts Curator Tania Harrison works on it all year round, devoting "most evenings to seeing new acts and shows"' (McLaren 2012). In Harrison's view 'we've become a festival that commissions great work as well as providing a showcase for existing art. Our unique set-up means we can commission site-specific pieces in places like the Faraway Forest, and this is typically the area that pushes most boundaries from year-to-year' (quoted in McLaren 2012). Latitude Festival presents work that ranges from the highest level Arts Council–funded work from significant UK arts organizations with national impact to impressive international acts to commissioned site-specific experimental work. I am not arguing that site-specific commissioned work is essentially novel. However, site-specific work that is shown, or performed, alongside such a broad range of other practices, with a captive potential audience of over 30,000, may bring challenges and innovation that do not occur in other contexts. I spoke to Harold Offeh who made site-specific work for Latitude Festival in 2013 and 2014. In 2013, he presented the Mothership project, a multidisciplinary performance art work based on imagery and ideas taken from the 1970s Afro-futurist movement and ideas of utopia. Mothership was made up of several concurrent performance art works: generating an alien language through crowd-sourcing, a family-focused workshop to create puppets for a puppet show, a soundwork and a midnight collective "soul train" performance through the woods. In 2014, Offeh worked with Latitude's theme of surveillance. He focused on replicating digital culture offline: physical tetris with wooden blocks, a performance where you could hire people to 'follow' you and document your festival experience and selfie Polaroid-style frames. He talked in some detail about the specific nature of the festival site, 'the festival space is unique because of the nature of the audience; an audience who have come specifically to the site to engage with the arts in its broadest sense'. He went on to describe the festival as a utopian space where 'people are emancipated from the everyday' and more open to engagement. Offeh described the impact of the festival on his own performance art practice: 'it's like a mini residency'; in other words it's not only immersive and utopian for the audience but it's immersive for the artists too. He went on to discuss Marisa Carnesky's Tarot Drome, a surreal immersive promenade of living tarot cards; part cabaret, part installation, part disco. In Carnesky's piece the audience interact with living tarot cards in order to get a personal card reading. Tarot Drome has been shown in the Old Vic tunnels, the Faraway Forest at Latitude and a roller disco in Vauxhall. Carnesky's works with site and with unusual spaces and draws on a huge range of creative practices. For Offeh this is where the innovation in practice lies, when artists are not constrained by a single genre or genealogy of practice. He stated that festival art works draw from club cultures, performance, durational art, circus skills, cabaret, experimental theatre, music. He said, 'I've been to things that have tried to do this, outside of festivals, but it doesn't always work because, people are like, well what is it? Is it dance?' So, the festival space makes the audience more open to engagement and it allows for cross-disciplinary innovation in practice that can develop both artists and practice itself. But is this kind of innovation happening at other festivals?

Impossible Lecture is a performance space at the boutique northern Beacons Festival, in Yorkshire, that has been running each year since 2009. In the publicity Beacons produced for their 2014 festival, Impossible Lecture is described as

> a theatre tent with a reputation for the unexpected, the anarchic and the sublime. Come and indulge your sensibilities with a packed line-up of salacious cabaret, gratuitous dance, provocative live art and welcoming workshops, all presented in the cosy confines of a cafe/bar atmosphere. Family friendly through the day, then drifting into 18 + around 9 p.m., Impossible Lecture twinkles into the night with guest art-house DJs such as the eminent TRACEYEMINSOUNDSYSTEM and select performances from the likes of STEAKHOUSE LIVE. With a fine selection of food and drinks on offer, you may be seduced into calling this tent your new home. (Beacons Festival website)

Impossible Lecture was established by Artistic Director Adam Young, working with a small stable management team. I interviewed Young to find out exactly what it is, how it developed and whether he feels that the Impossible Lecture space is generative of new practices and potentially new knowledge.

Impossible Lecture is a 'test space' for performers and artists, which requires immersion and investment from artists and audiences. It is also a space where the boundary between artist and audience is permeable. While Young does have a directorial or commissioning role in programming art work, much space and time is left for openness and experimentation: 'the best stuff is always the unplanned. This is the most innovative. We allow space for anything to happen; that's what's special about it, we give it permission. We encourage it.' Young acknowledges that Impossible Lecture has much in common with improv, but argues that generating improvised performance is not the central aim of the more unplanned sessions. For him, it is about 'activating the audience' (see Figure 23).

Interestingly, in Young's view there is something about Impossible Lecture which could only happen in the space-time of the festival, which is, as he puts it, 'some kind of a retreat, when people are going away from whatever their life is'.

> If we tried to do it in Leeds city centre, people would have all of that baggage of, come on, impress me, impress me. In their daily lives time is more precious; in a festival you've got all the time in the world. The only

**FIGURE 23** *The Impossible Lecture, Beacons Festival 2014.*

people that are clock-watching at a festival are the people who really want to see all the bands. And then there's all those other people that don't and that's who we cater for really. We don't cater for the hardcore music fans. We capture people. Different rules apply. Everyone gets a go, and people throw away their inhibitions. There was one point this year when there were about fifteen naked people on stage; and only about four were performers. Beacons Festival is not queer at all, it's a hipster festival; it's for people who are really into their music, so we made a point of queering the whole thing. This was a curatorial decision.

I'm going to go back to the idea of retreat. For the last few years we've run a retreat for artists. So, a group of artists come on site as the festival's getting built; a week early. They … make work for Impossible Lecture on site, and they see the festival getting built around them. Then they have this time slot and they share whatever they've made. You almost build a community before the festival starts, they own the field; eight each year. It's an open call for participation. The idea of retreat is really central but it's also that idea that you retreat towards something and have a retreat. So are you getting away from something or going towards something.

You go to another tent, programmed with maybe theatre, or comedy, or improv, and in the spaces in between the acts you might have a compere, someone keeping the show alive. But we have continuous programming, there are no gaps, anything can happen and all the artists are made aware of this. They are aware. No tech run, no changeover. The uncurated stuff; that what makes it special. (personal interview)

So, in what might appear a rather sanitized, music-oriented event like Beacons Festival, perhaps Impossible Lecture is offering the opportunity for re-engagement with the contemporary carnivalesque. As a response to increasing commercialization and the regulated space of the festival, Impossible

Lecture offers a kind of meta-carnival space. And it is possible to remain in this space, uninterrupted by the relative order and mainstream activity of the festival overall, for the entire 72-hour period of the festival itself.

Impossible Lecture re-introduces the carnivalesque; Adam Young's 'anything can happen' and joy in the uncurated is clear evidence of that. Much of the content of Impossible Lecture is relational performance; 'it requires dialogue, interaction or audience intervention to make it work' and furthermore Young explicitly cites this research. He also cites other theoretical and historical models including Filiou, a fluxus artist, and Joseph Beuys's lectures at university that went on as long as Beuys wanted (up to 8 hours). Adam Young is undoubtedly framing this project as research-informed practice; at least in terms of his role as Artistic Director. Some of the individual works at Impossible Lecture may well be innovation in practice and perhaps, with its continuous programming, the Impossible Lecture format is itself a new mode of practice.

If we consider both Offeh's work at Latitude and the Impossible Lecture, the art, film performance and other creative work can be argued to be original and significant and in some cases the work is rigorous and critically informed. I want to consider how knowledge is shared, managed and generated in festivals. According to Sharma, festivals offer 'not only outlets for celebration, but also encourage a desire to exchange ideas, to test skills' (Sharma 2004, 135). In *Situated Learning: Legitimate Peripheral Participation* Lave and Wenger (1991) describe communities of practice; these are groups of people who share interests or work together and acquire skills through social contact and spending time together. Often communities of practice evolve naturally, catalysed by common interests or professional contexts. In these groups members develop skills and knowledge by a process that Lave and Wenger call 'situated learning'. It is through the process of sharing information and experiences with the group that the members learn from one another, and have an opportunity to develop themselves personally and professionally. However, the details of this is explored further in Wenger's later work (Wenger 1998, 72–3). Through participation in the community of practice, members develop mutual engagement in order to establish norms and build collaborative relationships. They also create a joint enterprise, or shared understanding, of their common ground that is known as the 'domain' of the community; this domain becomes the 'statement of what knowledge the community will steward'. Finally, communities of practice produce a shared repertoire and it is in this shared repertoire that knowledge is located and passed on. This is what happens at Impossible Lecture's artist retreat and then these principles extend into the 72-hour performance which in itself constitutes a larger, broader and less rigorous community of practice.

Festival sites include a far-reaching range of arts practitioners: visual, performance, cabaret, comedy, film and so on, plus musicians, technical and security staff, festival managers, audiences and more. This kind of proximity to other knowledge bases rarely exists in the gallery or theatre space.

This can be seen as a community of practice where unusual collaborative relationships are built, shared understanding is generated and knowledge is shared (Figure 24). However, the festival site is a hugely complex system and one where the community of practice may consist of many smaller, sometimes overlapping, communities. Non-music acts at music festivals may form communities of practice; these communities share knowledge both within and between their communities and also more broadly. They also have the potential to generate new knowledge but this still does not answer the question about why the festival site can be a particularly fertile one. These sites are very different from traditional sites of art and performance production, galleries and theatres, but there is more to be said. Gallery and theatre spaces also house communities of practice and share bodies of knowledge, but the (comparatively) singular nature of the programming into these spaces means that these sites are policed in a way that constricts genuine innovation and novelty beyond the single discipline. The space of the music festival is, by programming non-music acts, constructing a multidisciplinary space. These types of music festival spaces make artists, audiences and festival organizers more open to risk-taking, more able to give artists permission to experiment, to work across art forms and more open to the unplanned.

This is where Bakhtin can once more be useful. Heteroglossia can be described as a complex mix of worldviews and languages that is fundamentally dialogic. By this I mean that each language is almost always viewed from the perspective of the others. This creates difficult unity, because meaning exists, floating, at a point between writer and reader, speaker and listener, artist and audience, maker and participant, production manager and director, practitioner and academic. This meaning can be floating internally, within an individual, between individuals, or within, or between groups. In this floating

**FIGURE 24** *'Unusual collaborative relationships are built' through non-music art and performance, at festival: Kendal Calling, 2010.*

space another process happens that Bakhtin calls hybridization, that is, the mixture of two different languages, or idioms, within a single utterance. For Bakhtin, hybridization happens in heteroglossia. Heteroglossia is not characterized solely by the ability to process multiple languages. It is not enough to quote, cite or simply reproduce those 'alien languages' (Bakhtin 1981, 366) that are incorporated into a text. What is vital is that the languages be viewed from each others' perspectives, that they be 'hybridized' so that an 'interminable' dialogue is created (Morson and Emerson 1990, 314).

The process of hybridization takes enormous amounts of effort. When hybridizing occurs in the space between music festivals and other forms of arts production (see Figure 25) we can think of it as 'a "broadening and deepening of the language horizon, a sharpening in our perspective of socio-linguistic differentiations" and a deepening of our sense of the potentials of languages' (Morson and Emerson 1990, 315). For Bakhtin potential is a core value. Heteroglossic languages are central to the growth and realization of potential. As multiple languages and complex beliefs interact and hybridize, potential is realized. In monologic writing this is almost impossible. A single language can only develop when provoked, or challenged, by another language. This type of language has no ability, or desire, to change in formal terms. It has no self-consciousness and no inherent reflexivity. When site-specific non-music art works are programmed in a music festival they import one, or more, new languages. In order for them to function successfully these languages need to interact with the language of the music festival and vice versa. The music festival site, because of the intervention of other art forms, and other creative and critical languages, allows all these languages to become reflexive, to evolve, to mutate, to see themselves, to take risks, to achieve potential and to see more potential in the future. It represents multiple, deliberate, self-conscious, messy and risky attempts to create an environment for dialogism and hybridization in the culture, practice and experience of festival.

**FIGURE 25** *Bill Drummond graffiti/artwork, Un-Convention, Salford, 2010.*

## Acknowledgements

Thank you to Adam Young, Artistic Director of Impossible Lecture at Beacons Festival, for the interview, which took place on 19 August 2014.

## References

Anderton, C. 2011. 'Music festival sponsorship: between commerce and carnival'. *Arts Marketing: An International Journal* 1(2): 145–58.

ACE website. 2014. Arts Council England. 'National portfolio organisations join Latitude line up. http://www.artscouncil.org.uk/news/arts-council-news/national-portfolio-organisations-join-latitude/. Accessed 10 July 2014.

Bakhtin, M. M. 1981. *The Dialogic Imagination: Four Essays*. Ed. Michael Holquist. Trans. Caryl Emerson and Michael Holquist. Austin: University of Texas Press.

Bakhtin, M. M. 1984. *Rabelais and His World*. Trans. Hélène Iswolsky. Bloomington: Indiana University Press.

Beacons Festival website. 'Impossible Lecture.' http://greetingsfrombeacons.com/impossible-lecture/. Accessed 3 August 2014.

Blake, A. 1997. *The Land Without Music: Music, Culture and Society in Twentieth-Century Britain*. Manchester: Manchester University Press.

Bourriaud, N. 2002. *Relational Aesthetics*. Dijon: Les Presses du Réel.

Gibson, C., and J. Connell. 2012. *Music Festivals and Regional Development in Australia*. Farnham: Ashgate.

Hetherington, K. 2001. *New Age Travellers: Vanloads of Uproarious Humanity*. London: Cassell.

Hewison, R. 1986. *Too Much: Art and Society in the Sixties, 1960-75*, London: Methuen.

Latitude Festival website. http://www.latitudefestival.com/. Accessed 10 July 2014.

Lave, L., and Wenger, E. 1991. *Situated Learning: Legitimate Peripheral Participation (Learning in Doing: Social, Cognitive and Computational Perspective)*. Cambridge: Cambridge University Press.

McLaren, J. 2012. 'Latitude Festival arts programmer Tania Harrison gives Run Riot the insider's story' *Run Riot*. http://www.run-riot.com/articles/blogs/interview-latitude-festival-arts-programmer-tania-harrison-gives-run-riot-insiders-st. Accessed 15 August 2014.

McKay, G. 2000. *Glastonbury: A Very English Fair*. London: Victor Gollancz.

Morson, G., and Emerson, C. 1990. *Mikhail Bakhtin: Creation of a Prosaics*. Stanford: Stanford University Press.

Mintel. 2006. *Music Concerts & Festivals – UK*. Mintel. August 2006. http://academic.mintel.com. Accessed 5 April 2013.

Mintel. 2008. *Music Concerts & Festivals – UK*. Mintel. August 2008. Mintel. http://academic.mintel.com. Accessed 5 April 2013.

O'Grady K. A., and Kill R. 2013. 'Exploring festival performance as a state of encounter.' *Arts and Humanities in Higher Education: An International Journal of Theory, Research and Practice*. 12(2–3) (April/July): 268–83.

Sharma, K. K. (2004). *World Tourism Today*. New Delhi: Sarup.
Stallybrass, P., and White, A. 1986. *The Politics and Poetics of Transgression*. Ithaca, New York: Cornell University Press.
Wenger, E. 1998. *Communities of Practice: Learning, Meaning, and Identity*. Cambridge: Cambridge University Press.

# CHAPTER SIX

# Photo-essay: Free festivals, new travellers and the free party scene in Britain, 1981–1992

*Alan Lodge*

*Glastonbury Green Gathering, Somerset, July 1982.*

*Cannock Chase, Staffordshire, July 1985.*

*Montgomery, Powys, July 1984.*

*Inglestone Common, Avon, July 1993.*

*Aktivator Festival, Tewkesbury, Gloucestershire, August 1988.*

*Pick Up Bank / Deeply Vale, Lancashire, August 1981.*

*Stonehenge, Wiltshire, June 1984.*

*Stonehenge, Wiltshire, June 1992.*

*Glastonbury Green Gathering, Somerset, July 1982.*

*Glastonbury, Somerset, June 1986.*

*Sizewell, Suffolk, September 1982.*

*Glastonbury, Somerset, June 1987.*

*Stonehenge, Wiltshire, June 1988.*

*Aktivator Festival, Tewkesbury, Gloucestershire, August 1988.*

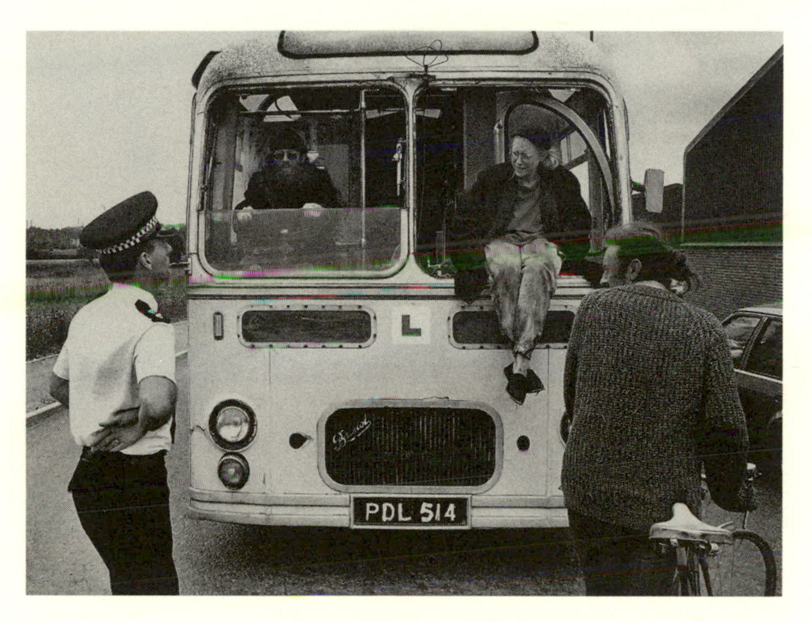


*Salisbury, Wiltshire, June 1988.*

*Stonehenge / Battle of the Beanfield, Hampshire / Wiltshire, June 1985.*

*Lechlade Rave / Festival, Gloucestershire, May 1992.*

*Castlemorton, Worcestershire, May 1992.*

*Castlemorton, Worcestershire, May 1992.*

*Castlemorton, Worcestershire, May 1992.*

# CHAPTER SEVEN

# Festival bodies: The corporeality of the contemporary music festival scene in Australia

*Joanne Cummings and Jacinta Herborn*

*... if you're a festival head, then you already know the plan*
*Go and pack up all your shit cause you're going on a trip*
*For those summer days.*

PEZ, FEAT. 360 AND HAILEY CRAMER, 'THE FESTIVAL SONG' (2008)

In this chapter we explore how the embodied experiences enabled or produced through participation in music festivals can create a sense of belonging and identification with a larger music scene, for festival-goers, while also exploring the Australian aspects of these experiences. The embodiment of the festival experience is grounded not only in the sensate dimensions of the physical, biological body, but is also connected and bound to the social and emotional aspects of the festival scene. These emotional, social and physical aspects of experience are all vital elements in festival-goers' identity formation and allow for affective social connections as well as the development of neo-tribal sociality. By examining the corporeality involved in the experience of the mosh pit, as well as the embodiment of heat, this chapter investigates the relationship between the body and the festival environment.

We draw on ethnographic research conducted at Australian youth-oriented music festivals between 2003 and 2014 to provide empirical insight into the corporeality festival-goers experience during a music festival. These events are considered youth oriented for several reasons; first, researchers observed primarily young people at the event, generally ranging in age from 18 to 30 years. Second, these festivals are clearly oriented towards young people which is shown in a range of details, including the styles of music, as well as the imagery and language used in the promotional material. For example, festival advertisements often incorporate imagery that clearly denotes youth and even childhood, such as a carnival, candy and cartoon pirates. The festivals researched included: Big Day Out, Homebake, Splendour in the Grass, Livid, Falls Festival, St Jerome's Laneway and Soundwave. These festivals vary in terms of the styles of music performed, the size of the audience, the size of the festival space and the environment in which they are each held.

Of course, fieldwork, in itself, is an embodied activity (Coffey 1999). The authors have drawn on their own embodied experience of participating in the Australian music festival scene, in addition to interviews with festival-goers. It is important to acknowledge the position of the authors in relation to this research particularly in terms of their 'insider status' (Bennett 2003; Cummings 2006). Both the authors are fans of the researched festivals, under thirty-five years old, Anglo-Saxon, able-bodied and female. Although some Australian music festivals, such as Soundwave, have male-dominated audiences, these are spaces filled predominantly with young, white bodies (as shown in Figure 26) and as such both researchers can be understood

**FIGURE 26** *The Australian festival space is 'filled predominantly with young white bodies': festival-goer at Future Music Festival, Sydney 2013.*

as insiders, holding the relevant knowledge, as well as possessing the 'normal' or 'usual' festival body. An examination of embodiment at festivals within Australia must first begin with a consideration of the theoretical underpinnings of this concept.

## Embodiment and popular music studies

For popular music studies an examination of the sensate experience and aesthetic ideological systems are essential to understanding the embodiment of musical festivals and the resultant community (Shank 1994). The concept of embodiment has been used to unravel entrenched dualisms, such as that of mind/body, nature/culture and subject/object, which suggests that experience and knowledge are always located in and produced by the body (Shilling 2007). As Levin (1999) discusses thinking takes place in our eyes, feet, hands – the flesh, which is lived and through which, cognition, action and behaviour are informed.

Here the body is not understood as a separate, static or contained entity, but instead transformed by culture and open to its surrounds. As Merleau-Ponty (2002) suggests, individuals know themselves only through their position in and interaction with the world. It is through our surrounds that we know our bodies and through our bodies that we know our surrounds. The body and environment unfold in a continual process of being and becoming. This inextricable entwinement of the body and its environment is experienced and understood through the senses. It is through sensorial experience that individuals are emotionally enmeshed with their environment, which, equally intricate and expansive, includes among other things the human and the non-human, the natural and the constructed, the permanent and the fleeting (Milton 2007). Indeed, all human life is bound to emotion – 'the relational flows, fluxes or currents between people, places' and things (Bondi et al. 2005, 3).

Fundamentally, bodies are bound not only to their environment, but also to the society and culture in which they exist. The senses demonstrate this relationship, considering the body's perceptual capacities to be bound to the five sense organs is not natural, universal or neutral (Classen 1993; Howes 2005). Rather, this conceptualization of the body emerged from the Aristotelian tradition and has continued to dominate Western thought. Within this tradition, perceptual experience is delegated to specific regions of the body – the eyes, ears, skin, nose and mouth. Moreover, sense experience and the information it generates are hierarchically ordered. This ranking of the senses creates what Classen (1993) describes as different modes of consciousness. The way in which we perceive, experience and understand our world and body is determined primarily through the mode of consciousness our society positions as dominant. In Western societies, sight is hierarchically positioned above hearing, touch, smell and taste (Ingold 2000). However, recent works in the field of embodiment, which focus specifically upon the senses, are 'supplanting other paradigms and challenging conventional theories of representation' (Cranny-Francis 2013, 10).

According to Cranny-Francis (2013, 10) the past decade has seen the emergence and development of 'sensory studies as a research field'. Significantly, 'contemporary theorists, psychologists and neuroscientists have specified other senses' such as vestibular sense or the sense of balance and proprioception which relates to the internal sense of the body's movement (Cranny-Francis 2013, 13). These developments are important as they open up the body for further investigation and allow for a broader and more in-depth understanding of how the body unfolds in its environment.

Despite the increased interest in the body and the increasingly complex conceptualizations of embodied experience that have been generated, the body remains absent in certain areas of contemporary inquiry – the study of popular music, and in particular the music festival is one such area. As Johnson (2013, 101) writes, a 'fundamental physicality' is involved in the experience of music. Yet, 'there are significant gaps in popular music studies', perhaps summarized best as 'the case of the missing body' (Johnson 2013, 106). One study which does incorporate the idea of the sensate dimensions of experience is Wendy Fonarow's (2006) ethnographic account of the British indie music scene. For Fonarow, embodiment relates to understanding human activities as an incorporation of the biological, psychological and cultural. She considers the body in terms of both the physical and the communicative aspects of interaction. She examined how the body is used and read by participants during music events. She observed the way bodies position themselves within the environment or space of the musical performance, for example, where audience members stand in relation to the stage during events. Younger people are at the front, where they can mosh and dance and be close to the band, whereas older people tend to stand towards the back where they can drink and watch the band. She also investigated non-verbal communication at these events; for example, the wearing of a back stage pass: is it displayed overtly or covertly? The overt display of the pass demonstrates the wearer's special connection privileges, while covert wearing suggests that the person is just another member of the audience.

A recent study by Duffy (2014) has captured how 'festivalization' may relate to the body. Festivalization refers to the processes through which communal ideas of identity and belonging are formed through the shared understandings and practices of agency, time and space (Duffy 2014). Duffy investigated the emotional ecology of two cultural music festivals in Australia. In particular, she examined how sound impacted on the body and what this meant in terms of the processes of subjectivity and identity formation. She argued that by attending the festivals participants engaged in an experiential process, which opens the body to the sights, sounds, smells, experiences and feeling aroused by the festival. She argued that emotional and affective responses are integral parts of identity formation and social

**FIGURE 27** *'The intensity of the festival experience creates a sense of connectedness and belonging': The crowd at Big Day Out, Sydney, 2013.*

connection for festival-goers. They are feelings and means by which 'we' create togetherness and a sense of belonging. Her study mainly uses the sense of 'sound' to explore this connection, as 'sound can be both participatory and alienating – it evokes a bodily way of being in the world, you can loose yourself in the music or feel isolated and disruptive by the music' (Duffy 2014, 231).

This 'we' is a type, which Maffesoli (1996) refers to as a neo-tribe or emotional community that are bonded together through collectively shared thoughts, feelings, emotions and experiences (Cummings 2006, 2007). For festival-goers festivals are not only about leisure and pleasure; these spaces contain meaning as the intensity of the festival experience creates a sense of connectedness and belonging to scene within which they can experiment and express their identity (Cummings 2007) (Figure 27). Festival-goers often express their identity through their physical bodies and spectacle, such as wearing certain clothing, adorning their bodies with tattoos and outrageous hairstyles (Finkel 2009). While the physical embodiment of youth culture or neo-tribal alliances has been well documented in previous studies (McRobbie 1994; Cummings 2006; Anderton 2009), little attention has been given to the embodied sensual experience of attending a festival.

## Moshing as part of the festival rhythm

*The crowd roared and cheered, clapping their hands above their heads as the band walked on stage. The lead guitarist struck the first chord and the music began. From my elevated position I surveyed the growing crowd, as they began to move. The mass of people were rising and falling like rolling waves in the sea. They sang as they jumped up and down in time to the music. Then, a lone sweaty body emerged from the ocean, elevated on the outstretched hands floating above the bouncing heads as he is passed along toward the stage. He stretched his arms toward the band, forming his hands into a sign language known only to him and then he gave an almighty shout, 'Rock and roll!' He was caught and dragged safely down over the front barricade by the security guards. As the song reached its crescendo, more bodies arose from the ocean of people. Girls and shirtless guys with tribal tattoos in black ink surfed above the crowd. Feet, legs, arms flew in every direction as the dust rose and engulfed the crowd. Finally the song ended and the dust settled for a brief moment as the sweat-saturated crowd cheered clapped, and grabbed a breath of air in anticipation of the next song.* (Field notes, JC, 2005)

Lefebvre suggests that the conscious and unconscious perceptions we have of our bodily rhythms means we think with our bodies 'not only in the abstract, but in lived temporality' (cited in Duffy 2014). As Ehrenreich (cited in Duffy 2014, 231) argues 'to submit, bodily, to the music through dance [or moshing as described above] is to be incorporated into the community in a way far deeper than shared myth or common custom can achieve'. It is this corporeal shared experience that creates a sense of sociality and feeling of belonging for festival-goers.

The mosh pit is an example of the embodiment of this sense of belonging, as Penny (festival-goer aged twenty-three) describes.

> It's funny [because] it's a kind, a communist sort of atmosphere, you're all in it together but at the same time it's very vicious like everyone's got their elbows out marking out their own space. I never saw anybody fall over without three hands reach down to pull [him or her] up. I suppose it's like self-preservation as well because if someone goes down and no one helps them up someone else is gunna fall over and it's gunna be terrible but yeah.

The contradictory nature of the mosh pit, as both a place of violence and solidarity, is interesting, as it contains a kind of mosh pit etiquette wherein the festival-goers look after one another and try to ensure a level of safety within the chaos, as Finn (festival-goer aged nineteen) notes:

> When they would start those circle moshes when people would just run wildly in the middle of a circle and bash into each other. But when someone would fall over and they would help them straight back up and I kind of thought I that's a bit weird like there trying to bash each other up but they're still looking out for each other.

Music provides individuals with an 'intensely subjective sense of being social' (Frith 1996, 273). This intense engagement with the music by festival-goers in the mosh pit can create a sense of neo-tribal sociality and belonging. Such behaviour, which transcends what is expected and acceptable in everyday life, such as wild running and bodies bashing and jumping into each other, while viewed by non-festival-goers as eccentric and inappropriate, does create a sociality for the festival-goers. The field notes starting this section demonstrate this sociality and embodied sense of being, in and with the crowd. Interestingly, crowd surfing is officially banned at many festivals, as the activity is extremely dangerous and often results in injury; yet the practice is still common place during festivals (Tsitsos 1999; Ambrose 2001). In 2001, at Sydney's Big Day Out the actual rather than potential danger of mosh pits was demonstrated with tragic consequences when festival-goer Jessica Michalik was killed in a crowd surge during a performance by American band Limp Bizkit (Figure 28).

Furthermore, the mosh pit is an extremely hot environment and the bodies as described above are often saturated in sweat. The embodied experience of heat, which occurs at many live music events, can be considered as one way in which Australia's environment is entwined with and experienced through many Australian music festivals. Heat provides or produces festival experiences that can impact significantly upon the embodied experiences of festival-goers and as such warrants examination here.

**FIGURE 28** *Soundwave Festival 2012, Melbourne. Limp Bizkit return to pay tribute to fan Jessica Michalik who had died as a result of injuries in the mosh pit at Big Day Out in 2001.*

## The Australian music festival scene

> Hand in hand, it goes together. It's hot, summer, have a nice cold beer or four or five. [Paul, festival-goer, aged twenty]

Contemporary Australian music festivals occur throughout the year, in a wide range of environments. They are held in both urban and rural (Gibson and Connell 2011) locations, from the sun-baked concrete and searing heat of urban festivals like the Big Day Out and Soundwave, to the tranquil bush campsites of rural festivals like Splendour in the Grass. The festivals are a mixture of one-day touring events such as St Jerome's Laneway and multi-day camping events like Falls festival. Moreover, the varied locations and times of year produce highly varied weather conditions; as such while researching these festivals the authors have experienced record-breaking heat, torrential rain, swamp-like fields of mud, icy winter nights and lightning storms. However, Australian music festivals are held mainly during summer, and so these events are commonly associated with the embodied experience of heat. This was evidenced through participant responses, which is examined here. Moreover, the association of heat with music festivals has occurred since festivals were first held in Australia.

The Australian festival scene dates back to the open-air festival of Love Peace and Music held on pastoral lands in Ourimbah New South Wales in 1970, which was a Woodstock-like festival heavily influenced by the counterculture of the 1960s. The next major Australian music festival, Sunbury (which took place annually from 1972 to 1974), was held on farmland near Melbourne, Victoria. Unlike its predecessor the festival was heavily dominated by 'heat, dust and hard sweaty guitar' (Cockington 2001). These environmental factors continue to contribute significantly to the experiences of festival-goers, often shaping their practices during the festival, as well as their memories of the event. The embodied experience of heat, at one and the same time, evidences the inescapable entwinement of individuals and their surrounds, pulls attention from those surrounds back towards the body, penetrates the body and reconfigures the festival-goer's emotional engagement with the space. Moreover, the experience of heat demonstrates the complexity and multiplicity of the corporeal capacity of touch and its inseparability from the body as a whole entity.

It must be noted that the embodied experience of heat is not simply an innate response to external stimuli. Rather, heat imprints upon different bodies in different ways. Two attendees who spoke to us about heat considered it to be only mildly irritating, though for several other participants, the embodiment of heat profoundly impacted upon the experience of these events. Thus, the experience of heat demonstrates the diverse ways in which the environment presses upon bodies and the diverse ways in which this interaction is felt and understood. Heat was discussed most commonly by participants in terms of negative experiences. The negative effect that heat had upon participants is not simply related to their individual physiological responses to heat, but instead evidences the body as a physical, social and emotional entity. The understanding of heat produced by Western cultures demonstrates entrenched concerns that relate to the relationship between individuals and certain aspects of the natural environment – perhaps exemplified outside an Australian context in the aptly named Burning Man gathering in the American desert.

The embodied experience of heat is most often associated with tactility and experienced through the skin. In recent years, as interest in the senses has grown, the corporeal capacity of touch has begun to receive significant scholarly attention. Despite this there seems to be few academic accounts of the embodied experience of heat. Further, although the skin enables and produces tactile experience, Benthien (2002) suggests this region of the body has been relatively neglected in scholarly texts. Indeed some recent examinations of the senses and touch focus more generally upon this corporeal capacity, without providing an in-depth account of the skin. Also, the weather, an element of our natural environment, which provides tactile stimulation, is often ignored in scholarly accounts that consider the interaction between the individual and the environment (Ingold 2000). In everyday life, through design and architecture, the weather is often experienced at a distance (Howes 2005; Waitt 2014); however, during a festival attendees are exposed to the weather for long periods of time. Indeed for some festival cultures, the impact of weather, its variability and capacity to change landscape, is a pivotal issue (we might think of Glastonbury Festival in England, divided in memory and public perception into the mud and the dry years – see Figure 29).

**FIGURE 29** *Glastonbury Festival 2007 – one of the 'mud years'.*

So, the weather does not merely swirl above, in the periphery; rather it shapes the experiences of festival-goers. When Marion (festival-goer aged twenty-six) was asked about negative experiences at live music events, she discussed the weather and in particular the heat of Big Day Out.

> It was boiling hot and I got sunburnt ... that made me feel weary throughout the day and ... [I was] just physically feeling exhausted from the heat ... it was just horrible.

At festivals the tactile neutrality of everyday life is replaced by dynamic weather conditions, unavoidable and uncontrollable. Extreme tactile stimulation was produced by the 'boiling hot day', and Marion's body is transformed by the space, made 'weary' and 'exhausted' by the heat. Tim (festival-goer aged twenty-five) reflected similar concerns through his discussion of heat. For him the tactile experience of the natural environment at festivals was particularly intense and deeply effected his emotional connection to the space.

> [At] outdoor festivals usually I'm cranky and sunburnt and hating all the shirtless men who are touching me ... I think at the summer festivals because it's so hot and so horrible to be out in the heat there's this underlying anger, like everyone's just walking around a bit angry.

Tim understands this embodied experience of the Australian summer at a festival to be a collective or shared experience. The way heat is absorbed by or impinges upon different bodies can vary immensely, yet Tim projects his own response to the weather conditions onto the bodies that surround him. Exposure to the sun simultaneously evidences the skin as a place of encounter, where an element of the natural environment – the sun – touches the body, and as a porous conduit through which heat enters and affects the body, physically and emotionally. Moreover, Tim's comments relating to shirtless men reflected a common concern for participants with bare skin and in particular sweaty skin.

## Sweaty bodies

> ... Squished together with 20,000–50,000 other sweaty people you don't know ... confronting yet uniting. (Howarth 2006)

At festivals thousands of bodies move throughout the event site, and at Australian festivals these bodies are often hot and sweaty. Personal space is often limited and so bare, often-sweaty skin comes into contact with the bodies of others. This physical interaction, between skin and sweaty skin, produced emotional responses by participants. Despite the commonality of sweat within these spaces, festival-goers often viewed sweaty bodies as undesirable and abhorrent:

> it hinders the rest of my experience ... the super-, super-sweaty people that just rub up against you, like if you're wearing a shirt that's fine, everybody's going to get a bit sweaty, but when it's the actual sweat coming straight off someone onto you, that puts a bit of a literal dampener on your experience. (Sally, festival-goer aged twenty-five)

Smith and Davidson's discussion of the nature/culture dualism in relation to bare skin is relevant here, as they believe a key facet of the modern Western symbolic order is the 'boundary it constructs and relies upon between nature and culture' (2006, 47). The primitive, disordered and often chaotic natural environment poses a threat to the civilized, ordered, modern self. Through the uninvited contact of certain elements of nature with bare skin, this threat is felt (Smith and Davidson 2006). Sweat could be understood here as posing a similar threat to the embodied experience of the self, particularly for contemporary youths.

According to Waitt, 'bodily fluids are often considered a dirty topic' (2014, 6). Indeed, within the social sciences sweat is commonly conceptualized as dirt; sweat is 'matter out of place' (Waitt 2014, 3). This substance, which oozes out from the inside, sits upon the skin and through touch can be transferred to another. As Waitt suggests, 'rendered as dirt, sweat is understood as a potential source of contamination' (2014, 3). This notion was reflected in the comments of Peter (festival-goer aged nineteen) who said, 'it's so hot and it's pretty disgusting there's so many people and they're all sweating'. This perception of sweat as dirty was also articulated by Eric (festival-goer aged twenty-one):

> you know Big Day Out is synonymous with sweaty people ... that's why you buy a new t-shirt when you go to Big Day Out mate, because you've just got fat people sweat all over you and you wanna get rid of that shit.

For Eric, sweat is both expected and unacceptable. He finds the sweat of others, particularly 'fat people', so undesirable he replaces his t-shirt in an attempt to 'get rid' of that which he understands as a contaminating element. So, within certain live music spaces, the touch of sweat from another's body is unavoidable and highly undesirable. Potential contact with sweat triggers feelings of disgust. The natural element of sweat represents the uncivilized, uncontrollable interior of the body and as such, contact with it transgresses the experience of the ordered, modern self. Festival spaces as sites in which everyday norms are transgressed has also been discussed in relation to the carnivalesque.

## Corporeality, the carnivalesque and the festivalization of everyday life

During music festivals attendees are exposed, for long periods of time, to a sensory environment that is rich and varied. Sensory engagement in everyday life is often mundane, routine and comfortable (Howes 2005). But the festival space is full of sounds, sights and bodily experiences that can be had only within the festival space. Festivals are replete with overwhelming stimulus. Music flows, rages or pumps through the space, the hum of the crowd is constant, bright lights flash, graphic artworks and huge media screens are seen throughout the site, aromatic smells from food stalls mix with that of stale beer, cigarettes and sweat, the tastes of Australian festival food such as gozleme, fairy floss and Bundaberg rum touch the tongue throughout the day, the skin registers the heat of the sun, the constant brushing and bumping into other bodies and in the stomach a twinge of excitement and joy may be felt as you watch your favourite act.

Festivals provide sensory stimulation unlike that experienced through everyday activities. The experience is understood as a kind of freedom from the mundane routines of everyday life and the heightened sensory environment provided by festival spaces has prompted some theorists to draw a connection between contemporary festivals and the carnivalesque. According to Anderton contemporary music festivals are 'a time during which the normal rules of social hierarchy and acceptable behaviour are suspended or inverted' (Anderton 2009). This is exemplified by the 'loud music, colourful and outlandish clothing, muddy fields, drugs, alcohol, sexual freedom and so on –which are both celebrated and denounced in the media portrayal and advertising of festivals to this day – offer carnivalesque liberation from social norms' (Anderton 2009).

However, although transgressions of social norms are tolerated within the festival space, following Bakhtin (1984), of course, with carnival there are limits and boundaries as to just how far that transgression can go. Festivals may appear to be the 'epitome of disorder' from the outside, but order is constantly 'provisional local and specific and not something that can be avoided all together' (Hetherington 2000, 57). Confirming some limits to carnival excess, festival-goer Sally discussed her understanding of the mosh pit etiquette:

> just being considerate, jump around and sing along, that's fine, but yeah just don't do anything out of the ordinary, like not being violent on purpose, if you're taller than someone and you can move to accommodate someone behind you then that's sweet.

Similarly, and with its own corporeal resonance, the long-standing Meredith Music Festivals overtly present what they term a 'no dickhead policy' (Meredith Music Festival 2014) through which festival-goers are encouraged to be self-regulatory, 'politely informing' their fellow festival-goers that certain behaviours are not admired or appreciated.

Although festivals provide unique (even if repeated) experiences, which vary significantly to that of everyday life, these experiences and the way in which they affect the individual, physically, emotionally and socially are not all contained to the festival site. Rather, embodied experiences triggered or enabled through festivals can occur beyond the time and space of the actual event. This festivalization refers to the process by which the boundaries between the festival event and its geographical and social context 'spill out' beyond its temporal and spatial boundaries (Roche 2011; Duffy 2014). Duffy suggests that 'festivalisation processes draw on collective understandings and practices of space, time and agency, which are then deployed so as to shape communal notions of identity and belonging' (Duffy 2014, 230). For Roche, events are internalized into a community's calendar of 'memorable and narratable pasts, with the sociocultural rhythm of life in the present, and with anticipated futures' (Roche 2011, 127–8). For the youth attending Australian music festivals, this incorporation of the festivals into their social 'calendar' is an example of the festivalization of the everyday. Thus festival-goers carefully plan festival attendance: saving up enough money for a ticket, buying tickets months in advance of the event, booking accommodation and all this before the announcement of the band line-up. There is a sense of anticipation, celebration, pleasure and fun that can be linked to the embodied experience of festival attendance. Before the event festival-goers share information, like or comment on festival pages on Facebook or follow festival organizers on Twitter, as well as share photos and videos, checking-in or updating their status both during and after the event, and as such the spatial and temporal boundaries of these events become increasingly fluid, by means which include social media.

Festivals, though providing distinct experiences from everyday life, are not contained events, easily separated from everyday life. Rather, the spatial and temporal boundaries of these events extend into the everyday. Recent academic accounts reflect this notion and add complexity to considerations of these events. Giorgi and Sassatelli (2011) assert the ways in which they are intimately embedded within the public sphere as normative and at times transformative processes. As the lyrics to Pez's Australian hit from 2008 'The festival song' (Pez 2008) used above demonstrate, there is an innate sense of community of 'festival heads' and 'knowing the plan'. This insider knowledge creates a sociality between festival-goers and their everyday lives as they both plan *and* remember their festival experience.

## Conclusion

Music festivals provide a space that draw attention to one's bodily experience and the bodies of others. Through the shifting, fleeting nature of the space, the body is enlivened within these spaces as 'live bodies perform for live bodies' (Johnson 2013, 101). The corporeal experience of the festival contains a distinctive temporality and spatiality, which creates a heightened sensuality that imprints upon the body. Music festivals are spaces which allow for the interaction of live bodies, between performers and the audience or among festival-goers themselves. The tribal nature of the festival space allows for a form of togetherness that draws attention to the entwinement of mind and body, thought and feeling. The sensory body allows a corporeal connection to the collective consciousness that lingers in the air at the festival, the feel or vibe of the event, that which is indescribable, yet palpable. As we have seen, with the rapid growth of contemporary music festivals in Australia and around the globe, researchers explore festival practices and histories as well as the festivalization of the everyday. Festival-goers develop sociality through the embodied experience of participating in a music festival. This sensate dimension is produced through a combination of affective responses to the sights, sounds, smells, experiences and feelings of the festival. In this chapter we have attempted to go beyond the literature, which privileges the discussion of body in response of the 'sound' of music. It has captured bodily response to the environment of the festival through the examples of moshing and the feel of sweat on the skin, which endeavours to add new understandings of the body in popular music studies.

## References

Ambrose, J. 2001. *Moshpit: The Violent World of Mosh Pit Culture*. Sydney, Omnibus Press.

Anderton, C. 2009. 'Commercializing the carnivalesque: the V Festival and image/ risk management.' *Event Management* 12: 39–51.

Bakhtin, M. 1984. *Rabelais and His World*. Bloomington: Indiana University Press.

Bennett, A. 2003. 'The use of "insider" knowledge in ethnographic research on contemporary youth music scenes.' In A. Bennett and M. Cieslik, eds. *Researching Youth*. New York: Palgrave Macmillan.

Benthien, C. 2002. *Skin: On the Cultural Border Between Self and World*. Trans. T. Dunlap. New York: Columbia University Press.

Bondi, L., J. Davidson and M. Smith, eds. 2005. *Emotional Geographies*. Aldershot: Ashgate.

Classen, C. 1993. *Worlds of Sense: Exploring the Senses in History and Across Cultures*. London: Routledge.

Cockington, J. 2001. *Long Way to the Top: Stories of Australian Rock and Roll*. Sydney: ABC Books.

Coffey, A. 1999. *The Ethnographic Self*. London: Sage.

Cranny-Francis, A. 2013. *Technology and Touch: The Biopolitics of Emerging Technologies*. Sydney: Palgrave Macmillan.

Cummings, J. 2006. 'It's more than a T-shirt: neo-tribal sociality and linking images at Australian indie music festivals.' *Perfect Beat* 8(1): 69–84.

Cummings, J. 2007. 'We're all in this together: the meanings Australian festival-goers attribute to their music festival participation.' *History of Stardom Reconsidered*: the referred proceedings of the inaugural conference of IIPC, International Institute for Popular Culture, University of Turku.

Duffy, M. 2014. 'The emotional ecologies of festivals.' In A. Bennett, I. Woodward, and J. Taylor, eds. *Festivalisation of Everyday Life: Identity, Culture and Politics*. Farnham: Ashgate, 229–49.

Finkel, R. 2009. 'A picture of the contemporary combined arts festival landscape.' *Cultural Trends* 18(1): 3–21.

Fonarow, W. 2006. *Empire of Dirt: The Aesthetics and Rituals of British Indie Music*. Middletown, CT: Wesleyan University Press.

Frith, S. 1996. *Performing Rites*. Cambridge: Harvard University Press.

Gibson, Chris, and John Connell, eds. 2011. *Festival Places: Revitalising Rural Australia*. Bristol: Channel View Publications.

Giorgi, L., and M. Sassatelli. 2011. 'Introduction.' In L. Giorgi, M. Sassatelli, and G. Delanty, eds. *Festivals and the Cultural Public Sphere*. London: Routledge, 1–11.

Hetherington, K. 2000. *New Age Travellers: Vanloads of Uproarious Humanity*. London: New York, Cassell.

Howarth, S. 2006. *Peace, Love and Brown Rice: A Photographic History of the Big Day Out*. Korea: Peace, Love and Brown Rice.

Howes, D. 2005. 'Skinscapes: embodiment, culture and environment.' In C. Classen, ed. *The Book of Touch*. New York: Berg, 27–49.

Ingold, T. 2000. *The Perception of the Environment: Essays on Livelihood, Dwelling and Skill*. London: Routledge.

Johnson, B. 2013. 'I hear music: popular music and its mediations.' *Journal of the International Association for the Study of Popular Music* 3(2): 96–110.

Levin, D. 1999. 'The ontological dimension of embodiment: Heidegger's Thinking of Being.' In D. Welton, ed. *The Body: Classic and Contemporary Readings*. Oxford: Blackwell, 122–49.

Maffesoli, M. 1996. *The Time of the Tribes. The Decline of the Individual in Mass Society*. London, Sage.

McRobbie, A. 1994. 'Different, youthful, subjectivities: towards a cultural sociology of youth.' In A. McRobbie. *Postmodernism and Popular Culture*. London: Routledge.

Meredith Music Festival. 2014. 'Dickhead Policy.' http://2014.mmf.com.au/what-goes-on/dickhead-policy/. Accessed 22 July 2014.

Merleau-Ponty, M. 2002. *The Phenomenology of Perception*. Trans. C. Smith. London: Routledge.

Milton, K. 2007. 'Emotion (or life, the universe, everything).' In H. Wulff, ed. *The Emotions: A Cultural Reader*. Oxford: Berg, 61–76.

Pez. 2008. 'The festival song' (feat. 360 & Hailey Cramer). Soulmate Records.

Roche, M. 2011. 'Festivalisation, cosmopolitanism and European culture.' In L. Giorgi, M. Sassatelli, and G. Delanty, eds. *Festivals and the Cultural Public Sphere*. New York: Routledge, 124–41.

Shank, B. 1994. *Dissonant Identities: The Rock'n'Roll Scene in Austin, Texas*. Middletown, CT: Wesleyan University Press.

Shilling, C. 2007. 'Sociology and the body: classical traditions and new agendas.' *The Sociological Review* 55: 1–18.

Smith, M., and J. Davidson. 2006. '"It makes my skin crawl" ... the embodiment of disgust in phobias of nature.' *Body & Society* 12(1): 43–67.
Tsitsos, W. (1999). 'Rules of rebellion: slamdancing, moshing and the American alternative scene.' *Popular Music* 18(3): 397–414.
Waitt, G. (2014). 'Bodies that sweat: the affective responses of young women in Wollongong, New South Wales, Australia'. *Gender, Place and Culture: A Journal of Feminist Geography*. 21(6): 666–82.

# CHAPTER EIGHT

# The Love Parade: European techno, the EDM festival and the tragedy in Duisburg

*Sean Nye and Ronald Hitzler*

Over the course of its 21-year history (1989–2010), the Love Parade grew to become, for a number of years, the largest and most famous electronic music event in Germany and all of Europe. The event was staged on a total of nineteen occasions in Germany – sixteen times in Berlin (1989–2003, 2006), the city with which the event remains most closely associated, and three times in the Ruhr Valley (2007, 2008 and 2010) (see Meyer 2001; Nye 2009a and, for images and interviews, Loveparade 2003). Over the course of this history, from 2001 on, the Love Parade name was globalized and used for affiliated mass events in numerous cities (Tel Aviv, San Francisco, Vienna, Cape Town, Santiago de Chile and Mexico City).

The Love Parade was also the first 'techno parade' event of its kind in Europe, and the most famous techno parade in the world. Techno parades are a specific form of electronic dance music (EDM) festival, consisting of a caravan of trucks that drive through the main streets of a major metropolitan area. The trucks are equipped with sound systems, from which DJs play techno, or EDM. The aesthetics of techno parades grew out of a combination of rave and free festival culture, while borrowing from the aesthetics and structures within the larger history of festival parades, such as Carnival and Pride Parades (Johnston 2005; Nye 2009a). Yet the Love Parade became its own original. The techno parades that followed in its wake, both in Germany, such as Generation Move in Hamburg and Reincarnation in Hannover, and internationally, such as the Street Parade in

Zürich and the Technoparade in Paris, borrowed extensively from the Love Parade's aesthetics and structures. It thus became the symbolic originator of a specific form of EDM party, primarily based in Europe, that saw its rise in the 1990s and decline in the 2000s.

On 24 July 2010, the Love Parade's history came, however, to a horrific and abrupt end. Several hours after the event began in the city of Duisburg, overcrowding at its main entrance resulted in a panic and stampede, which caused the deaths of twenty-one people and the injuring of hundreds more. With a tragedy of this magnitude, a shadow has been cast across the Love Parade's legacy. It now stands in the popular imagination as an exemplary annual event whose existence was perpetually in crisis and whose future was never certain, but which, in the end, lived beyond its time. When the definitive cancelling of the event by its de facto owner, Rainer Schaller, was announced the day after the tragedy, the debate regarding the Love Parade's definitive meaning for our time began (T-online Nachrichten 2010). The legal procedures regarding accountability and criminal actions occurring around the panic in Duisburg are also ongoing.[1] However, this chapter does not address these legal ramifications or criminal procedures. As authors who have experienced the Love Parade in Berlin and the Ruhr Valley, we seek rather to clarify how the Love Parade came to be held in the city of Duisburg and to provide an overview of the parade's history within the framework of pop festivals.

The chapter is divided into three sections. We begin with an introduction to the Love Parade's Berlin history and the transforming interests involved in moving the parade to the Ruhr Valley. We also explain the economic and cultural context of the Rhine-Ruhr metropolitan region. Second, we focus on the Ruhr Valley Love Parade history and the city of Duisburg. This investigation addresses Duisburg's hosting of the Love Parade in the context of the Ruhr Valley's status as the 2010 European Capital of Culture, under the title 'RUHR.2010' (see Hitzler et al. 2012, RUHR2010 website), as well as the tragedy of 24 July 2010. In the final section, we offer some conclusions regarding the Love Parade's history in the context of 'eventization' theory, to understand the role that mass gatherings such as the Love Parade play in marketing cities and regions with cultural capital and tourism, while also addressing the continuous and arguably increasing importance of EDM festivals in the twenty-first century.

## Love Parade history: Berlin, the Ruhr Valley and event economics

The Love Parade began on a rainy summer's day, 1 July, in the fortuitous year of 1989, just a few months before the Berlin Wall came down (on 9 November), which resulted in Germany's official reunification on

3 October 1990. A two-truck 'sound system', with 150 people attending this underground parade, announced a new form of party within the developing Berlin techno scene. The first parade (and subsequent parades until 1995) took place along the Kurfürstendamm, the main shopping street in West Berlin. The parade was thus established during the musical-historical crossroads following the 1988–89 acid house trend in West Germany (and West Berlin) and leading to the early 1990s techno-rave popular explosion in the newly united Germany. The idea of the 'Love Parade' derived from Dr Motte, a Berlin acid house DJ who wanted to have a free and open party on the streets where people could gather and 'be themselves' through dance, fun and spectacle. The partiers that year demonstrated under the quite playful slogan, 'Friede, Freude, Eierkuchen' (Peace, Joy, Pancakes), a discursive attitudinality that arguably reflected also the cheeky combination of 'Love' with the political and military traditions of 'Parade'.

It was hardly expected during this inauspicious beginning that the parade would develop into the flagship event for the German techno scene as early as 1991 (see Figure 30). During that year, the regional EDM scenes from across Germany (including Frankfurt, Cologne and others) gathered at *a single event,* the Love Parade, for the first time (see Meyer 2001; Sextro and Wick 2008). The parade grew rapidly from 6,000 participants in 1991 to an extraordinary 750,000 in 1996, which was the year the Love Parade transferred from the Kurfürstendamm in West Berlin to the Straße des 17. Juni. This rapid development also occurred in parallel with the establishing of Berlin techno clubs and parties along a new 'club mile', many of which were located in the free spaces that had opened up in East Berlin during the

**FIGURE 30** *The Love Parade, Berlin, 1998: 'The flagship event for the German techno scene'.*

early 1990s (Nye 2009a; Rapp 2009). The Straße des 17. Juni is a major thoroughfare; while still located in West Berlin, this street leads to the Brandenburg Gate, a monument along the former East–West border. On the other side of the Brandenburg Gate, the thoroughfare continues into former East Berlin under a more famous name: Unter den Linden. This move to the former border reflected in urban geography the symbolic development of the parade into the pop symbol of a newly united Berlin and a newly united Germany. The festival eventually grew to become the largest electronic music festival in the world, with a peak attendance of 1.5 million in 1999. Echoing Woodstock decades earlier, it was even described, in *Der Spiegel* newspaper, as the 'symbol of a generation' (Beyer et al. 1999).

Indeed, by the time of its move, the Love Parade had become a hybrid pop festival beyond its original form as a 'techno parade'. It retained a playful, and minimal, use of political language through official yearly mottos (1997's 'Let the Sunshine in Your Heart', or 1998's 'One World, One Future', for instance) and the legal designation of a demonstration through Dr Motte's annual, and short, speeches (often just a few minutes long) during the event. Along with the parade, media and cultural industries began to develop. For example, each year the parade was broadcast live on *VIVA*, Germany's music television equivalent to MTV; as a result, numerous videos of Love Parade DJ-sets remain available on YouTube. Various kinds of media were also produced in connection with the parade, from CD compilations to Love Parade 'anthems', to a feature film called *be. Angeled* (Nye 2009a).

The parade itself split into two parts. During the day, the parade format was retained to the extent that numerous sound systems, or 'love mobiles', sponsored by clubs, labels or pop media organizations, had DJs playing varieties of EDM. These would run along the Straße des 17. Juni and around a Prussian monument known as the Siegessäule (Victory Column), which was at the centre of the thoroughfare and thus became the de facto symbol of the Love Parade. Shortly before sunset, the various love mobiles were linked up with the main stage for the so-called *Abschlusskundgebung* (closing rally). The linked sound systems represented a symbolic experience of greater unity with the main stage at the Siegessäule. Sets by star DJs followed in rapid succession, with the main focus on the stage rather than the parade. The passage into night also allowed for an extraordinary light show to be broadcast both from the trucks and the main stage. The Love Parade developed into a kind of hybrid event that mixed parade, outdoor festival and media spectacle. The closing ceremony would be followed by the dispersing of the masses, usually to various techno parties, and the soundscape across Berlin itself that night made it feel like a techno city. Techno was played in all possible venues: restaurants, cafes, the U-Bahn and various impromptu DJ sound systems in the streets and parks. Numerous special club and rave events of the so-called Love Week were organized in the days leading up to and following the parade.

The parade's long history on the Straße des 17. Juni (1996–2003, 2006) had both symbolic and organizational benefits. First, it took place in front of the Brandenburg Gate, which had become a symbol of German and European division during the Cold War. Thus, the parade became associated with a monument identifiable to numerous German and international tourists (Nye 2009a). As seen in Figure 31, the party's pop play with these monuments is evident, for example, in the music video to an anthem with which the parade remains strongly identified: Da Hool's 'Meet her at the Love Parade' (Da Hool 1997). The Straße des 17. Juni is also located in the Tiergarten, Berlin's central park, which ensured that overcrowding was not a great concern. The park grounds allowed people to come and go from the parade as they wished. This use of space, however, also caused anger and debate regarding the damage to the gardens each year and the mass amounts of rubbish; indeed, the greatest criticism of the parade at this time focused on its commercialization and the antisocial behaviour, the mass beer consumption and resulting urine in the park.

For these and a variety of others (legal, economic and popular) reasons, conflicts regarding the event's presence in Berlin remained constant. Eventually, the possibility of holding the Love Parade in Berlin came to a definitive end in early 2007. Completing a long process of commercial distancing from the Berlin techno scene, the new organizer of the event was the Lopavent GmbH, a subsidiary of a German fitness club chain, McFit. The owner, Rainer Schaller, had set up Lopavent after he bought the Love Parade name from Dr Motte and four co-owners in 2006. Thereafter, the Love Parade became an event organized in order to promote the McFit brand. Lopavent still managed to organize the Love Parade in Berlin in 2006. However, by 2007, Lopavent became interested in moving the event to the Ruhr Valley, a major industrial area that was part of the metropolitan region of the Rhine-Ruhr. Consisting of roughly 11 million people, the Rhine-Ruhr is by far the largest metropolitan region in Germany; in fact, it is roughly

**FIGURE 31** *Da Hool, 'Meet her at the Love Parade' (1997) video: The Love Parade's 'pop play', dancing in front of the Brandenburg Gate.*

double the size of Berlin. The commercial and cultural benefits of moving the parade to the Ruhr Valley quickly became clear; in February 2007, the end of the long Berlin history of the Love Parade was finally announced, and a five-year plan for the Love Parade to tour different Ruhr cities each year (see Heissmeyer 2007 for the five-year plan).

Relocating around the Ruhr Valley seemed to offer many benefits for Lopavent's plans for securing the Love Parade's future. These involve three key aspects. First, this *polycentric* metropolitan region was markedly different from Berlin; it even necessitated that the Love Parade take place in various cities within the Ruhr Valley. This Berlin event thus transformed into a travelling carnival. In this way, Lopavent could avoid suspicion that, in leaving Berlin, it had to settle for a 'second best' German city (such as Hamburg or Munich). Indeed, the move to the Ruhr Valley seemed to be a conscious decision to fundamentally reimagine the Love Parade. Second, the negotiations confirmed that the managers from business, the media, politics and culture were interested in, indeed enthusiastic about, bringing the Love Parade to the Ruhr Valley. Third, the Ruhr region had already gained considerable prestige, because the city of Essen was to be the European Capital of Culture for 2010. The nomination of Essen was, in effect, the occasion for promoting the entire region as a cultural Ruhr Metropolis. By pooling their resources and embracing a marketing strategy of symbolic monocentrism, these cities could challenge the regional dominance of the Rhine cities (Cologne and Düsseldorf). Finally, it seemed as though the *Ruhrzeit* (so-called Ruhr time) had arrived.

The idea that had been manifested, the Ruhr Metropolis, appeared to be the ideal surroundings for the Love Parade. The following cities were chosen as its future sites: Essen (2007), Dortmund (2008), Bochum (2009), Duisburg (2010) and Gelsenkirchen (2011). This meant that a five-year plan now existed that would secure both the cultural promotion of the Ruhr Valley and, finally, the future of the Love Parade. After all, the Love Parade had been in various stages of crisis throughout its long history in Berlin, despite the economic and cultural benefits it had given the capital following unification. These crises included cancellations of the parade in 2004 and 2005, which almost ended the event permanently. In contrast, the Ruhr parades could securely garner anticipation, with the apparent support of welcoming cities, for a grand finale of the European Capital of Culture celebrations during RUHR.2010.

## The Ruhr parades and the Duisburg tragedy

On 25 August 2007, with the sloganizing certainty that 'Love is Everywhere', the parade's new advance through the Ruhr Metropolis began: first in Essen. As had happened during its Berlin years, the official figures of the Love Parade attendance were exaggerated. Yet, with pressure for success and marketing sensations, the Love Parade figures quickly increased to the point of systematic falsification during the Ruhr years.[2] It was widely reported in the media that up to 1.2 million party people attended the Love Parade in Essen (unofficial statistics of 400,000 are more reasonable). With a split structure comparable to the Berlin Love Parades, the love mobiles headed through the city during the day, up to the main square. A successful 'closing rally' at the prize-winning main stage helped to quell longings for a return to the Berlin Victory Column. By the end of the parade, worries that had been prominent in the media – such as that the parade could be a quantitative disaster in terms of attendees or a qualitative debacle in terms of party organization – proved unfounded.

Completely enthused by the precedent established by Essen, the Dortmund city authorities began to plan for 2008. For the 'Highway of Love', they blocked an entire section of the major route, the B1/A40. The start of the parade was delayed considerably by rain, but when it began, a resounding sound-exhaust was emitted along the Ruhr highway. The masses of partying people seemed endless, both on the freeway and in front of the two-storey main stage. With these great results, the extraordinary figure of 1.6 million visitors was announced, suspiciously 100,000 more than the 1.5 million record set by the 1999 Love Parade. While clearly a PR stunt (actual figures of 'only' 500,000 are more reasonable), the elation of the organizers was patent. However, after these successes in creating what looked like a successful new travelling tradition of the Love Parade, the following year it was suddenly cancelled when the Bochum city authorities withdrew their support and organization, daunted by the prospect of a reported 1 million party-goers turning up to their small city for Europe's largest rave.

For the numerous supporters of the Love Parade, including the organizers of the European Capital of Culture RUHR.2010 events, and those with a vision of the Ruhr Metropolis, this was a new and unexpected blow. After the Love Parade's future had finally seemed secure after years of crisis, it was once again cancelled. Thus, the thanks to Duisburg was considerable when the city confirmed it would indeed still host the 2010 Love Parade, as originally agreed, even though it also did not appear to have the capacity to handle the event. Duisburg was immediately swept up by supportive and powerful interests, so that the Ruhr Valley would not suffer the disgrace of rejecting one of the largest pop festivals in Europe during the same year as RUHR.2010. In the following months, the technical, logistical and financial wheels were set in motion to transform Duisburg, in particular, the ruins of the Duisburger Güterbahnhof (the Duisburg train depot).

This large industrial field, about a mile south of the Duisburg train station, was to be developed into a usable site for the 'Art of Love', the Love Parade 2010 (Figure 32). Observers and fans were at first irritated that no actual parade was planned through the city centre. Rather, a considerably reduced number of floats would drive in a circle around the massive industrial fields of the depot, which was itself to be fenced in because of a

**FIGURE 32** *The location for Love Parade 2010, on disused post-industrial ground behind Duisburg railway station.*

range of technical and legal reasons. In this form, it appeared that the Love Parade had finally diminished into the mere semblance of a techno parade. The official justification was that the compact urban structure of Duisburg did not allow for any alternative. The Güterbahnhof was the only site large enough to accommodate the anticipated mass of ravers and party-goers.

After Bochum, Duisburg was the smallest and the least recognizable city that had ever been considered for the Love Parade. The compact urban structure and lack of administrative resources thus presented considerable challenges and new risks. As charted above, the Love Parade ran smoothly for its many years in Berlin's *Tiergarten,* and it took place in the two major cities of the Ruhr Valley: Essen and Dortmund. Dortmund, especially, had developed a reputation for electronic music events that made its hosting of the Love Parade seem logical and practical. Since 1995, Dortmund's Westfalenhallen, or Westphalia Halls, were host to the oldest annual mega-rave in Germany: the Mayday. Similarly, an electronic music festival, Juicy Beats, had taken place annually in the Westfalenpark since 1996. Each of these sites was ideal for the after-hour parties following the Love Parade 2008.

Duisburg, however, was beset by considerable challenges. While the Ruhr Valley has suffered from a declining population and unemployment since the early 1960s, Duisburg had been particularly hard hit. These struggles aside, the importance of Duisburg as a logistic and industrial area should not be discounted. Duisburg is one of the world's major steel cities, home to Thyssen-Krupp, and it also boasts the largest inland harbour in Europe. Nevertheless, Duisburg provided challenges not present in Essen, Dortmund or Berlin. For a city with such economic and cultural issues, it was of utmost importance to Duisburg that the Love Parade be successful. The event was both a marketing platform in the effort to attract 'youth culture' and a source of considerable tourism for the industrial city. Moreover, this event was to take place in the year of RUHR.2010, which represented the opportunity for Duisburg to become fully integrated into the new Ruhr Metropolis, while stealing the spotlight from more prominent cities. In short, the pressures were extraordinary.

So in the early afternoon of 24 July 2010, despite many unanswered logistical issues, the arrival of the expected party masses in Duisburg began. Shortly after 4 p.m., there was an official announcement that 1.4 million visitors were expected. It seemed to be an extraordinary triumph for the city. The realistic figures are now estimated at around 300,000; nevertheless, until the moment the panic began at approximately 4.40 p.m., the jubilation in Duisburg seemed apparent. What followed was a chaotic unfolding of events and reports that were deeply troubling, even traumatic, for all who were personally involved in some capacity. As attendees tried to escape overcrowding by reaching a narrow staircase at the main entrance, a stampede resulted in hundreds of injuries and the deaths of twenty-one people.[3] This disaster also resulted in trauma for many of the survivors and, as mentioned, serious legal actions against multiple parties connected to the organizers, the police and the city government, which are ongoing.

Such a horrific end to the history of the Love Parade in the Ruhr Valley has further resulted in a plethora of cultural accusations and interpretations. It was later linked by many, including the original founder of the Love Parade, Dr Motte, to the gradual distancing of a cult-event from its original idealistic intentions (The Local website 2010). It had been transformed and reorganized to suit the complex materialistic calculations of entrepreneurs, media organizations and city politicians – as Dr Motte put it in the wake of the disaster, 'It is the fault of the organizers. ... It is just about making money; the organizers did not show the slightest feeling of responsibility for the people' (quoted in The Local website 2010).

In 2007 and 2008, the Love Parade had been the exemplary pop event representing the new cool cultural vision of the Ruhr Metropolis. This vision utilized the reputation of the Love Parade, following its internationalization in 2001, as an event linked to major global cities. However, the Ruhr officials and media organizations were also fooling themselves if they believed that the Love Parade would bring the Ruhr Valley cultural prestige. In fact, the Love Parade's move to the Ruhr Valley was at once an economic benefit and a cultural liability. Arguably, the prestige of the Love Parade had already run its course, and, for many EDM and carnival purists, it had become the object of ridicule for its commercial compromises. After all, they would point out, to maximize profits, sponsorship and media partnership deals (even with the notorious German tabloid, *Bild*) had been made, while for the McFit fitness chain itself, the Love Parade was seen as a marketing event suited for the chain – combining the twin-functionality of EDM as music for dance clubs and fitness clubs – while offering mainstream youth and other party-goers relaxing summer fun.

Yet the Love Parade, these criticisms aside, remained one of the few music events of such social-political dimensions as to claim the representative spotlight of an entire generation. That it became representative of the German techno scene during the 1990s was its achievement and its scourge. Indeed, in the 2000s, a gradual alienation occurred between the Love Parade and the techno scene, including its more popular wings. Dr Motte, the founder of the Love Parade, transformed already by 2006 into one of its most outspoken critics. It remained an EDM festival musically, yet many branches of the techno scene no longer identified the parade as a relevant techno festival. Rather, media attention during the 2000s became focused on Berlin club culture and its new international scene of 'easyjetset' tourism (Rapp 2009; Nye 2009b). The major techno magazines located in Berlin, primarily *Groove* and *De:Bug*, contained virtually no reports on the Love Parade following 2003, although regional ones, such as the Rhine-Ruhr-based *Raveline*, did continue to feature the Love Parade. The aura of the Love Parade appeared to have dissolved into a hollow ritual, where its pop fun had turned into a bad mix of cynicism and sarcasm.

Since the catastrophe, in which twenty-one people died, the question of the Love Parade's hollow aura has been heightened to include issues of self-deception in relation to both moral and legal responsibilities. Still, over the course of its twenty-one years history, it seemed almost miraculous that an annual event of this size was carried out eighteen times seemingly without a hitch. However, the transformation of the Love Parade into a travelling carnival ultimately posed new risks. The feature of constant geographic novelty meant that the Love Parade would take place on untested grounds and sites every single year. For an event of this size, this presented logistical challenges each year that eventually resulted in terrible mistakes at the Love Parade Duisburg.

## Eventization: The continuation of the EDM festival

Placed in the larger context of popular culture at the turn of the millennium, the Love Parade can be considered within the structure of 'events' (Gebhardt et al. 2000). An event, understood sociologically, pertains to social gatherings that are systematically marketed as necessary for people to attend in order to have a unique 'experience'. Entertainment industries, of which the Love Parade was a part, offer an 'experience' consisting of profane 'fun' that is marketed as self-expression free from specific rituals and political ties (Gebhardt et al. 2000). Mass events like the Love Parade operate on a double marketing strategy of connecting to specific scenes and traditions (techno and rave culture) while promising that the event will be a unique experience for all (we might here consider the 2,000 motto, 'One World, One Loveparade').

In whatever way the event is marketed, it is simply *not to be missed*. Cities and regions thus view events as ideal means to attract both media attention and visitors.

The Love Parade was an event with far greater potential for visitors than the mere techno scene itself offered. Indeed, in virtually every economic aspect and media practice, the Love Parade had been transformed into a *public event*. To be sure, aside from its early period (1989–91), the Love Parade had been a public event both in Berlin and the Ruhr Valley. It transformed within a few short years from a totally unobserved, small and alternative techno parade to a mass event that was reported on the world over. While the Love Parade changed its motto each year, it kept its basic idea: individuals from all corners of the world gather in a single place to party, dance and have 'fun'. The only limitation was the specific type of music on offer. This propagated a universal sense of what a 'participant' could be. It is important to remember that the Love Parade charged no entrance fee and had no door policy. In this sense, it was in its conception a public event in a fundamental form, although it did maintain links with the edgier techno scene: in Berlin, for example, as noted, there developed a Love Week of techno events that accompanied the Love Parade.

At mass events, there is always the potential that panic or other catastrophes can occur. A disaster on the scale of Duisburg might lead one to expect major changes in event planning. After all, the trust of city and local authorities would be shaken, especially the assumption that events are the best option for promoting economic growth and cultural prestige. However, the only major change in events that the Duisburg tragedy directly caused was the definitive cancelling of the Love Parade and a partial decline and avoidance by sponsors, of new techno parades; an attempted replacement, in particular the B-Parade proposed for Berlin in 2012, was itself cancelled. In fact, the Fuck Parade, a small anti–Love Parade started by the critical wings of the Berlin scene in 1997, is the only remaining 'techno parade' in Berlin (see Kutschbach 2013 for a report). Nevertheless, established techno parades of similar size, notably the Street Parade in Zürich, continue (see The Local website 2014 for a report on the 'million party-goers' at the 2014 Street Parade in Zürich).

Moreover, the Berlin Love Parade helped to establish the reputation of the Straße des 17. Juni as a place for mass events that continues to this day; recent and current events on this street include public screenings for major international football tournaments at the *Fanmeile* (fan mile), and Berlin's Pride Parade (the Christopher Street Day Parade), which boasts a considerable number of techno floats. One newspaper report of the football *Fanmeile* was even headlined: 'Like the Love Parade with football' (Brennberger 2012). Though the techno parade is now not the preferred form of event, the multi-day and midsized dance festival continues to have an extraordinary, and growing, presence throughout Europe. In part, this form is preferred because security and logistics can be better managed on long-established, ticketed and regulated festival grounds. In Germany alone, this includes major annual festivals: Mayday (since 1991), Time Warp (since 1994), Nature One (since 1995), Melt (since 1997), Fusion (since 1997) and many more. Dance festival polls and reports continue to be featured in techno magazines and online publications, from *Faze* to *Resident Advisor,* which has even included a *monthly* Top ten list of dance festivals since 2007 (Resident Advisor 2014). International EDM festivals have also grown immensely in recent years, from the United States to Brazil to Korea, which has caused increased competition, rising prices and critical reports in the German press (e.g. see Hartmann 2013; Waltz 2014).

For officials and local authorities, mass events, including EDM festivals, appear to remain the only alternative because everyday life in late modern society has already become *eventized*. Indeed, eventization has turned into a routine aspect of modernity similar in ways to pluralization (Berger and Luckmann 1995), individualization (Beck and Beck-Gernsheim 2002), optionalization (Gross 1994), commercialization (Prisching 2006), globalization (Beck 1999) and mediatization (Krotz 2007). Eventization is, in other words, the strongest manifestation of what the Bamberg sociologist Gerhard Schulze has called our 'experience rationality' (Schulze 1992), which he later analysed as an 'event culture' (Schulze 1999). In the German context, this has led to repeated critiques of the perceived problem of the hedonistic 'society of fun' (*Spaßgesellschaft*) (Hepp and Vogelsang 2003). These critiques against the amoral sale and consumption of abstract 'fun' arise, however, within a context in which events are the primary basis by which cities and regions, including the Ruhr Valley, market their worth and quality of life to their customer-citizens; for the music industry as well, the decline in recording profits has resulted in an increased emphasis, and dependence, on festival culture.

## Acknowledgements

This chapter is a revised and updated version of the following article: Hitzler, Ronald, and Sean Nye. 2011. 'Where is Duisburg? An LP postscript.' *Dancecult: Journal of Electronic Dance Music Culture* 2(1).

## Notes

1 Reports regarding official legal proceedings began in January 2011: http://www.badische-zeitung.de/panorama/loveparade-katastrophe-16-personen-im-visier--40204959.html. Accessed 14 September 2014. In July 2014, the first civil lawsuit was filed against three parties: the city of Duisburg, Rainer Schaller and Lopavent, and the state of North Rhine-Westphalia: http://www.zeit.de/gesellschaft/2014-07/loveparade-klage-duisburg. Accessed 14 September 2014.

2 http://www.rp-online.de/niederrheinnord/duisburg/loveparade/Alle-Loveparade-Zahlen-gefaelscht_aid_887726.html. Accessed 14 September 2014. A thirty-four-page report was released after the Duisburg catastrophe acknowledging the systematic inflating of attendance numbers during the Ruhr years.

3 For more information, a video 'documentary' by Lopavent contains images of the location and timeline of the events, though this should be viewed with the knowledge that it serves Lopavent's legal interests of assigning the blame to the police: https://www.youtube.com/watch?v=8y73-7lFBNE&list=UUlmsa1MvDRyVXsvCld8LMzQ. Accessed 14 September 2014. A more thorough documentary by *Der Spiegel* also exists: http://www.spiegel.tv/filme/loveparade-duisburg/. Accessed 14 September 2014.

## References

Beck, Ulrich. 1999. *What is Globalization?* Trans. Patrick Camiller. Cambridge: Polity Press.

Beck, Ulrich, and Elisabeth Beck-Gernsheim. 2002. *Individualization*. Trans. Patrick Camiller. London: Sage.

Berger, Peter L., and Thomas Luckmann. 1995. *Modernity, Pluralism, and the Crisis of Meaning: The Orientation of Modern Man*. Gütersloh: Bertelsmann Foundation Publishers.

Beyer, Susanne, Nikolaus von Festenberg, and Reinhard Mohr. 1999. 'Die jungen Milden.' *Der Spiegel*. 12 July. http://www.spiegel.de/spiegel/print/d-13950835.html. Accessed 14 September 2014.

Brennberger, Iris. 2012. 'Like the Love Parade with football.' *Berliner Zeitung*. 11 June. http://www.berliner-zeitung.de/berlin/em-public-viewing-wie-love-parade-mit-fussball,10809148,16343136.html. Accessed 17 September 2014.

Da Hool. 1997. 'Meet her at the Love Parade.' https://www.youtube.com/watch?v=KO4y3nkJXDA. Accessed 15 September 2014.

Gebhardt, Winfried. 2000. 'Feste, Feiern und Events: zur Soziologie des Außergewöhnlichen.' In Winfried Gebhardt, Ronald Hitzler, and Michaela Pfadenhauer, eds. *Events: Soziologie des Außergewöhnlichen*. Opladen: Leske + Budrich, 17–31.

Gebhardt, Winfried, Ronald Hitzler, and Michaela Pfadenhauer, eds. 2000. *Events: Soziologie des Außergewöhnlichen*. Opladen: Leske + Budrich.

Gross, Peter. 1994. *Die Multioptionsgesellschaft*. Frankfurt a.M.: Suhrkamp.

Hartmann, Andreas. 2013. 'Die vereinigten Raver von Amerika.' *Die Zeit*. 18 June. http://www.zeit.de/kultur/musik/2013-06/hakkasan-las-vegas-ibiza-edm. Accessed 27 September 2014.

Heissmeyer, Arno. 2007. 'Loveparade: Abhotten in Pott.' *Focus*. 21 June. http://www.focus.de/panorama/welt/love-parade_aid_64062.html. Accessed 14 September 2014.

Hepp, Andreas, and Waldemar Vogelgesang. 2003. *Populäre Events: Medienevents, Spielevents, Spaßevents*. Opladen: Leske + Budrich.

Hitzler, Ronald, Gregor Betz, Gerd Möll, and Arne Niederbacher. 2012. *Mega-Event-Macher: Zum Management multipler Divergenzen am Beispiel der Kulturhauptstadt Europas RUHR.2010*. Wiesbaden: VS.

Hitzler, Ronald, and Sean Nye. 2011. 'Where is Duisburg? An LP postscript.' *Dancecult: Journal of Electronic Dance Music Culture* 2(1). https://dj.dancecult.net/index.php/dancecult/article/view/303/289. Accessed 18 September 2014.

Johnston, Lynda, 2005. *Queering Tourism: Paradoxical Performances of Gay Pride Parades.* New York: Routledge.

Krotz, Friedrich. 2007. *Mediatisierung: Fallstudien zum Wandel von Kommunikation.* Wiesbaden: VS.

Kutschbach, Thomas. 2013. 'Laut, Lauter, Fuckparade.' *Die Berliner Zeitung.* 8 Sept.

The Local website. 2010. 'Love Parade founder Dr Motte blames new organizers for disaster.' 25 July. http://www.thelocal.de/national/20100725-28727.html. Accessed 17 September 2014.

The Local website. 2014. 'Zurich's Street Parade draws million party-goers.' 2 August. http://www.thelocal.ch/20140802/zuirchs-street-parade-draws-million-fans. Accessed 17 September 2014.

Loveparade. 2003. *Loveparade: Masses in Motion.* [Germany]: BMG (Ariola Media Gmbh).

Meyer, Erik. 2001. 'Zwischen Parties, Paraden und Protest.' In Ronald Hitzler, and Michaela Pfadenhauer, eds. *Techno-Soziologie: Erkundungen einer Jugendkultur.* Opladen: Leske + Budrich, 51–68.

Nye, Sean. 2009a. 'Love Parade, please not again: a Berlin cultural history.' *Echo: A Music-Centered Journal* 9(1). http://www.echo.ucla.edu/old/Volume9-Issue1/nye/nye1.html. Accessed 14 September 2014.

—. 2009b. 'Review of *Lost and Sound: Berlin, Techno, und der Easyjetset.*' *Dancecult: Journal of Electronic Dance Music Culture.* 1(1): 144–6. https://dj.dancecult.net/index.php/dancecult/article/view/279/248. Accessed 14 September 2014.

Prisching, Manfred. 2006. *Die zweidimensionale Gesellschaft.* Wiesbaden: VS.

Rapp, Tobias. 2009. *Berlin, Techno, und der Easyjetset.* Frankfurt a.M.: Suhrkamp.

Resident Advisor online. 2014. 'Top 10 festivals: each month we offer our essential festivals from around the globe.' http://www.residentadvisor.net/features.aspx?series=festivals. Accessed 17 September 2014.

RUHR2010 website. http://archiv.ruhr2010.de/en/home.html. Accessed 14 September 2014.

Schulze, Gerhard. 1992. *Die Erlebnisgesellschaft.* Frankfurt a.M. and New York: Campus.

—. 1999. *Kulissen des Glücks: Streifzüge durch die Eventkultur.* Frankfurt a.M. and New York: Campus.

Sextro, Maren, and Holger Wick, dirs., 2008. *We Call It Techno: A Documentary about Germany's Early Techno Scene and Culture.* DVD. [Germany]: Sense Music and Media.

T-online Nachrichten. 2010. 'Veranstalter: Es wird keine Loveparade mehr geben.' 25 July. http://www.t-online.de/nachrichten/specials/id_42361526/veranstalter-es-wird-keine-loveparade-mehr-geben.html. Accessed 14 September 2014.

Waltz, Alexis. 2014. 'Techno-Kapitalismus: so läuft der Tanz ums grosse Geld.' *Groove.* 5 September. http://www.groove.de/2014/09/05/techno-kapitalismus-so-laeuft-der-tanz-ums-grosse-geld/Accessed 27 September 2014.

# CHAPTER NINE

# Protestival: Global days of action and carnivalized politics at the turn of the millennium[1]

*Graham St John*

*In carnival the body is always changing, constantly becoming, eternally unfinished. Inseparable from nature and fused to other bodies around it, the body remembers that it is not a detached, atomized becoming, as it allows its erotic impulses to jump from body to body, sound to sound, mask to mask, to swirl across the street, filling every nook and cranny, every fold of flesh. During the carnival the body, with its pleasures and desires, can be found everywhere, luxuriating in its freedom and inverting the everyday.*

*WE ARE EVERYWHERE* (AINGER ET AL. 2003, 175–6)

## Introduction: Carnivalized politics

On 16 May (M16) 1998 a Global Street Party took place in thirty cities on five continents coinciding with the Group of Eight (G8) summit in Birmingham, England, and the following week's World Trade Organization (WTO) ministerial in Geneva. This was the first Global Day of Action, a transnational mobilization signifying the emergence of the alter-globalization movement. Called by those identifying with the People's Global Action (PGA; see Style 2004), the M16 Global Street Party was pivotal, since it signalled the re-emergence of a carnivalized cultural praxis which Brian Holmes – in a comprehensive testament to the activities and events of the alter-globalization movement, *We Are Everywhere* – deems a 'carnivalesque ritual' (2003, 346; see also Yuen et al. 2004).[2] Momentous in this regard, the 1960s has been identified as an experimental laboratory of emancipatory cultural politics (see Stephens 1998). A context for the emergence of guerrilla theatre and other nascent tactical media practices associated with an anti-disciplinary protest in which a 'new parodic political language' (Stephens 1998, 25) was being forged, the period was the 'privileged era of carnivalized politics' (Stam 1988, 136). In the interventions of the Situationist International, the Youth International Party (Yippies), the Diggers (an offshoot of the San Francisco Mime Troupe) and other avant-garde, theatrical and political groups the carnival's 'perennial repertoire' of gestures, symbols and metaphors had, according to Robert Stam (1988, 135), been 'deployed to give voice to desire for social and political justice'. But while the carnivalesque possesses deep historical roots, and the repertoire adopted and translated by social movements in the 1970s and 1980s, it would experience an explosive resurgence as the Carnivals Against Capital (and For Global Justice) mounted on numerous Global Days of Action from the late 1990s provided vivid proclamation of the emergence of a movement mobilizing against neoliberalism and war and for autonomy and peace. Massive anti-capitalist and anti-war convergences signalled the emergence of the *protestival* as a variegated complex of action performances enabling exposure and revelation.

'Protestival' is a term coined by radical technician John Jacobs[3] and offers a useful heuristic for contemporary events simultaneously negative/positive, transgressive/progressive, aesthetic/instrumental. Becoming virulent in a period which has seen an increase in political mobilizations deviating from those conventional to social movements, these events constitute a creative response to the traditional political rituals of the left: those 'ritual marches from point A to point B, the permits and police escorts, the staged acts of civil disobedience, the verbose rallies and dull speeches by leaders' (Ainger et al. 2003, 174). Embodying the increasingly attractive principles of 'diversity, creativity, decentralization, horizontality, and direct action', such events would thus hold principles found at the heart of what is understood to be an ancient form of cultural expression: the carnival (Ainger et al. 2003, 174). The carnival seems to provide an apposite framework for contemporary activists since it is a potent and diverse storehouse of cultural and political possibility. Carnival is understood to perform multiple tasks: 'as political action, as festive celebration, as cathartic release, as wild abandonment of the status quo, as networking tool, as a way to create a new world' (Ainger et al. 2003, 180). Importantly, as Stam (1988, 135) recognizes, while constituting 'a demystifiying instrument for everything in the social formation that renders collectivity impossible: class hierarchy, sexual repression, patriarchy, dogmatism and paranoia', carnival is simultaneously 'ecstatic collectivity, the joyful affirmation of social change, a dress rehearsal for utopia'.

This chapter explores this polyvalent tactic as it has been reclaimed by the alter-globalization movement. The locations and times that transnational financial organizations and political elites are most visible (i.e. G8 summits, WTO ministerials and World Economic Forum meetings) are also where/when global neoliberalism becomes most vulnerable. Such manifestations become contexts for the concentration of enmity and dissent, where accumulated grievances resulting from economic injustice and political oppression are expressed and mediated. These centres/summits provide occasions in which participants in the alter-globalization movement can converge, either on location (such as 'convergence spaces' during G8 summits) or in-simultaneity (such as the Carnivals Against Capital, and For Global Justice).[4] Thus, as Crossley (2002, 685) observes, it may be 'the emergence of a more identifiable structure of power within the global field that has created conditions conducive to the emergence of protest activities and movements within it'. The most visible sites of neoliberal globalization then become the most obvious sites for dissenting voices. These sites have become the context for 'transnational collective rituals' (Routledge 2003, 341) such as summit sieges, autonomous convergences and other reflexive 'plateau events' (Chesters 2003, 49) where the globally aggrieved are drawn to challenge, momentarily, the 'crushing inevitability of history' (Butigan 2000, 46). These mobilizations build on the meta-political tactic of 'heightening the visibility of power' located in the 'symbolic challenge' posed by new social movements (NSMs) (Melucci 1989; Bartholomew and Mayer 1992, 146); however, only now they do so within a renewed climate of opposition to neoliberalism illustrated, for instance, by the popularity of the ideas of Hardt and Negri (2000) and the global resurgence of autonomism, anarchism and direct action. Exposing the mechanisms of power and oppression at these powerful, albeit vulnerable, sites – or indeed in absentia – becomes highly innovative, and the carnivalized/festal tactics employed within the contexts of these increasingly popular transnational rituals are the subject of this chapter.

## From festival to protestival

It is first worth exploring the role of the festal within counterculture, as it would come to bear on the cultural politics of the present. In the wake of the 'privileged era of carnivalized politics', dissidents, utopians, freaks and other descendants of the 1960s 'happening' were actively reviving, re-creating and re-inventing semi-nomadic traditions through free festival cultures. These invented traditions were as much efforts in maintaining or reclaiming a folk culture, often embracing indigenous worldviews and expressing re-enchantment with the natural world, as they were efforts at forging a new, alternative culture. In the United Kingdom, those sometimes named 'New Age' Travellers (though rarely self-identifying as such) sought temporary exodus from modern Britain in the Stonehenge Summer Solstice festival, the early Glastonbury Festival and other events (McKay 1996, 2000; Hetherington 2000). From the early 1970s in the United States, the Rainbow Family would hold major annual (eventually international) free gatherings (Niman 1997). In Australia, counterculturalists first journeyed to the Aquarius Festival at Nimbin in 1973, a precursor to the annual ConFest (St John 2001).[5] The countercultures were seeking autonomous sites, laboratories for experimental discourse and practice and the forging of alternative lifeways. These festal realms were alternative cultural heterotopias, contextualizing the exploration of proliferating and sometimes conflicting alternatives to patriarchy, militarism, capitalism and 'monophasic' consciousness. They would threaten property and propriety, circumstances provoking the state's efforts to eliminate or contain them, as in the British Conservative government's crushing of the mobile seasonal alternative travellers known as the Peace Convoy en route to the Stonehenge Summer Solstice Festival in 1985 (Worthington 2005),[6] or inspiring capital's insidious capture and recuperation of the 'cool' alternative.

Achieving their fullest expression in the festal, in the 'temporary autonomous zone' (or TAZ; Bey 1991), these counter-tribes seemed to exemplify those micro-cultures that Maffesoli (1996) holds as symptomatic of a post-Second World War society characterized by a voluntary, passional, networked and unstable neo-tribalism, the principal commitment of which is 'being together'. While this may be the case, the actual characteristics of their 'empathetic sociality' (Maffesoli 1996, 11) need circumscribing. Such contexts would be arenas in which official culture is intentionally transgressed and subverted. And since radical creativity would flourish within the context of a self-identified *tribalism*, an empathetic counter-sociality reputed to accommodate diverse differences, these were contexts perhaps more accurately articulated via the radical conviviality of Hakim Bey's 'Immediatist' (see Bey 1994) philosophy than Maffesoli's 'orgiasm' (see 1993). Yet attending to the rootless, fragmented and tragic characteristics of the present, such perspectives neglect the *movement* in sociality, discounting the activist subject who, like Tim Jordan's (2002) 'Activist!', is passionate and morally committed, albeit not unexposed to the fragility and impermanence of contemporary social life. On the heels of a useful though troubled effort to comprehend the fluid and empathetic character of contemporary society, one can detect a 'passional' sociality pervading the present which, given the emergence of 'post-citizenship' movements (Jasper 1997, 7), is morally purposed and motivated by a *cause* other than its own reproduction.[7]

Cultural and performance traditions are known to be integral to social movements (on music, see Eyerman and Jamison 1998; Mattern 1998; on theatre; see Kershaw 1992; Cohen-Cruz 1998; Moser 2003). Appropriately nuanced research on 'cultures of resistance' (McKay 1996), protest subcultures (Martin 2002), 'individualized and extended milieus' (Jowers et al. 1999, 114) and performative politics with regard to protest ritual (Szerszynski 1999) or the alternative reconfiguration of space in opposition to free-market strategies (Nield 2006) offer useful paths forward. The particular activist subjectivity that Tim Jordan discusses is 'transgressive'. Unlike reactionaries who press reinterpretations of the past into present efforts to forge a future, or reformers who 'pit the present against the present in order to shape the future', transgressive movements and subcultures look to the unknown future for their inspiration (Jordan 2002, 40). A desire to *reclaim the future* is performed by living the 'future in the present', a tendency particular to autonomists and anarchists, whose practices – social centres and other experimental autonomous spaces – experienced a resurgence globally in the mid-1990s (see Shantz 1999, 60–1; Day 2005). Inheriting from feminist, environmental, peace, post-colonial, sexuality and disability movements, a 'global anarchism' recognized the complex character of power (Bowen and Purkis 2004, 5), those movements' struggles for autonomy and self-empowerment often juxtaposed with traditional modes of contestation and protest in a sea of flags and banners and a cacophony of chants and protest mantras apparent within the new protest environment. Here, *the cause* (such as local autonomy, global justice and peace) contextualizes and characterizes the non-hierarchical TAZ, the 'convergence space', and the *being together* of participants, itself constituting an effort 'to form the structure of the new world in the shell of the old' (Shantz 1999, 61).[8] Since counter-tribes would harness a future-directed anarcho-liminality, the Maffesolian perspective (of transgression for transgression's sake) should be approached with caution (see Martin 2002; St John 2003). While the earlier free festival 'happenings' had served as sites of *indirect action*, the TAZ would be mobilized in pursuit of the cause, often mounted in direct opposition to the circumstances which compelled (by choice or otherwise) participants towards a festal life (to live as 'travellers', itinerants, 'feral') in the first place.

The temporary festal would become a critical tool in the activist repertoire (Figure 33). In European traditions, since the Roman Saturnalia, the Feast of Fools and the Greek Dionysia, festival has been a time of inversion, intensification, transgression and abstinence – a theme, and term, commonly interchanged with 'carnival'. A season of festive events culminating in two or three days of massive street processions, carnival is rooted in Roman Catholic pre-Lenten festivities occasioning 'release from the constraints and pressures of the social order, generat[ing] relationships of amity even among strangers and allow[ing] forbidden excesses' (Cohen 1993, 3). Integrated into twentieth-century social movements, these occasions for excess and intense participation would become implicated in direct action at least as far back as the late 1950s.

According to McKay (2004, 430), amidst a carnival atmosphere and eventually propagating a 'youth lifestyle protest movement', the Campaign

**FIGURE 33** *Reclaim the Streets, street party flyer, London, May 1995: 'The temporary festal as critical tool in the activist repertoire'.*

for Nuclear Disarmament's (CND) annual marches to Britain's nuclear weapons research facility at Aldermaston were significant in this regard. While the Aldermaston march of Easter 1958, and later CND-related events, saw a carnival of protest travel from the 'imperial centre of London to the countryside', around twenty years later the Greenham Common peace camp in Berkshire signified a similar passage from the city (McKay 2004, 431). Peace camps such as those at Greenham (Roseniel 1995; Cresswell 1996) and Seneca in New York State (Krasniewicz 1994) would become a protest template where women made spectacular vigil upon the military industrial apparatus, their often uncovered bodies forming an abject contrast to the phallic nuclear missiles harboured behind the wire. The grotesque and undisciplined body was emigrating to contested locations on the margins, and at remote sites such as nuclear airbases, uranium mines (e.g. Australia's Jabiluka) and migrant detention centres (the outback detention centre at Woomera) participants found ever newer ways of attracting sympathetic media (rather than withdrawing from the media). Drawing from *Bomb Culture* (1968), in which Nuttall discusses the presence of jazz and the 'spontaneous and creative interventions' of the beats in early CND activity, McKay (2004, 431) declares that the association between protest and festivity had gathered pace by the early 1960s. (For further discussion on the historical merger of music subcultures and political activism, see McKay 2007 on street music and marching bands.) The association developed as counter-tribes were taking their grievances – *and their carnivals* – back to the city and centres of power. Indeed, in the year after the first Aldermaston march, the route was reversed, with the festival descending upon Trafalgar Square, a tradition which would continue (and which would see 100,000 CND marchers and supporters occupy Trafalgar Square in 1961, the numbers growing throughout the decade as opposition to the Vietnam War escalated: McKay 2000, 88–9). In 1970, raising opposition to the ongoing war in Vietnam, carnival was launched on the lawns of the White House (Kershaw 1997, 261–4). Having flourished at the margins, the habitué(e)s of the autonomous carnival were reassembling in the (city) centres and, with regard to the United Kingdom, Scott and Street (2001, 43) afford insight into how this transpired. Identifying how 'carnival seems now to have been elevated to the defining characteristic of the [protest] event, transplanting the language of the mid 1980s hippie convoys and free festivals into an urban context', unlike efforts by travellers to reclaim marginal sites like Stonehenge at the summer solstice, or contest remote places, the new protest tribes of the 1990s – those that the then British prime minister Tony Blair would derogate as an 'anarchist travelling circus'[9] – would directly contest the meaning of powerful and iconic sites, such as the City of London.

Described as a performance where 'the poetic and pragmatic join hands' (Jordan 1998, 132–3; see also Luckman 2001), Reclaim the Streets (RTS) was instrumental in such spatial contestation. Emerging in London in 1995, immediately downstream from the anti-road protests and rave and free party culture, and providing the platform for disparate groups uniting against the Criminal Justice and Public Order Act, 1994, RTS proliferated across Europe and around the world with the assistance of the communications and organizing capabilities provided by the internet (Figures 34 and 35). RTS had targeted that most conspicuous symbol of material wealth, fossil fuel consumption and critical source of carbon emissions – the motor car – obstructing its progress along major thoroughfares of the contemporary metropolis, the temporary autonomous carnivals disrupting traffic and business as usual. Avoiding conventional and increasingly uninspired forms of mobilization such as *the demonstration*, RTS and successive anarchist 'dis-organizations' (such as London's Wombles: White Overalls Movement Building Liberations through Effective Struggle, named after a 1970s children's television series) were effectively subverting the normative function of space through a kind of carnivalesque hacking. Here, the most overt and immediate (local) expressions of transnational (global) power are effectively 'dis-alienated' or 'de-reified' (Uitermark 2004, 711). What Uitermark calls the 'de-programming' of space offers a revelatory mobilization, and we witness one critical path towards comprehending the protestival. The festival as hacking event. Here, the *hack*, not exclusively a negational practice, is

**FIGURE 34** *A 'two-day festival of resistance', Reclaim the Streets, London, 1997.*

radically creative since it involves the intentional disruption, disorientation and de-programming of 'consensus' reality. Just as the protestival is an intervention which is more than a blockade or obstruction, the hack is not confined to blocking, erasing or destroying information, but potentiates the re-programming of reality. Festal hacktivism is a ritual of de-reification which renders power and contradiction visible at its most central and reified sites, practices which enable the performance and construction of lived alternatives.

Such festal re-programming is orchestrated variously – from women-only Reclaim the Night rallies, to RTS occupations of the High Street, to the disruption of 'summits' and meetings of 'peak' transnational financial and political bodies. When the 'pulsing, computerized, hyper-competitive brain of the beast' – the London International Financial Futures and Options Exchange (or LIFFE) building, which houses the largest derivations market in Europe – was hacked on 18 June (J18) 1999 during the Carnival Against Capital (activists bricked up the building: Blissant 2006); or when the WTO was successfully hijacked on 30 November (N30) 1999 in the 'Battle of Seattle'; and when the 'jugular vein of consumer capitalism', Oxford St., was re-represented along with other London landmarks on the Wombles' May Day Monopoly brochure distributed prior to the May Day protests

**FIGURE 35** *Berlin 'street-rave', 1997: Reclaim the Streets – 'celebrating temporary liberation from the established order'.*

in 2001 (Uitermark 2004, 717), we witness the festal rupturing of critical sites of capitalist representation. Efforts to lobotomize 'the brains of the beast' or rupture the 'jugular vein' of capital are performed at the sites of its vital organs, at its most visible/vulnerable points, which become magnetic to diverse actors who are compelled to seek out the source of their oppression, misery and discontent. Targeting 'centres' whose visibility is exploited in the effort to expose its 'truths', to de-legitimate its ideology, festal hacktivism corresponds to that which we know as 'culture jamming'. From the performative hijacking of 'flagship' stores to the 'liberation' of billboards and websites at focal points in the urban landscape (and indeed the global cyberscape), such activities flourish within the context of the protestival. The journey to the centres, and spectacular focal points of neoliberalism, those summits where its power is reaffirmed and extended, is likened to a pilgrimage for those who intend to jam its otherwise unperturbed flows of meaning, destabilize its agendas and challenge its hold on 'reality'. Claiming that Seattle was the context for the emergence of a 'new politico-religious pilgrimage' consistent with earlier journeys from bondage to freedom (such as that of Gandhi), Ken Butigan presciently observes that

> the urgency of this journey came from a deep intuition that the great web of violence in which we are caught today is spun by large economic and

> political forces, and that the instructions for this 'web design' for the next decades were about to be codified in a very few short days on the shores of Puget Sound. (2000, 46)

This 'journey to the centre' would enable an armada of aggrieved pilgrims and pirates to hack the design.

## Intentional carnivals: Against capitalism and for global justice

Signifying the growing popularity of direct action/democracy, RTS was an emergent flourishing of anarchistic logic providing the template for Carnivals Against Capitalism (CAC) and other festivals of resistance proliferating across the global North from the late 1990s and converging on local centres and conspicuous symbols of global capital. The first CAC, on J18, occurred on the heels of the Global Street Party of 16 May 1998 (and would be the immediate precursor for N30, Seattle). Like M16, J18 was a 'Global Day of Action'[10] called by the People's Global Action and would coincide with the G8 summit in Köln. While leaders of the International Caravan for Solidarity and Resistance paraded through the city at the end of a month's protest tour of Europe, there were street parties in twenty cities around the world and actions in another twenty. One of the largest J18 turnouts was naturally in London where the carnival had been reclaimed by anarchists as a tactic of resistance and insurrection, and where the Barking Bateria marching band took to the streets.[11] It is understandable that RTS and CAC activists would adopt the carnival as a medium for action, since – without hierarchy, determined by principles of self-organization, direct democracy, conviviality and noise – the carnival is an anarchist demesne whose legacy can be discerned in British youth subculture. In his analysis of the 'cultural anarchism' expressed in post–Second World War UK youth subcultures, Nehring (1993) discusses how the medieval marketplace, the carnival clown and the transgressive power of the carnivalesque were transmuted into 1970s punk. The contumacious and irreverent character of punk possessed a *form* of response to the social order consistent with Mikhail Bakhtin's (1968) carnival: emerging from below, from the folk, from the working class, society is forgotten. According to Nehring, punks served the function that Bakhtin attributes to clowns in carnival: 'the clown sounded forth, ridiculing all "languages" and dialects [in] a lively play with the "languages" of poets, scholars, monks, knights, and others'. This play was parodic, 'aimed sharply and polemically against the official languages of its given time' (Bakhtin, quoted in Nehring 1993, 318). Yet, in a development Nehring neglects, while the 'guerrilla semiotics' of punk are known to have contributed to the formation of a 'hardcore', or authentic, punk identity, the progressively motivated transgression which came to be concentrated within the UK *anarcho-punk* scene (McKay 1996) would see the carnival (and the expository character of the carnivalesque) adopted in more specifically emancipatory – that is, 'hardcore activist' – endeavours (St John 2010).

As carnival's deep historical roots were recognized, its reclamation united contemporary habitué(e)s with those hardcore compatriots imagined to have occupied such 'worlds' throughout history – an underworld or interzone of fellow insurrectionaries such as those of the Paris Commune of 1871. As has been acknowledged (Grindon 2004), anarchists and other activists enthused by such identifications appear to have invented a 'tradition of carnival as liberatory insurrection', with those organizing and facilitating contemporary events drawing on and synthesizing the ideas of theorists and practitioners of the carnivalesque in order to build such a tradition. Appropriating the writing of Bakhtin, RTS anarchists valorized the carnival not as an entertaining sideshow but as something of a temporary autonomous breach in which occupants are empowered to participate in the forging of 'a new world'. As RTS themselves put it in their document 'The Evolution of Reclaim the Streets', a carnival

> *celebrates temporary liberation from the established order; it marks the suspension of all hierarchy, rank, privileges, norms and prohibitions.* Crowds of people on the street seized by a sudden awareness of their power and unification through a celebration of their own ideas and creations. (RTS 1997; emphasis added)

Yet cultural critics have long been sceptical about the role of the carnival/festival, questioning its countercultural or emancipatory value. Is it an instrument of political opposition *or* 'ritual of rebellion' (Gluckman 1954), an artificial revolution like Fasnacht at Basle, 'a savage form of class struggle' which 'enables the underprivileged class to make revolution without really performing it' (Weidkuhn 1976, 44)? Are carnivals temporary outlets ultimately ensuring the maintenance of structures of privilege (see Eagleton 1981)? Would they be evidence of 'repressive desublimation', which Marcuse thinks allowed 'just enough freedom to disrupt and integrate discontent – but not enough to endanger the discipline necessary for a stable industrial order' (quoted in Roszak 1995, xxii)? As Bruner (2005, 140) infers, ruling authorities may actively endorse such events since, as official periods of 'sanctioned transgression', they are 'capable of "magically" reinforcing the normal moral and political order by revealing the limits of that order in more positive ways than outright physical and/or ideological repression'. Would RTS, CAC and neo-Situationist enthusiasm function as 'safety valves' permitting participants' 'revolution' before returning to their consented roles at school, in the office, on the footpath? Are TAZs the privilege of middle-class rebels practicing 'lifestyle anarchism' (Bookchin 1995)?

While the Situationists and Bey have been challenged for being privileged white male elitists promoting a 'bourgeois deception', this did not deter J18 activists from distributing 50,000 metallic gold flyers featuring a line attributed to Raoul Vaneigem, and smacking of Bey: 'to work for delight and authentic festivity is barely distinguishable from preparing for general insurrection' (from Blissant 2006). The adoption of such language signalled an earnest sympathy with the Situationist practice of recapturing utopia as a process of becoming, a process believed to be 'already geographically realizable within the interstices of everyday urban practice' (Swyngedouw 2002, 161).

But in the attempt to answer the above queries and challenges, it must be recognized that carnival is essentially polyvalent. There are varied reasons why people participate in carnivals, as Stam attempts to outline in relation to its attraction to the left. Thus, the carnival is

> (1) a valorization of Eros and the life force (appealing to a Reichean left) as an actualization of the ancient myths of Orpheus and Dionysius; (2) the idea, more relevant to the left generally, of social inversion and the counter-hegemonic subversion of established power; (3) the idea, attractive to poststructuralists, of 'gay relativity' and Janus-faced ambivalence and ambiguity; (4) the notion of carnival as trans-individual and oceanic (appealing ambiguously to the left and right alike); and (5) the concept of carnival as the 'space of the sacred' and 'time in parenthesis' (appealing to the religiously inclined). (Stam 1988, 135)

Others regard carnivals as ambivalent, featuring complex subtexts of manipulation and desire. According to Notting Hill Carnival ethnographer Abner Cohen, carnival is poised between genuine opposition *and* means of domination. Like a 'grand joking relationship', carnival/festival is characterized by 'both conflict and alliance' (Cohen 1993, 128). Moreover, sweeping statements, dismissive or celebrational, are unhelpful since each event, and each occurrence is, as Stallybrass and White (1986) and Stam (1988) concur, characterized by 'shifting configurations of symbolic practices whose political valence changes with each context and situation' (Stam 1988, 135).

With regard to CAC, it ought to be recognized that these events are acts of civil disobedience, neither sanctioned nor tolerated by official culture (as were the medieval carnivals inspiring Bakhtin). These are direct action festivals, often, and certainly in the case of RTS, driven and organized by anarchist principles, and thus hardly sanctioned by the state, and not becoming easily recuperable. In Grindon's view (2004, 160), dismissing or embracing the carnival unequivocally is less productive than 'examining it as a heterogeneous set of theories that at the very least offer a valuable cultural approach to the prefigurative societies that are so common in contemporary anarchist thinking'. The contribution to *We Are Everywhere*, with more than a hint of Vaneigem and Bey, appears to respond to some of this criticism:

> The revolutionary carnival may only last a few hours or days, but its taste lingers on. It is not simply a letting-off of steam, a safety valve for society, enabling life to return to normal the next day. It is a moment of intensity unlike any other, which shapes and gives new meanings to every aspect of life. The everyday is never the same after one has tasted a moment that is ruled only by freedom. Tasting such fruit is dangerous, because it leaves a craving to repeat the exhilarating experience again and again. (Ainger et al. 2003, 182)

In a true reflection of the internal dynamic of carnival as both negative/positive, transgressive/progressive, by 11 September (S11) 2000 – when Melbourne hosted the Carnival for Global Justice on the occasion of the meeting of the World Economic Forum (WEF) at Kerry Packer's Crown Casino – the carnivals on the Global Days of Action would be acknowledged to be as decidedly *for* 'justice' as *against* neoliberalism. This mood would become clearer in the wake of 9/11, and the subsequent global 'War on Terror'. Thus, by 18–20 March 2006, when protests marked the third anniversary of the beginning of the war in Iraq, the Global Day of Action template had become instrumental to a transnational movement united against war and for peace (see St John 2008).

## The domain beyond starts here: Towards another world

Protestivals are designed to make a difference in the world. Themselves 'other worlds', they constitute pragmatic efforts to render 'the official world' transparent, while simultaneously demonstrating that 'Another World is Possible'.[12] Appropriating the cultural legacy of 'the people's second world', as anarchistic laboratories and storehouses of action far from unofficial domains residing comfortably adjacent to business as usual, the Carnivals Against Capital and For Global Justice are autonomous convergence sites. By aesthetically and collectively de-reifying high streets, corporate centres and summits of power, re-inscribing such places in the name of 'the people', 'democracy', 'peace', 'justice' and so on, such reclamations seek fundamental alterations in the composition of the official world (neoliberalism) (see Figure 36). Here, the 'culture of laughter' and the language of the carnival are not related in a regenerational fashion to official culture, since it is intended to be generative of an alternative future.

'Another world' comes to life during the other world of the carnival. As protest dramas these events would resemble those which Kershaw

**FIGURE 36** *Tent city at Climate Camp, G20 summit, London 2009 – from festival to protestival.*

(1997, 264) identifies as being 'increasingly aimed to produce for both participants and spectators an image of an experience that gave a glimpse of the future as pure freedom from the constraints of the real, a hint of utopia'. The Global Days of Action and other convergence spaces would constitute a *freedom from* corporate fundamentalism enabling a *freedom to* experiment with alternatives. The inversion generated in these 'plateau events' (Chesters 2003) makes possible a subversive or subjunctive mood. In the context of a 'progressive public transgression', the inversion of hierarchies, the reversal of binaries and the wearing of masks are 'ultimately capable of serving a much greater purpose: allowing subjects to enter a liminal realm of freedom and in so doing create a space for critique that would otherwise not be possible in "normal" society' (Bruner 2005, 136, 140). As N30 in Seattle and ensuing events effectively problematized the ideology of 'free trade', breaking 'the spell of inevitability and unquestioned authority of global capital' (Butigan 2000, 47), they would become heavily mediated moments for the exploration and dissemination of alternative approaches. At convergence after convergence, familiar patterns emerged. At S11 Melbourne (11–13 September 2000), activists 'embraced the power of the carnival to "de-naturalize" the rhythms and expectations of everyday life ... upsetting conventional expectations' with regard to appropriate behaviour around Crown Casino (Scalmer and Iveson 2001, 229). At the convergence space dubbed the 'hori-zone' (since it was a horizontal space) at Gleneagles for the 2005 G8 summit, temporary autonomous neighbourhoods facilitated, through direct action, spokescouncils,

Indymedia and the preference for 'direct' over 'representative' democracy (and 'revolutionary' politics), a 'living alternative to capitalism' (Pickerill and Chatterton 2006, 9), in a way not unlike the squats, housing cooperatives, social centres, health clinics and other autonomous projects which 'allow an unpacking of the power working at different levels through governments, corporations and local elites' (2006, 7). Only now, like a spectacular anarchist carnival.

As an unpredictable intervention, the 'other world' of carnival envelopes and destabilizes neoliberal centres and spectacles. A protestival most apparent in the Global Day of Action, it has flourished in recent history in the face of efforts to repress it. While this action template inherits much from the 'symbolic challenges' posed by post-1960s social movements, the contemporary challenge is performed within the context of a complex confrontation with neoliberalism, signified by the resurgence of global autonomism, anarchism and direct action. Scholars have indicated that summit sieges, autonomous convergences and other recent reflexive events constitute transnational 'carnivalesque rituals', politico-religious 'pilgrimage' destinations and alternative spatializations critical to the renewed opposition to capitalism. In this contribution to the study of the performative dimensions of contemporary protest, I have suggested that the idea of 'protestival' provides a suitable heuristic to enable comprehension of carnivals of protest; those moments which are simultaneously transgressive and progressive, against and for; which are ultimately expositional and revelatory of the workings of capital and war-bent administrations; and which demonstrate the legacy of the avant-garde – from the practices of the Situationist International, and alternative theatre, to RTS and the extreme performances of the Carnivals Against Capitalism and For Global Justice. Tactics of the margins and the marginal, these protest carnivals are a means through which 'centres' are targeted and 'summits' scaled, through which the vulnerabilities of the powerful are exploited, contradictions exposed and truths unmasked – means all the more important in a period (post-9/11) when fear-based ideologies are successfully mobilized to legitimate violence (war and repression) and mask the systemic acquisition and control of finite global resources.

## Notes

1 This chapter was originally published in full in *Social Movement Studies* (St John 2008) and references to the 'present' or 'contemporary' refer to events at the turn of the millennium. Readers are encouraged to consult that article for a detailed account of 'protestival' as it was conceptualized at that time.

2 Signalling the tradition of radical history, the title reproduces that of American counterculture activist Jerry Rubin's 1971 book, *We Are Everywhere*.

3 Personal communication. John Jacobs has been heavily involved with numerous anarchist and artistic projects in Sydney, including the Jellyheads alternative music project, Vibe Tribe, Sydney Reclaim the Streets, Catalyst community activist technology project and Wheelie Good Sound System (http://wheeliebinsoundsystems.com/)

4 Paul Routledge (2003, 341) calls the former 'localized global actions' where different movements and resistance groups coordinate around a particular issue or event in a particular place, and the latter 'globalized local actions' – initiatives that transpire in different locations around the globe in support of particular local struggles, or against particular targets (which may or may not occur simultaneously).

5 These transhumant pilgrimages to rural, remote or exotic locations would become the signature of more recent festal cultures, such as the European and North American techno music festivals known as 'teknivals' (St John 2009), Nevada's Burning Man (Gilmore & Van Proyen, 2005), or the psychedelic trance festivals whose antecedents journeyed the Eastern-oriented 'hippie trail' (especially that terminating in the former Portuguese colony of Goa) (St John 2012). Other examples and writings are found through this book.

6 The incident, known as 'the Battle of the Beanfield', transpired a decade after police brutally repressed the Windsor Free Festival, with both events, as McKay (1996, 33) points out, following Conservative action taken against striking miners.

7 Unless by this we mean its own survival (as in a human species whose perpetuity is reliant upon the maintenance of ecological balance and harmonious inter-ethnic relations).

8 Shantz paraphrases the Preamble to the Constitution of the syndicalist Industrial Workers of the World (IWW).

9 The comment came following protests at the EU summit in Gothenburg, Sweden, in June 2001. The phrase was subsequently adopted by protestors.

10 For an incomplete (as in not updated) Global Days of Action list, see http://www.nadir.org/nadir/initiativ/agp/free/global/index.htm

11 A precursor to the 'tactical mobile rhythmical unit', the Infernal Noise Brigade (INB), which formed for N30. The INB is addressed by McKay (2007) in a discussion of the politically regressive and progressive characteristics of protests.

12 The slogan embraced by participants of the World Social Forum, first held in January 2001 in Porto Alegre, Brazil (when the annual World Economic Forum met in Davos, Switzerland).

## References

Ainger, K., Chesters, G., Credland, T., Jordan, J., Stern, A. and Whitney, J., eds. 2003. *We Are Everywhere: The Irresistible Rise of Global Anticapitalism.* London: Verso.

Bakhtin, M. 1968. *Rabelais and His World.* Cambridge, MA: MIT Press.

Bartholomew, A., and Mayer, M. 1992. 'Nomads of the present: Melucci's contribution to "New Social Movement" theory.' *Theory, Culture, & Society* 9: 141–59.
Bey, H. 1991. *TAZ: The Temporary Autonomous Zone – Ontological Anarchy and Poetic Terrorism.* New York: Autonomedia. http://www.hermetic.com/bey/taz_cont.html. Accessed 27 September 2014.
Bey, H. 1994. *Immediatism.* Edinburgh: AK Press.
Bookchin, M. 1995. *Social Anarchism or Lifestyle Anarchism: An Unbridgeable Chasm.* Edinburgh: AK Press.
Bowen, J., and Purkis, J. 2004. 'Introduction: why anarchism still matters.' In J. Purkis and J. Bowen, eds. *Changing Anarchism: Anarchist Theory and Practice in a Global Age.* Manchester: Manchester University Press, 1–19.
Bruner, L. M. 2005. 'Carnivalesque protest and the humorless state.' *Text and Performance Quarterly* 25(2): 136–55.
Butigan, K. 2000. 'We traveled to Seattle: a pilgrimage of transformation.' In K. Donaher, and R. Burbank, eds. *Globalize This! The Battle against the World Trade Organization and Corporate Rule.* Monroe, ME: Common Courage, 44–7.
Chesters, G. 2003. 'Shapeshifting: civil society, complexity and social movements.' *Anarchist Studies* 11(1): 42–65.
Cohen, A. 1993. *Masquerade Politics: Explorations in the Structure of Urban Social Movements.* Berkeley: University of California Press.
Cohen-Cruz, J., ed. 1998. *Radical Street Performance: An International Anthology.* New York: Routledge.
Cresswell, T. 1996. *In Place/Out of Place: Geography, Ideology and Transgression.* Minneapolis: University of Minnesota Press.
Crossley, N. 2002. 'Global anti-corporate struggle: a preliminary analysis.' *British Journal of Sociology* 53(4): 667–91.
Day, R. 2005. *Gramsci is Dead: Anarchist Currents in the Newest Social Movements.* London: Pluto Press.
Eagleton, T. 1981. *Walter Benjamin or Towards a Revolutionary Criticism.* London: Verso.
Eyerman, R., and Jamison, A. 1998. *Music and Social Movements: Mobilizing Traditions in the Twentieth Century.* Cambridge: Cambridge University Press.
Gilmore, L., and Van Proyen, M., eds. 2005. *AfterBurn: Reflections on Burning Man.* Albuquerque: University of New Mexico Press.
Gluckman, M. 1954. *Rituals of Rebellion in South-East Africa.* Manchester: Manchester University Press.
Grindon, G. 2004. 'Carnival Against Capital: a comparison of Bakhtin, Vaneigem and Bey.' *Anarchist Studies* 12(2): 147–61.
Hardt, M., and Negri, A. 2000. *Empire.* Cambridge, MA: Harvard University Press.
Hetherington, K. 2000. *New Age Travellers: Vanloads of Uproarious Humanity.* London: Cassell.
Holmes, B. 2003. 'Touching the violence of the state.' In K. Ainger, G. Chesters, T. Credland, J. Jordan, A. Stern, and J. Whitney, eds. *We Are Everywhere: The Irresistible Rise of Global Anticapitalism.* London: Verso, 346–51.
Jasper, J. 1997. *The Art of Moral Protest: Culture, Biography and Creativity in Social Movements.* Chicago: University of Chicago Press.

Jordan, J. 1998. 'The art of necessity: the subversive imagination of anti-road protest and Reclaim the Streets.' In G. McKay, ed. *DiY Culture: Party & Protest in Nineties Britain*. London: Verso, 129–51.

Jordan, T. 2002. *Activism! Direct Action, Hacktivism and the Future of Society*. London: Reaktion.

Jowers, P., Durrschmidt, J., O'Docherty, R. and Purdue, D. 1999. 'Affective and aesthetic dimensions of contemporary social movements in South West England.' *Innovation: The European Journal of Social Sciences* 12(1): 99–118.

Kershaw, B. 1992. *The Politics of Performance: Radical Theatre as Cultural Intervention*. London: Routledge.

Kershaw, B. 1997. 'Fighting in the streets: dramaturgies of popular protest, 1968–1989.' *New Theatre Quarterly* 51(3): 255–76.

Krasniewicz, L. 1994. *Nuclear Summer: The Clash of Communities at the Seneca Women's Peace Encampment*. Ithaca, NY: Cornell University Press.

Luckman, S. 2001. 'What are they raving on about? Temporary Autonomous Zones and "Reclaim the Streets."' *Perfect Beat* 5(2): 49–68.

Maffesoli, M. 1993. *The Shadow of Dionysus: A Contribution to the Sociology of the Orgy*. Albany: State University of New York Press.

Maffesoli, M. 1996 (1988). *The Time of the Tribes: The Decline of Individualism in Mass Society.* London: Sage.

Martin, G. 2002. 'Conceptualizing cultural politics in subcultural and social movement studies.' *Social Movement Studies: Journal of Social, Cultural and Political Protest* 1(1): 73–88.

Mattern, M. 1998. *Acting in Concert*. New Brunswick, NJ: Rutgers University Press.

McKay, G. 1996. *Senseless Acts of Beauty: Cultures of Resistance since the Sixties*. London: Verso. McKay, G. 2000. *Glastonbury: A Very English Fair*. London: Gollancz.

McKay, G. 2004. 'Subcultural innovations in the Campaign for Nuclear Disarmament.' *Peace Review* 16(4): 429–38.

McKay, G. 2007. 'A soundtrack to the insurrection: street music, marching bands and popular protest.' *Parallax* 13(1): 20–31.

Melucci, A. 1989. *Nomads of the Present: Social Movements and Individual Needs in Contemporary Society*. London: Hutchinson Radius.

Moser, A. 2003. 'Acts of resistance: the performance of women's grassroots protest in Peru.' *Social Movement Studies: Journal of Social, Cultural and Political Protest* 2(2): 177–90.

Nehring, N. 1993. *Flowers in the Dustbin: Culture, Anarchy and Postwar England*. Ann Arbor: University of Michigan Press.

Nield, S. 2006. 'There is another world: space, theatre and global anti-capitalism.' *Contemporary Theatre Review* 16(1): 51–61.

Niman, M. 1997. *People of the Rainbow: A Nomadic Utopia*. Knoxville: University of Tennessee Press.

Nuttall, J. 1968. *Bomb Culture*. London: MacGibbon & Key.

Pickerill, J., and Chatterton, P. 2006. 'Notes towards autonomous geographies: creation, resistance and self management as survival tactics.' *Progress in Human Geography* 30(6): 1–17.

Reclaim the Streets (RTS). 1997. 'The evolution of Reclaim the Streets.' *Do or Die* 6 (Summer 1997). http://rts.gn.apc.org/evol.htm. Accessed 27 September 2014.

Roseneil, S. 1995. *Disarming Patriarchy: Feminism and Political Action at Greenham.* Buckingham: Open University Press.
Roszak, T. 1995 (1968). *The Making of a Counter Culture: Reflections on the Technocratic Society and its Youthful Opposition.* Berkeley: University of California Press.
Routledge, P. 2003. 'Convergence space: process geographies of grassroots globalization networks.' *Transactions of the Institute of British Geographers* 28: 333–49.
Scalmer, S., and Iveson, K. 2001. 'Carnival at Crown Casino: S11 as party and protest.' In G. St John, ed. *FreeNRG: Notes from the Edge of the Dancefloor.* Altona: Common Ground, 233–6.
Scott, A., and Street, J. 2001. 'From media politics to e-protest? The use of popular culture and new media in parties and social movements.' In F. Webster, ed. *Culture and Politics in the Information Age.* London: Routledge, 32–51.
Shantz, J. 1999. 'The New World in the shell of the Old.' *Arachne*, 6(2): 59–75.
St John, G. 2001. 'Alternative cultural heterotopia and the liminoid body: beyond Turner at ConFest.' *Australian Journal of Anthropology* 12(1): 47–66.
St John, G. 2003. 'Post-rave technotribalism and the carnival of protest.' In D. Muggleton and R. Weinzierl, eds. *The Post-Subcultures Reader.* London: Berg, 65–82.
St John, G. 2008. 'Protestival: global days of action and carnivalized politics in the present.' *Social Movement Studies: Journal of Social, Cultural and Political Protest* 7(2): 167–90.
St John, G. 2009. *Technomad: Global Raving Countercultures.* London: Equinox.
St John G. 2010. 'Making a noise – making a difference: techno-punk and terra-ism.' *Dancecult: Journal of Electronic Dance Music Culture* 1(2): 1–28.
St John, G. 2012. *Global Tribe: Technology, Spirituality and Psytrance.* Sheffield: Equinox.
Stallybrass, P., and White, A. 1986. *The Politics and Poetics of Transgression.* London: Methuen.
Stam, R. 1988. 'Mikhail Bakhtin and left cultural critique.' In A. Kaplan, ed. *Postmodernism and its Discontents.* London: Verso, 116–45.
Style, S. 2004. 'People's global action.' In E. Yuen, D. Burton-Rose and G. Katsiaficas, eds. *Confronting Capitalism: Dispatches from a Global Movement.* New York: Soft Skull Press, 215–21.
Swyngedouw, E. 2002. 'The strange respectability of the situationist city in the society of the spectacle.' *International Journal of Urban and Regional Research* 26(1): 153–66.
Szerszynski, B. 1999. 'Performing politics: the dramatics of environmental protest.' In L. Ray, and A. Sayer, eds. *Culture and Economy after the Cultural Turn.* London: Sage, 211–28.
Uitermark, J. 2004. 'Looking forward by looking back: May Day protests in London and the strategic significance of the urban.' *Antipode* 36(4): 706–27.
Weidkuhn, P. 1976. 'Carnival in Basle: playing history in reverse.' *Cultures* 3(1): 29–53.
Worthington, A. 2005. *The Battle of the Beanfield.* Teignmouth: Enabler.
Yuen, E., Burton-Rose, D. and Katsiaficas, G., eds. 2004. *Confronting Capitalism: Dispatches from a Global Movement.* New York: Soft Skull Press.

# CHAPTER TEN

# Alternative playworlds: Psytrance festivals, deep play and creative zones of transcendence

*Alice O'Grady*

The story of psytrance and its journey from the dazzling beaches of Goa to numerous cities, fields, forests and deserts across the globe has been documented most notably and insightfully by ethnographer Graham St John. In one of his books, *Global Tribe*, St John comprehensively gathers the experiential qualities of a transnational phenomenon that revels in technology, spirituality, communality and transformational experience under the umbrella of the visionary arts festival (2012). As I sit here writing on a grey, wet Friday during a fairly typical British summer, many of my friends and thousands of other people from around the world are making their way to Lake Idanha-a-Nova in Portugal where the mother ship of psytrance is about to launch into the cosmos once more. Boom, a biennial festival that hosts this 30,000-strong party, is commonly regarded as the epicentre of psyculture and provides the blueprint for countless other festivals across continents where collective dancing represents a vital way of being together, playing together and, as St John points out, '*being altered together*' (2012, 8; emphasis original). On a different pilgrimage, I travelled to rural Goa in 1991 to celebrate my twenty-first birthday amidst the sounds of 'a mutant dance music culture' (St John 2012, 3) that became known as Goa Trance and which eventually developed into a psychedelic trance, or psytrance as its commonly known today. While parties were in short supply that year because of our arrival just as monsoon was finishing, the memory of hearing 'Charly' by The Prodigy drifting out of a nearby café as I looked out across the Indian Ocean is one that will never leave me. Some 22 years later I returned to a very different, improved and bustling Goa for New Year celebrations. Despite the Indian government's Y2K restrictions on noise that prevents the large-scale beach parties of yesteryear, we managed to find a beach in Anjuna where we could dance to the looping sixteen beat bass line that has been the soundtrack to my life since that first trip in the early 1990s.[1] The space in between those encounters with Goa has been filled with countless outdoor parties, indoor club nights, free parties, gatherings, events and festivals where the audio-visual tapestry of psytrance culture has mediated the way in which I have engaged with each occasion, entered its dimensions and been a player in its midst.

The booming, vivid, welcoming, often scruffy, ragbag world of psytrance has kept me sustained for over 25 years largely because of its particular offer of 'reflexive raving' (St John 2012, 279), its commitment to collective play and the opportunities it provides for grassroots creativity for those who want it. With its distinctive visual aesthetic, the countercultural terrain of psytrance offers its participants an instantly recognizable playing space or what St John calls an 'imaginal geography' (2003, 74) that subscribes to a 'horizontality of participation' (Gaillot 1999, 60) which is both alluring in its promise and deeply satisfying in its realization. By providing a context for play and the opportunity to present a persona that exceeds that of the routine self, in this 'playful arena' (O'Grady 2012) individuals are given the license to embrace the 'freaky self '(St John 2009, 47) or, in my model, the 'ludic self'. Associated with having fun, messing around, cutting loose, making believe, experimenting, imagining, becoming someone else, creating something else and, ultimately, learning how to be with other people in the present moment through improvised sociabilities, the concept of 'play' is instrumental in framing how we view and interpret what happens on the trance floor and in the surrounding fields of the psytrance festival. Play offers a useful way of reading festival behaviour and provides an appropriately malleable means by which we might understand the intangible processes of transformation and transcendence that underpin both the ethos and aesthetic of psytrance events as they exist on the festival circuit today.

Play is transformational. It has the ability to lift us out of and beyond our immediate circumstances while, simultaneously, providing us with the means to confront our everyday reality. The transitional, transformational and transcendent qualities of psytrance are integral to its makeup and, while the often soggy fields of British festivals may seem worlds apart from the beaches of Goa and the dust beds of Portugal, the instantly recognizable sounds and decorative, visual aesthetic of psytrance (see Figure 37) have become enduring features of the more alternative end of the UK festival

**FIGURE 37** *Nature Lovers Society Solstice Gathering, 21 June 2014.*

circuit with many events dedicating at least part of their programming to this particular manifestation of electronic dance music. While notionally 'a clandestine phenomenon' (Lindop 2010, 119) that actively resists incorporation into the mainstream, psytrance can be found at mainstream and larger-scale festivals past and present such as Glastonbury, Glade and BoomTown Fair but is more typically placed within smaller events such as Bearded Theory, Nozstock, Sunrise, Waveform, Eden, Noisily and Alchemy that all feature dedicated psytrance areas. Far fewer, but highly prized by followers for their intimacy, are dedicated psytrance events such as Shamania, Triplicity, Magikana, Black Pearl and Sunset where capacity may be limited to a few hundred tickets but the vibe is closer to a free party or gathering and the original roots of psyculture. Though psytrance can be heard across the country on most weekends during the summer months, the scene continues to be branded 'uncool' by the dance music media (Lindop 2010, 119), the popular press and on social media sites where psytrance parodies are common.[2] While psytrance may not have (or want) a voice in these forums, it finds its natural home at outdoor festivals largely because of its association with hippie culture and the DIY ethic of the rave movement, free parties and the so-called New Age travellers of the mid- to late-1980s where occupying outdoor space was undertaken and understood as a political act of resistance against encroaching laws restricting civil liberties (see McKay 1996, 1998). True to its countercultural roots and grassroots ideology and in opposition to mainstream commercialism, the psytrance scene is fiercely protective of what Timothy Taylor calls its 'hidden little culture' (2001, 165), adopting a set of strong visual codes that mark out its distinctiveness while simultaneously embracing difference in the form of alternative dress codes, belief systems and lifestyles. While musical scenes frequently fracture, mutate and develop into something 'other', psyculture as an aesthetic entity expressed through artwork, clothing and design is curiously resistant to change despite there being an ever increasing number of musical variants under its umbrella, such as full on, dark, progressive, psybreaks, psyambient and so on. As Robin Lindop argues,

> Psytrance maintains a hermetic existence that ensures the continuation of its identity, while simultaneously allowing for outside influence. … Psytrance's distinct visual identity, style, textile fashions, discourse and practices, serve to offer participants a unified cultural experience. If desired, every aspect of life can be lived through an aesthetic that is unique to psytrance. In this sense, psytrance can be viewed as a cultural 'movement', where the music is connected to ongoing cultural, political and spiritual causes. (2010, 127–8)

The dominance of repeated and familiar visual aesthetics is one means by which the 'lifeworld' (Berlant and Warner 1998, 558) or, in my analysis, 'playworld' of psyculture is communicated. It is the reassuring sameness of the audio-visual terrain of psytrance that enables participants to immerse themselves fully in its landscape, to utilize it as a recognizable, and by association, 'safe' playing space where they might experience *the deepest play of all* in order to achieve the transformational qualities that underpin the scene's meta-narratives.

## Underground play and festival space

The idea that clubbing can be understood as a form of play is not a new one and has been explored in depth elsewhere (Malbon 1999; Buckland 2002; O'Grady 2012). By extension, club and festival spaces can be read as adult playgrounds that have both physical and psychical properties that keep them hedged off and marked out as 'special'. A theatrical analogy is useful here to determine the way in which the spatial-temporal conditions of festival space operate under the guise of play. Performance practitioner and director of interactive theatre Garry Izzo uses the Greek word 'temenos' to denote a sense of the sacred circle that wraps play and its players in order to keep both safe and separate from the routine world. He suggests this sacred circle can exist both in the physical world as well as in the mind of the players (1997, 9), a notion not lost on festival organizers who co-opt the idea of the playground as a way of marketing their events and signalling the way in which the space is to be utilized by its participants. A collection of psytrance, progressive and electro musicians and artists based in Wales and the West of England who go under the name of Triplicity use the strap line 'Psychedelic Playground' on all their flyers. They are explicit in conceptualizing their events as otherworldly, adult spaces of play where new discoveries might be

**FIGURE 38** *Flyer for the Psychedelic Spring Gathering, 2014.*

made within its borders. Their 2014 flyer (Figure 38) not only has the strap line 'The Psychedelic Playground' but features other areas called variously 'The Playground of Life', 'The Alternative Playground' and 'The Healing Playground', echoing the psytrance sensibility where dancing, well-being and healing go hand in hand.

Triplicity is not alone in using this analogy. Noisily Festival of Electronic Music and Arts, located in rural Leicestershire, describes itself as 'an exciting woodland playground ... where hedonism and escapism can flourish and thrive' (Noisily 2014). The woodland playground, away from the city and the world of work and the responsibilities it denotes, is significant in relation to the psytrance psyche insofar as it represents a geographical marginality that chimes with the broader desire to escape into and occupy the idealized liminal world of the forest. The preferred location of psytrance festivals, within the United Kingdom at least, is rural. Connecting to nature, immersing oneself in the natural landscape, forms part of the process of transition from daily self to festival self and the alteration of consciousness that might accompany that passage. The more remote the location, the more protected the party, its play and its players. For psytrancers the concept of the woodland playground is used to denote a marked off place, deep in the forest of childhood imagination, out of sight of authority where play can occur in relative freedom. It represents a return to nature and a return to an idealized, simpler way of life where the act of being and dancing together in the woods becomes imbued with magical properties that further stimulate the psytrance imagination. With strict licensing laws, health and safety regulations, tight security controls and an ever diminishing rural landscape in Britain, the reality of this autonomous rural idyll can often be very different but, nonetheless, the deliberate construct of the remote, natural playground as a notional TAZ or temporary autonomous zone (Bey 2003) is a significant framing device for festivals of this kind and assists in establishing the activities that occur within them as expressions of play.

Glade festival, which last took place in 2012, took its name from its location in the wooded area within the main site at Glastonbury Festival before it began as an electronic dance music festival in its own right in the summer of 2004. While not solely dedicated to psytrance, the perceived special properties of the wooded area at Glastonbury became intimately associated with Glade as an event, and its various incarnations from that point were often judged by festival-goers on the strength of the sites used thereafter. At the 2012 event, stages were set up deep within the wooded areas, a programming strategy that gave a significant amount of cover in terms of noise pollution, allowing music to be played almost continuously throughout the weekend (see Figure 39). Pathways and routes to these areas were lit in a way that drew attention to the natural setting and further contributed to the illusion of rurality and seclusion (see Figure 40) despite being located within the easily accessible grounds of Houghton Hall in Norfolk.

In contrast to this relatively large-scale EDM event but with a similar emphasis on the importance of location is Magikana Festival, a 'unique magikal gathering' that takes place over a continuous four-day period in the Cambrian Mountains in Wales. Starting as an underground free gathering in 2002, it has been fully licensed since 2012 but in the summer of 2014 had to postpone the event because of the transition from a small to a large festival license caused by a planned increase in its 500-strong capacity. Maintaining balance between growth and intimacy, access and seclusion are common concerns for psytrance party organizers who are explicit about their green credentials and commitment to sustainability and eco-politics. Nonetheless, set and setting are primary concerns for psytrance festival promoters, organizers and participants and act as a signifier of ethics as much as musical taste.

**FIGURE 39** *Outdoor stage at Glade Festival 2012.*

**FIGURE 40** *Woodland area at Glade Festival 2012.*

## Categories of festival play

Play that occurs at festivals is as diverse and as varied as the events themselves and the many thousands of players involved. Festival play can be individual or collective, private or public, structured or improvised, or in fact, can slide between categories to evade precise definition and capture (Figure 41). A brief scan of the countless online photo galleries associated with individual events, however, reveals the more visible forms of play and indicates the extent to which cutting loose, playing, having fun have become big business for the festival industry. Increasingly, promoters are striving to outdo one another in terms of providing more elaborate and sophisticated opportunities for play that can include official fancy dress policies, organized games and competitions, fairground rides, roller discos, installations, mazes, water zorbing, bungee rides, interactive art, participatory performance and so on.

However, in order to help identify play as it manifests within psytrance, a scene that tends to reject the more commercial 'fairground model', it is useful to consider the continuum of play as determined by Caillois (2001, 13). In Caillois's model, the way people play can be situated between

**FIGURE 41** *An invitation to play at Alchemy Festival, 2012.*

two opposite poles. At one extreme is *paidia*, a type of uncontrolled fantasy where free improvisation, turbulence, diversion and carefree gaiety are dominant. At this end of the spectrum, instances of festival play associated with improvisation, looseness and freewheeling might include inclusive forms of social and ecstatic dancing, trance, the play of multiple social interactions and Bey's notion of 'radical conviviality' (1994). At the other end of the spectrum is *ludus*, characterized by more rule-bound activity that requires greater effort, patience, skill or ingenuity. *Ludus* sits in contrast to the anarchic spirit of *paidia*. While one might assume that the playing space of the psytrance festival subscribes more to the ethos of *paidia*, particularly given the concept of the woodland playground where freedom abounds, it is interesting to note that both categories are well represented with perhaps a greater emphasis on skills acquisition through play than at other types of festivals. Circus performance is a notable feature of many psytrance parties with festivals offering various workshops, demonstrations and performances over the course of the weekend in types of physical play that have a spectacular or theatrical edge and which require some measure of skill and mastery. These include, for example, juggling, contact juggling, poi twirling, hoop twirling, fire staff and fire poi.

Play, and its association with the theatrical world, is of course, apparent in various different guises within festival spaces of all kinds. Professional and semi-professional performers are often programmed into festivals as walkabout performers, musicians, living statues and stilt walkers, their presence lending smaller events the air of a medieval fayre or pageant. In addition to performers contributing to the visual culture of the festival, festival-goers themselves adopt a playful refashioning of self through the use of costuming, disguise and masquerade. While fancy dress is a common feature of many festivals, including large commercial events such as Bestival, the psytrance attitude to dress is rather different. While most prevalent is a utilitarian dress code that facilitates dancing for long periods, some individuals go to great lengths to create bespoke outfits that chime with the core psytrance aesthetic of alternative culture and difference. Resonances with the natural or spirit world in the form of fairies, angels and insects are common as well as other fantastical or otherworldly types of dress, representing forms of display often associated with carnivalesque inversion and grotesque realism (Bakhtin 1998). Whether handmade creations or outfits purchased at the countless stalls selling garments bedecked with Om signs and images of Shiva, multi-pocketed belts, flowing dresses and floral head dresses, the psytrance dress code is a means by which players establish identity and undergo processes of identification for the duration of the event. Costume and dress contributes to the overarching scenography of psytrance festivals and provides another way of establishing the space as an alternative playworld where creativity, self-expression and an attention to the visual can run riot. The transcendence of time and place and the cyclical spiralling as it occurs within the music is echoed in the psytrance aesthetic and repeated in projections, hangings, posters, flyers and film where mandalas, fractals and Eastern symbolism are common symbols. Other recurring visual and aesthetic echoes include references to the Hindu culture, Buddhism, Shamanism, Native American culture, hippy culture and psychedelia, the occult, aliens, extraterrestrials and moonscapes, all of which contribute to what Robin Lindop calls a kind of 'psytrance rubric' (2010, 115). Visuals, music and dance work in conjunction with one another to create a network of signs and conventions that represent a cohesive psytrance imagination. A shared and repeated aesthetic code acts as a gateway for individual and collective expressivity and sets in motion a deliberate blurring between performer and participant that facilitates access to the construct of the alternative playworld. With participants subscribing to a shared aesthetic, the ethos of 'no spectators' is underlined and facilitates creative engagement and play.[3] The relationship between design and action, performance and participation, play and pleasure contributes to the overall schema of the festival experience. Describing their event as a 'pleasure portal', Sunset Festival collective describes what is on offer as a confluence of music, art, display, relaxation, therapy and game:

> Well four main music stages offering up just about every kind of psychedelic music except country and western. The return of the Sunset

> cafe ... a chillout and healing area ... a kids area filled with tranquility ... an esoteric cinema showing informative films ... an art gallery displaying hypnotic psychedelic art ... beautiful fairy's providing massage and good conversation ... Kozmicare to keep you safe and warm ... market traders to display their exotic creations ... workshops to learn new skills ... troupes of flying fire hoop juggling trapeze artists to thrill you with death defying feats of origami ... the most exquisite compost toilets ever to rest your bottom ... more sparkly light bulbs than Heathrow airport ... some pretty impressive lasers ... and finally (we saved the best to last) ... a new Sunset festival sign! (Sunset Festival 2014; spelling original).

Less visible instances of festival play and performance, but perhaps more significant as we move towards an understanding of deep play, are the instances of risky play or what Stephen Lyng calls 'edgework' in which certain types of extreme recreational pursuits, for example, might provide a 'means of feeing oneself from social conditions that deaden or deform the spirit through overwhelming social regulation and control' (2005, 9). Instances of this within psyculture might include experimentation and sensation seeking along and across the edges of experience in order to achieve a sense of transportation and reconfiguring of self achieved, at least in part, through the consumption of psychedelic drugs and other psychoactive substances. Drawing heavily on 1960s counterculture, the psytrance aesthetic involves repeated use of psychedelic images and symbols on flyers, posters, textiles and within the music itself, mainly through the use of vocal samples, or 'nanomedia' (St John 2012, 101), where reference to drug use and altered states of consciousness taken from film, television and documentary sources sail over the 4/4 beat, reinforcing the sense of journey, discovery and transcendence that might be achieved in moments of deep play. Arguments relating to criminality, morality and well-being will always circulate around the use of illegal substances, particularly in the context of youth or countercultures that challenge or threaten authoritarian structures. Nevertheless, playing with reconstructed realities through a variety of means (including but not exclusively those that are pharmacological) is a significant part of the psytrance sensibility and offers a route to reforming 'the spirit' that Lyng suggests social conditions may have damaged. For Graham St John,

> Not unlike other realms of extreme recreation, psychedelic trance and other EDM scenes facilitate the encounter with 'experiential anarchy', with psychedelic festivals optimized fairgrounds of experience in which transcendent states are guaranteed to those who 'make the sacrifice'. Unlike BASE jumping, however, the risk of physical 'death' is remote in psytrance, for rather than death *per se*, one faces a 'little death', or 'ego death', the dissolution of self in the context of others. (St John 2012, 265)

Although mindful of the epidemiological risks, St John is careful to point out that here, rather than posing any significant danger to life, the risks encountered within the context of the trance party are better conceived as performative constructs adopted by participants as a way of giving themselves over to the vibe of the party and as a means of gathering social capital among peers. This is a playful toying with risk in the presence of others, an intentional dramatized act that functions as an antidote to the strictures imposed by what Sean Afnan Morrissey calls 'societies of caution' (2008, 403). Performance of risk might include playful experiments with sex, sexuality, gender and identity as well as the consumption of psychoactive substances that serve to push at the edges of experience a little in order to establish or reaffirm a sense of belonging and position within the tribe. However, as Bromley notes, 'the key to creating empowerment and control in spiritual edgework is to identify connections to the transcendent that appear to pose extreme danger but are not as dangerous as they appear' (2007, 301). Engaging in types of creative practice coupled with practices of the self such as yoga, meditation or achieving trance-like states through prolonged dance is one way to achieve this.

> Creativity is ultimately a field of risk in which artists negotiate new aesthetic terrain. For 'in form', 'top of their game' or avant-garde artists across the spectrum of disciplines of performance, such experiments have long held the potential for self-exaltation and transcendence. (St John 2012, 269)

In a similar way, the creative, playful space of the psytrance world is positioned to offer festival-goers a potential route to well-being and self-actualization through a process of 'letting go', not only of the strictures of the everyday world they have temporarily left behind but also of themselves and their ego as they 'make the sacrifice' in favour of the party. Through a variety of technologies and practices, and with the express purpose of 'liberating the self' (St John 2012, 145), the alternative playworld created and inhabited by psytrancers offers opportunities for spiritual transcendence, letting go or, simply, *losing it* on the trance floor.

## The deep play of psytrance

And what of deep play? According to anthropologist Clifford Geertz in his description of Balinese cockfighting from 1972, the best or deepest play is when the match is so close the owners of the cocks are locked in a vicarious battle and immersed in the moment where the stakes are immeasurably high and the outcome uncertain. Furious betting ensues, tempers ride high, inhibitions are lost, the world outside the cockfight recedes as both players experience an all encompassing sense of being 'in over their heads'

(Geertz 1972, 15). In Geertz's formulation, the characteristics of deep play include the production of emotional intensity and a profound sense of liveness, of being fully in the moment. While Balinese cockfighting might be a curious place to linger when thinking about festival culture, it is the analogy with expressivity that is of significance here. As he argues, 'any expressive form lives only in its own present – the one it itself creates' (1972, 24). Allowing the outside world to recede, immersing oneself fully in the moment, being swept along by the tide of emotion – these are all common traits associated not only with deep play but also with the oceanic feeling of 'ecstasis' attributed to peak Maslow's peak experiences (1970) which, in turn, chimes with the trance floor experiences of many psytrancers.

According to author and poet Diane Ackerman, deep play is a 'special dimension of adult play ... akin to rapture and ecstasy' (1999, 12). For her, deep play is transcendent play and embodies the quest for altered states:

> Deep play is the ecstatic form of play. In its thrall, all the play elements are visible, but they're taken to intense and transcendent heights. Thus, deep play should really be classified by mood, not activity. (1999, 12)

She goes on to say that 'creativity, psychotherapy, sensation-seeking – are all ideal playgrounds for deep play' (1999, 13), and it is this particular trinity that brings us back to the psytrance festival. While music is the score that characterizes each festival, in an echo of Schechner's web of performativity (2002) play, creativity, artistic endeavour, ritual, performance and healing are all found in abundance in this context where various categories are fused under one cohesive aesthetic tradition. Virtually all festivals that have a significant psytrance presence pride themselves on the diverse range of additional talks, workshops, activities, crafts that are provided which often include alternative technologies dedicated to sustainability and green issues or which advocate the resurgence of traditional crafts such as blacksmithing, leatherworks, woodcarving and leather-making that, in turn, do much to imbue the festivals with a sense of nostalgia for the past and a desire to return to a simpler, more rural way of life (see Figure 42).

The intersections between the arts and community-building, creativity and consciousness, well-being and healing make frequent appearances in much of the literature and advertising that circulate around psytrance parties, indicating that attendance is a conscious lifestyle choice as well as an articulation of ethics that goes beyond mere musical choice. A recent flyer (Figure 43) for a charity fundraiser event entitled 'Something Different' in 'celebration of the psytrance community' encapsulates the constituent parts that are integral to the spirit of the psytrance festival, represented here as three progressive phases of the event.

> Friday will celebrate community and unity and the gathering of like-minded people with common beliefs.

**FIGURE 42** *Stalls offer a variety of different types of healing and alternative therapies as part of festival programming. Alchemy 2013.*

**FIGURE 43** *Something Different flyer. Artwork by Darren Nailer.*

> Saturday will celebrate life, consciousness, creativity and the rhythms of life that bring us together.
>
> Sunday celebrates healing and positive energy.

It is this particular blend of communal celebration, creativity and self-improvement that promises the potential for deep play and world-making that may be achieved through a number of complementary channels provided by the broad sociocultural architecture of the festival.

While psytrance may be a relatively marginal musical scene within the current landscape of UK festivals, it nonetheless has significant representation towards the more alternative end of the spectrum, is present across the globe and offers a particular blend of musical preference, aesthetic cohesion and ethical sensibility that surmounts cultural and geographical borders. Seen through the frame of play, it can be read as a space in which potentialities, imaginings and alternatives are made possible, where difference is realized and embraced and where transformation can take effect in a boundaried playworld built not in bricks and mortar but in signs, visual codes and conventions that are often rooted in the past but find their place in a liminal present where transit and transformation are made possible.

## Acknowledgements

Many thanks to Darren Nailer for supplying images of the flyers for the Psychedelic Spring Gathering and Something Different.

Note: This chapter has developed from previous research and includes some material that first appeared in *Dancecult: Journal of Electronic Dance Music Culture* under the title 'Spaces of play: the spatial dimensions of underground club culture and locating the subjunctive' (April 2012) 4(1): 86–106.

## Notes

1 The Noise Pollution (Regulation and Control) Rules that came into force in Goa in 2000 stipulate that 'no one shall beat a drum or tom-tom or blow a trumpet or beat drum or sound any instrument or use any sound amplifier between 10.00 p.m. and 6.00 a.m.' (see 'Noise pollution rules').

2 For an example, see Future Ducks of London, 'Why Psytrance has become shit', which can be viewed on YouTube (Future Ducks of London 2013).

3 The 'no spectators' philosophy stems from Burning Man's mission statement which is best summarized by the Ten Guiding Principles written by Burning Man founder, Larry Harvey, as guidelines for the Regionals Network in 2004 (see Burning Man website). This overarching ethos has been adopted by a number of other festivals that want to encourage participation and self-expression as part of their event.

## References

Ackerman, Diane. 1999. *Deep Play*. New York: Random House.

Bahktin, Mikhail. 1998 [1968]. *Rabelais and his World*. Trans. Hélène Iswolsky. Cambridge, MA.: MIT Press.

Berlant, Lauren, and Warner, Michael. 1998. 'Sex in public.' *Critical Inquiry* 24(2): 547–66.

Bey, Hakim. 1994. *Immediatism*. Edinburgh: AK Press.
Bey, Hakim. 2003 [1985]. *TAZ: The Temporary Autonomous Zone – Ontological Anarchy, Poetic Terrorism*. 2nd revised edition. New York: Autonomedia.
Bromley, David. 2007. 'On spiritual edgework: the logic of extreme ritual performances.' *Journal for the Scientific Study of Religion* 46(3): 287–302.
Buckland, Fiona. 2002. *Impossible Dance: Club Culture and Queer World Making*. Middletown, CT.: Wesleyan University Press.
Burning Man website. 'Ten principles of Burning Man.'
http://www.burningman.com/whatisburningman/about_burningman/principles.html#.VAR_vM3TxQM. Accessed 27 August 2014.
Caillois, Roger. 2001 [1958]. *Man, Play and Games*. Trans. Meyer Barash. Urbana and Chicago: University of Illinois Press.
Future Ducks of London. 2013. 'Why psytrance has become shit.' https://www.youtube.com/watch?v=kIjFMQsb2S4. Accessed 28 August 2014.
Gaillot, Michel. 1999. *Multiple Meaning Techno: An Artistic and Political Laboratory of the Present*. Paris: Editions des Voir.
Geertz, Clifford. 1972. 'Deep play: notes on the Balinese cockfight.' *Daedalus* 10(1): Myth, Symbol and Culture (Winter): 1–37.
Izzo, Gary. 1997. *The Art of Play: The New Genre of Interactive Theatre*. Portsmouth, NH: Heinemann.
Lindop, Robin. 2010. 'Re-evaluating musical genre in UK psytrance.' In Graham St John, ed. *The Local Scenes and Global Culture of Psytrance*. London: Routledge, 114–30.
Lyng, Stephen. 2005. *Edgework: the Sociology of Risk-Taking*. New York: Routledge.
Malbon, Ben. 1999. *Clubbing: Dancing, Ecstasy and Vitality*. London: Routledge.
Maslow, Abraham H. 1970. *Religions, Values, and Peak-Experiences*. New York: Viking Press.
McKay, George. 1996. *Senseless Acts of Beauty: Cultures of Resistance since the Sixties*. London: Verso.
McKay, George, ed. 1998. *DiY Culture: Party & Protest in Nineties Britain*. London: Verso.
Morrissey, Sean Afnan. 2008. 'Performing risks: catharsis: carnival and capital in the risk society.' *Journal of Youth Studies* 11(4): 413–27.
'Noise pollution rules'. 2000. http://envfor.nic.in/downloads/public-information/noise-pollution-rules-en.pdf. Accessed 28 August 2014.
Noisily Festival. 2014. http://www.noisilyfestival.com. Accessed 26 August 2014.
O'Grady, Alice. 2012. 'Spaces of play: the spatial dimensions of underground club culture and locating the subjunctive.' *Dancecult: Journal of Electronic Dance Music Culture* 4(1): 86–106.https://dj.dancecult.net/index.php/dancecult/article/view/331. Accessed 24 August 2014.
Schechner, Richard. 2002. *Performance Studies: an Introduction*. London: Routledge.
St John, Graham. 2003. 'Post-rave technotribalism and the carnival of protest.' In David Muggleton, and Rupert Weinzierl, eds. *The Post-Subcultures Reader*. London: Berg, 65–82.
St John, Graham. 2009. 'Neotrance and the psychedelic festival.' *Dancecult: Journal of Electronic Dance Music Culture* 1(1): 35–64. http://dx.doi.org/10.12801/1947-5403.2009.01.01.03. Accessed 26 August 2014.

St John, Graham. 2012. *Global Tribe: Technology, Spirituality and Psytrance*. Sheffield: Equinox.

Sunset Festival. 2014. http://www.sunsetcollective.org. Accessed 26 August 2014.

Taylor, Timothy D. 2001. *Strange Sounds: Music, Technology and Culture*. London: Routledge.

Triplicity 2014. Triplicity: the Psychedelic Playground. http://triplicitybiz.ipage.com. Accessed 26 August 2014.

# CHAPTER ELEVEN

# No Spectators! The art of participation, from Burning Man to boutique festivals in Britain

*Roxy Robinson*

By examining the American event Burning Man and a selection of festivals that have drawn influence from its approach to production, this chapter shows how British festivals have adapted and integrated a 'No Spectators' ethos. I discuss a wider scene of participatory music festivals in Britain, though I draw upon interviews and ethnographies centred on two in particular, which are both staged in the south of England. These festivals are BoomTown Fair (Hampshire) and Secret Garden Party (Cambridgeshire) and they offer the most significant UK-based examples of systemic audience integration in creative programming. Through this, the British sector is shown to be developing new and hybridized alternatives to concert-style festivals, which primarily award performative emphasis to musical line-ups. Though the festivals examined draw some influences from the Burning Man, relinquished is a decisively articulated ethical code. They are not politically forthright, nor do they present their ethos as a compulsory doctrine. Instead, a DIY ethic is reconfigured into something new, and, perhaps, something quintessentially British. This cross-pollination of ideas has, however, lead to the construction of environments similarly focused on delivering audience members from the role of spectators, by providing them with opportunities for autonomy in the process of consumption. In the project of defining the roles that regulate the media, scholars in the fields of cultural studies and social theory have criticized the concept of spectatorship, and indeed, essentialist couplings like production/consumption, activity/passivity (Levy and Windahl 1985, 110; Biocca 1988, 51; Gottdiener 2001, 6). I argue that, while such terms are not without flaws, they are crucial to understanding the constructs meaningful to 'boutique' festival culture. The events examined intentionally promote audience activity in a raft of ways, many of which have adopted a principle of physical involvement that, outside of festival, similarly guides immersive theatre and art towards co-authorship (Bishop 2006, 11; Bourriaud 2002). Their commercial success, and the broader shift towards themed environments and popular theatricality, illustrates a desire on the part of audiences to perform, collaborate and change their consumption practices: this change is key to understanding how and why festivals are a meaningful way to understand larger movements in the economies of pleasure.

## Burning Man and the art of participation

There is a rapid exchange of ideas accelerating the development of British music festivals, particularly with regard to their visual and participatory milieu. By this, I mean complex décor, concept staging,[1] installation artworks, novel games and encampments and the theatrical clothing worn by performance artists and ordinary festival-goers. The emergence of surrealist and scenographic spaces also embodies an aesthetic allied to the guiding principles of Nevada's Burning Man, a 50,000-strong gathering first held in 1986. There, a 'No Spectators' ethos is heavily reinforced by festival publicity and spatial arrangements. The fusion of practices based around this ideal obligates festival-goers to contribute to such an extent, that perceptible differences between the producers and consumers of the event are largely eliminated. Despite an abundance of music there is a meaningful absence of advertised artist billings, which is a purposive adjustment, intended to level the performative playing field. The anonymity has an equalizing effect, temporarily immunizing participants from the divisions inherent in line-up-focused festivals that require celebrity, and virtuosity, to perform.

In fact, the relationship between allied festivals and the politics of Burning Man stems from, among other things, mutually experienced perplexities regarding line-up-focused, 'concert-model' festivals. There is a sense that by focusing mostly on the main stage and its reception, such festivals present an allegory of the world outside; mimicking its flaws, instead of subverting them, limiting the potential of audiences and reinforcing an entrenched and spatially reinforced separation between them and the performers on stage. As a response, a codified doctrine enshrines systemic participation as a remedy to these ills while the notion of spectatorship, on the contrary, is denigrated as the symbol of an outside dystopia. At Burning Man, festival-goers are themselves invited to build and animate the event space. In the idealizing discourses relating to the festival, spectatorship is replaced with the idea of 'prosumption' (Chen 2011, 570–95). The festival attempts to maximize the potential for the audience's self-determination, and tangible action, in the process of consumption. The importance of audience agency is made explicit: event publicity describes Burning Man as 'more of a city than a festival, wherein almost everything that happens is created entirely by its citizens' (Burning Man website). With a singularity almost religious, the spatial, organizational and aesthetic arrangements of the celebration each resonates with this position. A monolithic main stage is conspicuously absent; instead, there is a semi-circular configuration of small tents, stages and geodesic structures, which are littered in close proximity across the sand (Figure 44). Teams of virgin and veteran 'Burners' build themed encampments, which are the result of their written proposals to the festival, and often, many months of advance planning. Symbolically placed at the centre is the wooden effigy – the Man. During the charged bacchanal on the Saturday night of the festival, he is ceremoniously burnt to the ground.

Nicknamed Black Rock City, Burning Man creates a 'para-urban' context and civic infrastructure, intentionally conferring onto festival-goers' social responsibilities associated with the status of *citizen* (Gilmore 2008, 216). The event's emphasis on citizenship has coincided with the development of a highly unusual organizational structure. There is a massive volunteer workforce that, for the most part, comprised ticket buyers. Most of them pay between $300 and $400 for entry, plus the cost of travel that can run into thousands of dollars, and undertake tasks that elsewhere would be shouldered by workers paid with a monetary fee and/or free entry into the event. Burning Man is unconventional in its ability to motivate

**FIGURE 44** *Burning Man, 2012: 'A semi-circular configuration of small tents, stages and geodesic structures'.*

ticket buyers to labour. The effects of the policy are twofold: by resisting an economically based divide between volunteers and ticket buyers, it prevents attendees from enjoying an easy purchase – or, in Burner-speak, a right to passivity. While there is no penalty for behaviours that could pass for passivity, the fact that ticket buyers are encouraged to volunteer means that buying a ticket does not come with immunity from the call to participate – and, in any case, many attend to experience this ethos in action. And, the policy also allows Black Rock City LLC, the festival's organizing entity, to democratize creative production without forfeiting organizational income. It would not be difficult to cast this as exploitative profiteering on the part of Burning Man's owners, as was implied by the original co-founder John Law while attempting to sue the festival in 2007.[2] P. J. Rey has also pointed out, in a piece titled 'Burning Man is the new capitalism', that 'the Burning Man experience is the product of tens (or even hundreds) of millions of dollars flowing into the consumer economy and is inextricably linked to disposable incomes of Silicon Valley's digerati' (Rey 2013). However, my view is that these interpretations of affairs do not alter the fact that ultimately, the arrangement is essential to the practical realization of a large-scale, participant-produced festival within a financially sustainable framework. With the bulk of creative minutiae left within the remit of participants, the organization focuses instead on finance and administration, legal duties, basic infrastructure build, recruitment and the safety and quality controls required to stage the event. Volunteers can also get involved with these areas if they have a particular skill set, and the workforce includes some highly specialized workers labouring for free. Donated labour is common and supported through the repetition and reinforcement, via various media, of values conducive to collective productivity. The decree 'No Spectators' is aligned with a broader repertoire of principles that amplify a sense of duty as well as social freedoms and experimentation: 'Civic Responsibility', 'Communal Effort', 'Decommodification', 'Radical Self-Reliance', 'Radical Inclusion', 'Radical Self-Expression' and 'Gifting' are statements found in festival literature. They help cultivate the attitudes necessary to building what is cast as a parallel society with redemptive qualities. The principles also respond to a perceived social malaise, supporting a Mannheimian critique of American culture and society as problematically conducive to wastefulness, passivity, anonymity and isolation (Fortunati 2005, 153).

Set against the featureless desert, elaborate costumes, art installations, theme camps and decorated vehicles known as art cars each contributes to form a uniquely spectacular landscape (see Figure 45). A synthesis of functionality and aesthetics, as the art cars in particular exemplify, marks out an inclusive interpretation of art by confusing its norms of qualification and authenticity. In the spirit of 'Radical Inclusion', a challenge to the remote position of 'the artist' is made in the attempt to transform festival-goers into the theme camp, installation and art car creators. This confluence

**FIGURE 45** *An art car and the Temple of Burning Man, 2012.*

of ideals and practice suggests a critique of how art is both judged and co-opted by commercial forces in American society (Clupper 2007, 229; Doherty 2004, 176). It is also implicitly tied to the politics of the festival's founder, Larry Harvey. His vision for the festival is stated as 'redefining and expanding the notion of who "artists" are, and what their social role could be in the psychological and institutional context amidst which they and others work and live' (Fortunati 2005, 163). Extending the concept of the artist to all participants, Harvey asserts an egalitarian principle that stems from his own critical perception of a compartmentalized and spectator-inducing external world. It is significant that Burning Man's publicity intentionally avoids using the term 'festival', as if the word has come to denote the very principles Harvey seeks to reject. 'Burning Man is', as stated on its website (2014), 'not like usual festivals where big acts perform on massive stages'. The critical tone of these assertions points to the founder's attempt to reclaim what he sees as *true* participation – a form that destroys the very concept of an audience by placing it, hypothetically, on centre stage. As the festival has grown over the years, its potential mixture of civic assembly and idealized participation has prompted speculation that knowledge of its success will instigate changes in the 'way people organise' (Chen 2005, 126). Online imagery and videos have also globalized this once-obscure gathering, contributing to its vanguard status among event enthusiasts around the world. As a result, it has developed into a celebration with international reaches and partner events: the Burning Man Network represents over fifty offshoot regional burns in locations as far afield as South Africa, Israel and China. These are festivals that follow the blueprint established by Burning Man and signal the establishment of Burner communities across the globe. The continued growth of the Network suggests that Burning Man should not be defined by the parameters of its secluded desert location, but rather, as a growing and international diaspora.

## Co-production and British boutique festivals

The first available reference to British *boutique* music festivals was made by Knight et al. in the *Observer* newspaper, in June 2003. The article described them as 'compact, stylish and intimate' (Knight 2003). Featured events, which included the Big Chill, Green Man and a concert on the grounds of Somerset House in London, appeared to be chosen on the basis that, while hosting notable line-ups of live bands and DJs, they were small, 'arty' and relatively unknown.[3] After 'boutique festivals' proliferated in the media's parlance, industry analysts defined them in another way: Mintel claimed that they represented a counter-trend to the growing commercialism found elsewhere in the festival's industry (Mintel 2008). This definition is at odds with the way that 'boutique' today signifies premium options, such as luxury camping, yet the emergence of these so-called boutique festivals did seem to herald a new, utopian zeitgeist within the sector. Within this social milieu, a format of collective production is growing in ways that both draw on, and depart from, the practice and politics of participation at Burning Man.

With a collective capacity of approximately 160,000, Secret Garden Party, Bestival, Beatherder, BoomTown Fair ('BoomTown' hereafter) and Shambala are among those that form an assemblage of UK events cultivating a 'No Spectators' ethos. Their event designs have taken a civic and surrealist turn: embellished venue facades, ambitiously scaled art and stylized infrastructure animate themes and invite festival-goers into scenographic shantytowns. For some, this has sidelined the centrality of line-ups, which now form the soundtrack to more integrated, theatrical productions. In the task of understanding these developments, it is worth pointing out that the experimentalism that Burning Man's break with line-up convention affords, together with its ticket-selling power, is a seductive prospect for British promoters. They have struggled to overcome challenges presented by dependency on big name artistes, such as soaring fees, the imposition of artist exclusivities by competing festivals and the general shortfall of ticket-selling artists able to play their stages. Yet this US anomaly interests them not only for economic reasons, but also because of the ideals embedded in its participative system of production. Though Secret Garden Party and BoomTown are nuanced in music focus, branding and style, there is an affinity in how their founders value this aspect of Burning Man. Co-founded by Freddie Fellowes, and hosted on the land of his father, Secret Garden Party was first staged with 1,000 guests in 2004 and subsequently followed a steep trajectory of growth. By the start of the global financial crisis in 2008 it was attracting 6,000 attendees. Seemingly immune to the economic instability which had begun to affect the market elsewhere, the festival doubled its capacity during 2009 to 12,000. Throughout this time, a participatory ethos was central to the development of Secret Garden Party's position in the marketplace, and in many ways this was directly inspired by the format of Burning Man. As Fellowes put it to me in an interview, 'Burning Man has shown you all the things you can do when you're not bound by a preconception of what a festival is' (personal interview, 2009). For nine consecutive years, he took a team of volunteers to the Nevada desert to create a theme camp, complete with a free bar and disco. His aim was, in his own words, to bring a touch of 'British tomfoolery' to Burning Man's proceedings. Another interviewee, who organized performance art at Secret Garden Party, described the outcome of the 2005 trip:

> The bulk of the Garden Party went. It was a real eye-opener for most of them, it's such a completely different format and they came back with loads of ideas. The Garden Party's really changed as a shift towards that. (Personal interview, 2009)

Fellowes later introduced schemes at Secret Garden Party to democratize production that bore close resemblance to the Nevada gathering. With his team he launched volunteer-led theme camps, renamed 'action camps', which are today publicized as central to the ethos of the festival. They offer a conspicuous avenue towards working as part of the production team, and they are open to anyone to apply. Advertised prominently on the festival's website, a central tab labelled 'participate' allows users to access an online application form which requires applicants to mastermind unique proposals for the festival – a novel game, perhaps, or an interactive performance piece related to that year's particular theme. As the 2014 application form stated:

> The Action Camps are the lifeblood of Secret Garden Party. They are created by you, for you. We have had a record amount of applications in 2013; some bold, some understated, but all of them dreamed up and designed by your fellow gardeners. (Secret Garden Party website 2014)

As can be seen, with its festival-goers called 'gardeners', Secret Garden Party has even drawn on Burning Man for its citizenship naming. The sorts of action camp proposals that are selected are usually hair-brained and tantamount to high levels of interactivity on site. In the past, these have included numerous fancy dress and make-up boutiques (Wot's a Curling/Banjax Banditos), concept stages and performance spaces (Dance-Off/Bearded Kitten), and the various art installations scattered across the site. Pictured in Figure 46, the Dance-Off exemplifies the way in which the action camps erode the distinctions between producers and consumers in two ways. The first of these is systemic: fans of the festival are able to become producers of distinct features (the Dance-Off is run by a group of friends who started out as litter pickers). Secondly, the creative outputs of fans are often aligned with the principles of participatory art in promoting audience agency – distributing

**FIGURE 46** *The Dance-Off at Secret Garden Party, 2014.*

the means of suggestion, among the many (Haggren et al. 2005, 5). Dance-Off performers include some professional dancers, though they are mostly ordinary festival-goers.

Some action camp producers are motivated by improved career or portfolio prospects, though many are simply rewarded with pleasure and a sense of community. As acknowledged by Fred Turner in his discussion of participants at Burning Man, they also enjoy a form of status in seeing creative projects *visibly* realized in front of their peers (Turner 2009, 76). The introduction of similar schemes at other festivals indicates that Fellowes was not alone in the view that a 'No Spectators' ethos should be championed in the United Kingdom. BoomTown's founder Lak Mitchell, soon after staging his own first festival, also travelled to the Nevada desert. During my interview with him, he acknowledged that Burning Man 'blew [him] away'. This was evidently a pivotal experience with emotional gravitas: 'I got a little upset actually', he remarked, 'because I thought we'd never get there in the UK' (personal interview, 2014). These words imply a perspective of Burning Man as some kind of achieved utopia, an ideal model that other festivals are gradually evolving towards. BoomTown has also implemented bursary schemes, though it has taken a different approach to achieving the goals of escapism and participant ownership. The division of the site into nine 'Districts' awards occupants with citizen status and an intra-festival identity. These zones are styled in ways that echo districts found in contemporary cities: there are areas characterized by immigration, with vaguely exotic themes implied by the Districts of Barrio Loco and ChinaTown; the Old Town simulates an historic area, and a high-class, gentrified zone can be found at Mayfair Avenue. These areas constitute invitations to tribalize and contribute in ways aligned to these thematic titles.

For both festivals, the process of deploying fan contributions has been made possible through the formalization and transparency of recruitment. Online application forms can be accessed from anywhere in the world, and many other music festivals have developed similar application procedures that assist in the democratization of production. To take a broader perspective, there are several core congruencies in the relationship between the organizers of Secret Garden Party and BoomTown, and their experience at Burning Man. They each attended during the early years of staging their own events, awarding it a vanguard status. They came to place great importance on audience participation, and as a practical extension of this view, diversified their arts programme and introduced public-facing bursary schemes. 'No Spectators', though only semi-articulated in their own promotional texts, is an idiom that guided the tangible development of their events. It should be noted that music billings remained, however, paramount to press coverage and ticket sales: they integrated only those elements that would *add value*, re-modelling the 'No Spectators' ethos to fit within their own economic frameworks.

## Theming the festival

In the United Kingdom, the promotion of festival themes has become increasingly popular. Hence it has transpired that popular theatricality – that is, a theatrical *audience* – is today a noticeable feature of contemporary British festival culture. British festivals reconfigure what is an enshrined and symbolically loaded practice at Burning Man into a more casual mode of play. From *Desert Island Disco* (Bestival) to *Fact or Fiction* (Secret Garden Party), themes form aesthetic umbrellas under which the makers of costume, art and décor find unity and stimulus. Festivals that engineer richly themed environments do so by saturating their virtual and physical spaces with symbols that allow them to masquerade in chosen forms. In stylized settings, festival fashion and full-blown costumes constitute the co-production of spectacle and, like carnival's inversion, the event becomes a stage on which festival-goers perform. Many also invent their own themes. Figure 47 shows festival-goers in space-style costume at Secret Garden Party 2014, which was themed *Goodbye Yellow Brick Road*.

Outside of music festivals, theming has been critically theorized in commercial terms as a function allowing restaurants, amusement parks and shopping centres to simulate more interesting environments. The increased enjoyment resulting from the added layers of meaning have proved to be, for many franchises, conducive to increased consumer expenditure. In his work on Disneyization, Bryman argues that otherwise 'lacklustre' environments are able to introduce 'a veneer of meaning and symbolism' (2004, 15). Walt Disney also cited more practical motivations for his theme parks: he wanted

**FIGURE 47** *Revellers in fancy dress at Secret Garden Party, 2014.*

to create clean, less tawdry versions of the amusement parks he visited in his own childhood (2004, 21). Disney's parks pioneered the use of theme, but they constituted a distinctly sanitized form of escapism. By contrast, festivals offer a more spontaneous and bacchanalian thematic milieu. The spontaneous element is a ward of the audience, for they represent an unpredictable aspect of the show. Festival-goers convey considerable enjoyment in becoming part of the fantasy, immersing themselves in the surreal atmosphere by adapting the signifiers of bodily display. That is not to say that there is no connection between festival culture and the sprawling thematic environments of amusement parks. Indeed, the co-founder of BoomTown acknowledged taking inspiration 'straight out of Disneyland' (Lak Mitchell, personal interview, 2014). The festival's title – BoomTown – itself denotes a mythical setting: the township of Boom. In the festival's online presence, a town history mingles fact with fictional events (BoomTown website). This detailed fantasy spans a sequence of chapters, engaging festival-goers in an imagined metropolis long before they reach the fields. The sense of narrative is reinforced by a civic-style site design (see Figure 48). It is not coincidental that the popularity of BoomTown's carnivalized and richly themed environment parallels its growth: at the time of writing, BoomTown is currently the fastest-growing independent festival in the United Kingdom.[4]

It has been claimed that all 'workable' themed environments relate to a limited set of concepts (Gottdiener 2001, 176; Schmitt and Simonson 1997, 138). According to Gottdiener, these include status, tropical paradise, the Wild West, classical civilization, nostalgia, Arabian fantasy, urban motif, modernism and progress (2001, 176–83). The following breakdown demonstrates that although music festivals were not referenced in the formation of his typology, many themes found at music festivals coincide with the spaces that were. Like amusement parks, restaurants and other

**FIGURE 48** *'Streets' at BoomTown Fair, 2014.*

public contexts, music festivals are recycling the thematic motifs that pre-exist in popular culture.

### *Music festivals as themed environments*

*'Status'*

- Superheroes (Y-Not Festival, 2013)
- Rock Stars, Pop Stars and Divas (Bestival, 2011)
- TV Shows and DVD Box Sets (2000 Trees, 2014)
- Kendal Calling goes to the Movies (Kendal Calling, 2013)

*'Modernism and progress'*

- Kendal Calling goes Beyond the Stars (Kendal Calling, 2014)
- BoomTown Fair goes to Outer Space (BoomTown, 2012)
- Frontiers of the Future (Beacons Festival, 2013)

*'Nostalgia'*

- Decades (Blissfields, 2010)
- Thrift Shop and Vintage (Rockness, 2013)
- Empires (Beacons Festival, 2014)
- 80s Movies (2000 Trees, 2013)

*'Tropical'*

- Desert Island Disco (Bestival, 2014)
- 30,000 Freaks Under the Sea (Bestival, 2008)
- The Seas of Shambala (Shambala, 2014).

Some themes overlap and relate to more than one overarching concept, and a few do not relate to this typology at all. However, the majority do convey a sense of place, in space or time, enhancing the symbolic, immersive and hyperreal qualities of festival space. Gottdiener disparaged what he saw as an inevitable corporate preference for themes that speak to the 'lowest common denominator' (2001 176, 178). It is true that from the perspective of promoters, the choice of themes is necessarily limited because it is bound by the criteria that determine levels of engagement: they must be broad enough to suggest multiple avenues to creative participation, but clear enough to be of interest to the majority of their festival's clientele. That is why festival themes invite imitation, and numerous iterations of the same concept are reconstructed as organizers try to avoid obvious plagiarism or repetition. In this crowded scene, theme *names* are also important. A clever turn of phrase (like *Desert Island Disco,* Bestival, as opposed to *TV Shows and DVD Box Sets,* 2000 Trees) increases the likelihood a theme will be remembered, and thus, the likelihood of audience response. They are also connotative, triggering mental associations that allude to imagined settings. For example, *Desert Island Disco* connotes sunshine, sand, Hawaiian shirts, grass skirts, disco balls and multicoloured parrots. These material associations are first introduced with brand imagery, before physical realization on the festival site (which happens to be a resonant festival island, the Isle of Wight). Theme *type* is also becoming a mark of distinction. For example, themes like *Beyond Belief* (2003) and *Evolution* (2009) at Burning Man challenge participants to consider loftier, more conceptual associations. Testament to its allegiance to the festival, Secret Garden Party's themes are similarly abstract, with theme titles such as *Superstition* (2013) and *Standing on Ceremony* (2012) poised to appeal to a well-heeled, intellectual and bohemian demographic. Like pop stars that continually reinvent themselves through adopting new assemblages of sounds, style and dress, this tactic allows festivals to preserve their novelty through continuous renewal. Audience involvement is a key component in this process, providing animation for scenery that is primed for action with stylized décor. The approach generates colourful imagery that is posted online, guiding the expectations of newcomers and becoming a self-fulfilling prophecy for next year's event. As we have seen, the core architects of the UK festivals most conducive to popular theatricality via theming have each attended Burning Man and expressed affection for the model of systemic democratization it exemplifies. Their work must be regarded, however, as the manifestation of an ideal that also offers a practical solution to the pressures of the marketplace. Promoters are cultivating their own version of the 'No Spectators' ethos for it supplements event content with the creative imaginings of participants. With such an increased quantity of boutique festivals jostling for notice among festival-goers, and limited means for securing top artist billings, the engagement that theming promotes has become crucial to achieving industry status and a loyal relationship between festivals and their fans.

## Conclusion

This chapter evidences a surrealist turn in the production of festival space. Participative arts, audience theatricality and themed environments are increasingly popular within what may be described as the 'boutique' festival sector. In addition to raising the overall levels of visual stimulation on site, this is likely because the status of audiences is raised through the open legitimization of their contributions. Much like differing carnival traditions, these festivals also show that certain presentations of virtual and physical space promote 'patterns of theatricality' (Cremona 2004, 74). Of course, not every festival-goer finds enjoyment in costumes, 'dance-off' competitions or creating themed encampments, and there will always be a strong market for 'concert-model' festivals. Yet activities like this are becoming more common, and as well as the events discussed in detail in this chapter, the trend towards immersive event design is increasingly perceptible within large swathes of Glastonbury (in particular, Shangri-La) and at other independent music festivals, including Kendal Calling, Bestival, Standon Calling, Y-Not and 2000 Trees. They are owned by conventionally structured companies, with a very small nucleus of full-time organizers, though it is clear that the mobilization of fans to create content has become (for Secret Garden Party and BoomTown in particular) crucial to their success in the marketplace. Outside the United Kingdom, the ways in which Fusion festival (Germany) and Tomorrowland (Belgium, Brazil and the United States) have incorporated contrasting expressions of immersive design shows that this phenomenon is not specific to the United Kingdom or United States and is now found within both overtly commercial and 'anti-commercial' frameworks.

It is interesting to observe that, while a 'No Spectators' ethos is shaping UK music festivals, *spectacles* are a presiding characteristic. Complex spectacles, together with challenging notions surrounding spectatorship, are reconciled by the fact that participants help *produce* the spectacle. This is not the first subcultural context to have contested modes of spectatorship: 1990s DJ and rave events were thought to offer a meaningful relief from theatrical spectacle (Huq 1999, 17). DJs, unlike watching live bands, did not seem to be predicated on watching stylized personalities on stage. Here the very removal of *watching*, and the repositioning of the DJ as the medium, rather than the message, seemed to challenge the spectator-inducing facets perceptible in the performances of live music. If DJ-centred culture offered a replacement of the live music spectacle, the festival cultures discussed in this chapter restore spectacle, though on more democratized grounds. It is important to remember, however, that inter-festival rivalry has helped drive this development. For many years, festival ticket buyers have logically expected loaded programmes of music; on the contrary, features such as art, décor and theming are added values. Because of this, they are areas of rapid evolution. The relationship between Burning Man and UK festivals must be considered within this competitive context, as an allegiance supported by the cultural economics of organizer beliefs as well as incentives (Anderton 2008, 42). This is an important observation because commercial incentives have a habit of transforming appropriated content. The burning of sculptures, for example, with the symbolism that accompanies such ceremonies at Burning Man, is to a certain extent de-radicalized through its co-option in the United Kingdom. Electric Picnic, the former Glade and Secret Garden Party have each created comparable moments of intrigue by burning sculptures down during the celebrations, though they are not framed in the same terms. This is also true in a wider sense: the literature of BoomTown, for example, does not reflect on its own importance as a social experiment, or conjecture as to how its form of social organization might influence the world outside. At Burning Man, its more conscious approach has been described as a self-righteous and forced attempt to increase 'impact and meaning' – which has not always been viewed as positive (Mason, in Doherty 2004, 164–5). The United Kingdom's appropriation has resulted in a dilution of 'earnestness' (164), and through this process, has ushered in a new festival hybrid. The phrase 'No Spectators' is largely absent and perhaps it is the implicit, as opposed to explicit, delivery of its ideal that renders the festivals discussed accessible to a wider audience. This chapter has drawn upon the influences and actions of festival organizers, and it would be easy, though ill advised, to forget that the success of their initiative is fully reliant on meaningfulness to the festival-going community. The shift towards democratized models of production is not an isolated phenomenon: considering contemporary forms of online leisure and sociality, evidence for the ubiquitous popularity of fan-produced content is everywhere. Festivals like Secret Garden Party and BoomTown did not grow into popular events *because of* Burning Man, but because, like Burning Man, they have engaged with the human impulse to connect with the apparatus of cultural production. This may not have the same chaotic force as the 1960s and 1970s counterculture that energized early British festivals, but it does suggest that there is more than a hint of DIY zeal shaping the scene today.

## Acknowledgements

Thanks are owed to Lak Mitchell, who was interviewed for this study on 8 February 2014, and to Freddie Fellowes, who was interviewed on 17 January 2014. I also interviewed performance artist Daniel Winch for my doctoral thesis on 20 March 2009, which I have re-quoted in my discussion of Secret Garden Party.

## Notes

1 Concept staging is a phrase introduced by the author to refer to performance spaces with a highly stylized sculptural form. An early notable example is the Pyramid Stage at Glastonbury. The original was built out of scaffolding and metal sheeting in 1971. As specialized production teams are developing their techniques, concept stages are now emerging as distinct features of smaller British festivals. For example, Lancashire's Beatherder hosts a stage resembling a fortress, while BoomTown has introduced one stage built to represent a gold mine, and another, a Mayan temple. Skills developed in the set design of film and theatre productions are often utilized in the build of concept stages, which add to the repertoire of scenery animating the thematic, festival space.

2 This was a lawsuit relating to the festival's ownership, involving its founders John Law, Larry Harvey and Michael Mikel. The case was settled out of court on undisclosed terms, in 2008.

3 The only capacity size listed in the article is 2,000 (for Green Man), though the festival reportedly sold just 300 tickets that year. The 2008 *Music Concerts and Festivals* report by Mintel claimed that festivals branded as 'boutique' had an approximate capacity of 5,000. Since the publication of the report, many of the festivals that featured have outgrown this capacity figure. Consequently while 'boutique' still connotes intimacy in the festival sector, this does not always equal small scales in actual terms.

4 This is based on a survey of fifty independent outdoor music festivals in the United Kingdom, conducted by Dr Emma Webster for this study. BoomTown has grown at a rate of 660 per cent between 2010 and 2014, from a capacity of 5,000 to almost 40,000. The growth of the festival, when compared with the rest of the market, is unusual in that it has been very rapid, and in the sense that the festival exists outside of both the corporate festival sector (i.e. not owned by Live Nation, Mama Group, etc.) and, to some extent, the independent festival sector (it has never been a member of the Association of Independent Festivals, for example). It has also refrained from participating in the annual UK Festival Awards, rendering its surge in popularity somewhat unrecognized by industry standards.

# References

Anderton, Chris. 2008. 'Commercializing the carnivalesque: the V Festival and image/risk management.' *Event Management* 12(1): 39–51.

Biocca, Frank A. 1988. 'Opposing conceptions of the audience: the active and passive hemispheres of mass communication theory.' *Communication Yearbook* 11: 51–80.

Bishop, Claire, ed. 2006. *Participation*. London: Whitechapel.

BoomTown Fair website. Town History. http://www.boomtownfair.co.uk/tourist-info/town-history. Accessed 10 April 2014.

Bourriaud, Nicolas. 2002. *Relational Aesthetics*. Trans. Simon Pleasance and Fronza Woods, with the participation of Mathieu Copeland. [S.I]: Les Presse Du Reel.

Bryman, Alan. 2004. *The Disneyization of Society*. London: Sage.

Burning Man website. Burning Man. http://www.burningman.com/. Accessed 4 September 2014.

Chen, Katherine K. 2011. 'Artistic prosumption: cocreative destruction at Burning Man.' *American Behavioural Scientist* 56(4): 570–95.

Clupper, Wendy. 2007. 'Burning Man: festival culture in the United States – festival culture in a global perspective.' In Temple Hauptfleisch et al. eds. *Festivalising! Theatrical Events, Politics and Culture*. Amsterdam: Rodopi, 222–41.

Cremona, Vicky-Ann. 2004. 'Carnival as a theatrical event.' In Vicky-Ann Cremona, Peter Eversmann, Hans van Maanen, Willmar Sauter and John Tulloch, eds. *Theatrical Events: Borders, Dynamics, Frames,* New York: Rodopi, 69–90.

Doherty, Brian. 2004. *This is Burning Man: The Rise of a New American Underground*. New York: Little, Brown.

Fortunati, Allegra. 2005. 'Utopia, social sculpture, and Burning Man.' In Lee Gilmore, and Mark Van Proyen, eds. *Afterburn: Reflections on Burning Man*. Albuquerque: The University of New Mexico Press, 151–70.

Gilmore, Lee. 2008. 'Of ordeals and operas: reflexive ritualising at the Burning Man festival.' In Graham St John, ed. *Victor Turner and Contemporary Cultural Performance*. New York: Berghahn Books, 211–26.

Gottdiener, Mark. 2001. *The Theming of America: Dreams, Media Fantasies, and Themed Environments*. Colorado: Westview Press.

Haggren, Kristoffer, Elge Larsson, Christoffer Lindahl, Andie Nordgren, Leo Nordwall, and Gabriel Widing. 2005. *Interacting Arts: International Issue*. Vol. 5. http://issuu.com/interactingarts/docs/ia-international-05. Accessed 8 May 2013.

Huq, Rupa. 1999. 'The right to rave: opposition to the Criminal Justice and Public Order Act 1994.' In Tim Jordan, and Adam Lent, eds. *Storming the Millennium: The New Politics of Change*. London: Lawrence & Wishart, 15–33.

Knight, Robin, Vikki Miller, Dee O'Connell, Lucy Siegle, Ian Tucker and Polly Vernon. 8 June 2003. 'A-Z of Summer (Part One)'. *Observer*. http://www.guardian.co.uk/lifeandstyle/2003/jun/08/ethicalliving1. Accessed 20 November 2013.

Levy, M., and Windahl, S. 1985. 'The concept of audience activity.' In Karl Erik Rosengren, Lawrence A. Wenner and Philip Palmgreen, eds. *Media Gratifications Research: Current Perspectives*. California: Sage, 109–22.

Mintel Report. 2008. *Music Concerts and Festivals*. http://reports.mintel.com/display/280413/#. Accessed 3 September 2014.

Rey, P. J. 2013. 'Burning Man is the new capitalism.' *The Society Pages* (5 September 2013). http://thesocietypages.org/cyborgology/2013/09/05/burning-man-is-the-new-capitalism/. Accessed 3 September 2014.

Schmitt, Bernd. H., and Simonson, Alex. 1997. *Marketing Aesthetics: the Strategic Management of Branding, Identity, and Image*. London: Free.

Secret Garden Party website. 2014. Participation Grants Application 2014. http://www.secretgardenparty.com/2014/forms/SGP_Participation_2014.pdf. Accessed 10 May 2014.

Turner, Fred. 2009. 'Burning Man at Google: a cultural infrastructure for new media production.' *New Media and Society* (February/March 2009) 11(1–2): 73–94.

# CHAPTER TWELVE

# Musicking in motor city: Reconfiguring urban space at the Detroit Jazz Festival

*Anne Dvinge*

For the 2009 International Detroit Jazz Festival, a video spot, vox-pop style was produced, promoting the festival. A series of jazz musicians were filmed in non-performance situations (talking to friends in the backstage area, passing from one place to another), all praising and recommending the festival. The spot opens and closes with bass-player Christian McBride's exclamation that 'It's all here. It's all here, baby'.

This is not the statement that first springs to mind when conversation falls on Detroit. The economic downturn that began in 2007 took a particularly hard toll on the car industry and other heavy industries, hitting the economy of cities like Detroit hard. The media has consistently narrated a tale of woe; of economic, social and cultural decline. It told of a city that never managed to get a foothold in the post-industrial economy, of a city whose nickname, Motor City, today no longer evokes the American infatuation with the car as a strong symbol of freedom and mobility, but rather the crisis and subsequent bailout of an industry that had behaved like a cross between a dinosaur and an ostrich – unable and unwilling to adapt.

The decline of Detroit is possibly accelerating in the current economy, but the disintegration of the city has been in process since the 1950s, with a steady depopulation from 1,849,568 in 1950 to an estimated 688,701 in 2013 (US Census Bureau 2013). One of the most visible products of the depopulation is the proliferation of abandoned and derelict buildings, as well as empty plots where structures were torn down to make room for new builds in the name of a progress that never arrived. Many of them now serve as temporary – but often vacant – parking lots. The eerie emptiness of the city is not just an effect of the abandoned buildings and paved over building plots. Detroit is a city built to contain 2 million people, now housing just a third of that.

The devastation of Detroit has been slow, but continual. Though happening over decades rather than overnight, it is perhaps as complete and inevitable as the one that New Orleans faced in 2005 after Hurricane Katrina and the breach of the levees. The images of broken windows, leaning houses and peeling walls bear resemblance. And as in New Orleans, there is a sense of defiance, of cultural heritage and community among those who chose to stay, as well as those who arrive in the city looking for artistic and entrepreneurial openings (notwithstanding that the narrative of entrepreneurship from 'outsiders' or non-native inhabitants remains a contested one, in both Detroit and New Orleans). Music – and jazz – plays a strong part in both cities' cultural heritage.

Unlike New Orleans, Detroit was never invested with the preservation of the past, but rather kept its eyes firmly fixed on the future. Nevertheless, jazz still plays a part as cultural repository and once a year, on Labor Day weekend in early September, Detroit celebrates itself and jazz with the giant block party that is Detroit Jazz Festival (Figure 49). With three-quarters

**FIGURE 49** *Detroit during the festival: Woodward Avenue towards Campus Martius.*

of a million people in attendance over four days and with such headliners as Chick Corea, Wayne Shorter, Wynton Marsalis, Sonny Rollins, Dave Brubeck, Jimmy Heath and Hank Jones, this has become the largest, free jazz festival in the world (Poses 2010), that is, free as in 'no-cost', not as in 'avant-garde'. This point is by no means moot. The 'no-cost' as well as the largely mainstream programming are crucial factors in the festival's connection to the city of Detroit.

In the following pages, I investigate these and other aspects of Detroit Jazz Festival. I wish to argue that the festival is intimately tied to the cultural and economic history and geography of Detroit. It functions as a marker of identity as well as a creator of radical space. Issues of production and economic gain, of tourism economy and commercial interests are central, but so are issues of participation and community that transcend the boundaries of the festival and its locale while being rooted in both place and tradition. I outline this history and development through three perspectives – the urban concept city, the role of music and the festival's connection with both. I finally offer a reading of the festival with Christopher Small's concept of musicking – music as a verb rather than an object – in mind. That is, a ritual that functions as 'a form of organized behaviour in which humans use the language of gesture ... to affirm, to explore, and to celebrate their ideas of how the relationships of the cosmos operate, and thus, how they themselves should relate to it and to one another' (Small 1998, 95). Thus, the jazz festival performs a complex vernacular play and ritual that ultimately celebrates and connects Detroit with its past, present and future. Any city festival may achieve a temporary transformation of the urban; here I show how joy takes root annually in Detroit, and I also discuss the specific contribution of the musical practice that is jazz to making a particular kind of festival and transformation.

## Concept city

A plethora of writing on the rise and fall of Detroit has surfaced over the past decade, from the coffee-table books that depict the post-industrial ruins of Detroit in all its decay and visual splendour, to article series in magazines and newspapers (often swerving wildly between 'ruin porn' and urban agro-romanticism), to historical analyses of 'what went wrong'. It is tempting to slip in to hyperbole, telling the tale of Detroit as a modern parable of the decline of the one-industry town and industrial society in general. But as each investigation of Detroit offers its respective analysis of the causes of depopulation and blight, it becomes clear that simple explanations or facile analogies do very little in terms of grasping the complexity of Detroit's history and current life. I deliberately use the term 'life' to counter the 'failed state' rhetoric of much of the current writing. Throughout this writing, puzzled commentary on the continued optimism and perseverance of Detroiters paint a different, albeit fragmented, image of a city made habitable by the people who live and work there. Thus, the declaring of Detroit as dead, somewhere between the 1970s oil embargo and the city's filing for bankruptcy in 2013, may have been premature.

Notwithstanding the complexity of the history of Detroit, for the purpose of this chapter's analysis of Detroit Jazz Festival as an urban phenomenon, two interconnected elements are particularly relevant: race and the design of the urban environment. Pervasive segregation, then and now, has formed the socio-economic and cultural geography of the city, while urban planning decisions have reinforced and widened the gap, creating a metropolitan area divided between largely white suburbs and a black downtown.

As Detroit grew into an industrial hub from the 1870s to the first half of the twentieth century, the influx of African American workers from the South and other ethnic immigrants placed a strain on its housing and social infrastructures. The black population was confined to small and overcrowded areas (Sugrue 1996, 23). Official and unofficial policies such as deed restrictions, 'neighbourhood improvement' associations, selective rentals, sales and viewings from real estate agents cemented the segregation: the black population was first pressed into specific neighbourhoods and as its groups spilled out into other areas of the city, whites fled to the suburbs (Farley et al. 2000, 144–54). Simultaneously, segregation in the workforce and unequal access to well-paying jobs meant that median incomes in the white and black population differed starkly, creating a divide between city and suburb along congruent lines of race and class (Farley et al. 2000, 49–52).

The freeway system in Detroit has both aided and abetted this pattern of racially segregated urban sprawl and the decentralization of both businesses and housing in the Detroit metropolitan area. Federal aid programmes and the automobile industry's dominance in Detroit meant that mass transit solutions were left behind in favour of freeways (Foglesong 2003, 263). Neighbourhoods were split down the middle or erased completely, such as Black Bottom and Paradise Valley, the vibrant African American business and entertainment districts, situated where the Chrysler Freeway runs today. The freeway system offered rapid transit between suburbs, eliminating the need to develop the downtown area. Today it is hemmed in on three sides by the Chrysler, John C Lodge and Fisher freeways (Detroit River being the fourth border), functioning as physical and mental barriers to any organic cohesion with the surrounding areas.

Various plans for urban development and redevelopment for the city of Detroit have focused the city in (macro) economic and demographic terms, what cultural critic Michel de Certeau has called the 'concept city'. However, not only is the concept city decaying, but also is the way that we talk about the city, using symbols or metaphors, creates discourses around the city that elude the systematic discourses of the concept city (de Certeau 1984, 95,

105). This explains why, in the face of economic and demographic decline, historians, sociologists and urban theorists remain puzzled by the fact that 'Detroit remains a place of surprising – if often misplaced – optimism' (Martelle 2012, 233). They consistently overlook un-systematic and symbolic discourse, de Certeau's 'local authority', which in turn is linked with stories that are intimately bound with neighbourhoods, families and individuals and so remain fragmented (de Certeau 1984, 106, 108).

Some of these stories have in part been co-opted by media and city council PR, such as the urban farming movement, an influx of 'the creative class' as revitalizing the city and the idea of turning the fascination of the ruins of Detroit into a tourism industry. They are part of what Mark Binelli refers to as 'the Detroit comeback narrative', which proved to have a particular allure as the entire nation sank deeper into recession. But Binelli also points to the power of anecdotal evidence, small instances of resistance to master plans and stories of people using the cracks and open spaces, literally and metaphorically, in the fabric of Detroit-the-concept-city, creating a 'DIY city' (Binelli 2012, 53, 289–92). In Detroit it becomes increasingly obvious that as the strategies fail, only tactics are left standing. Thus, the stories of the DIY city represent 'local authority', a 'crack in the system that saturates places with signification' (de Certeau 1984, 106).

Omnipresent in the stories of Detroit are the presence of memories of what used to be, when envisioning a tomorrow. As one of Binelli's interviewees states, 'Detroit isn't some kind of abstract art project. It's real for people. These are real memories. Every one of these houses has a story.' Another suggests that memories of a place have different signification for different generations: 'I didn't grow up with that post-nineteen-fifties drop to compare everything to, so from my perspective, Detroit has always been improving. … If you come to Detroit, you're probably someone who likes challenges' (each quoted in Binelli 2012, 285, 298).

## Music city

In Detroit, music history and its cultural importance run as undercurrents in many of the more anecdotal and inspirational stories of Detroit as a placeholder for memory and community. They form a discourse that goes counter to the tales of woe, yet is intricately linked to the city and its history – to that which is memorable of Detroit. The music cultures of Detroit are connected with the city through the same elements that shaped its history in the twentieth century: race, labour and geography. And, as Suzanne Smith has argued, this was not just a matter of socio-economic and cultural factors influencing the music, but also of the music and the institutions built around the music, reflecting, critiquing and shaping those factors (Smith 1999, 10).

One of the most common and powerful musical associations with Detroit is undoubtedly Motown. Barry Gordy, the founder of Motown, insisted that his approach to record production and the sound of Motown was inspired by the assembly line of the Ford factories. However, adopting those means of production also meant adopting the capitalist system they were part and parcel of. Musicians on Barry Gordy's roster became labourers, often underpaid. Gordy's first hit single, 'Money (that's what I want)' indeed made millions, but Barrett Strong, the singer and possibly also the man behind the piano riff of the song, never saw a cent of royalties (Rohter 2013). According to Smith, Motown Records followed the automobile industry in a 'gradual process of corporate decentralization, relocation, merger, and buy-out'. She also points out that Motown matured as the racial and class divides of Detroit deepened. The music of Martha and the Vandellas, Marvin Gaye and Aretha Franklin became the sound of the civil rights struggle and the violence that erupted in Detroit (and across the United States) in the late 1960s (Smith 1999, 8, 254). In the 1970s, the decline of industry was reflected in the rise of counterculture and rock music with MC5, the White Panther Party and the magazine *Creem*. Later still, in the post-industrial Detroit of the 1980s, Detroit Techno was inspired not by a landscape of industry, but by the bleakness it left behind (see here 'Juan Atkins interview' 2011).

By contrast, Detroit's association with jazz is one anchored in the boom years of the first half of the twentieth century. The rise of the car industry and the Great Migration converged in Detroit to create one of the nation's strongest black urban centres for decades from the 1920s on. Detroit has fallen out of the simplified narrative of an evolutionary jazz history that focuses on New Orleans, Kansas City, Chicago and New York. But jazz was the dominant music culture when Detroit was at its peak. Jazz was here a music of modernity, of industrialization and migration. The automobile industry drew black migrants to Detroit and created a middle class that had the means to seek out entertainment. The outbreak of the Second World War brought on a demand for labour that gave black workers a foothold in the industry, which coincided with the rise of bebop. The 1940s and 1950s were golden years, not just for the heavy industries in Detroit, but also for the jazz scene of Detroit. And just as the car factories provided vehicles for all of the country, the rich jazz community in Detroit provided musicians for the jazz scene both nationally and internationally.

Bebop is also a music associated with what Guthrie Ramsey refers to as 'midcentury Afro-modernism' (2003, 97ff), and Anthony Macías argues for Detroit as a city that 'facilitated the evolution and explorations of bop-inspired jazz', mainly through black cultural institutions (2010, 56). The scene in Paradise Valley, church music and strong music programmes in the high schools fostered a generation of talented, skilled and dedicated musicians: Tommy Flanagan, Kenny Burrell, Pepper Adams, Barry Harris, the brothers Elvin, Hank and Thad Jones, and Yusef Lateef, to name a few. Geographically, as the black community expanded north, so did the venues. Even Woodward Avenue, which had been a white entertainment centre, slowly opened up to African American audiences and black-owned or -managed clubs. Black and tan clubs meant integration of audiences and increased opportunity for black musicians, making Detroit (according to the *Michigan Chronicle* in 1947) 'the sepia entertainment center of the nation' (quoted in Bjorn and Gallert 2001, 73). More informal sessions at after-hour clubs, schools and private homes also expanded the community of artists in and around the music – and helped foster a sense that being from Detroit mattered. Poet Phillip Levine discovered through jazz that 'it was possible to be a kid from Detroit & an artist. And that if you worked hard enough at your art you could create original, beautiful works and just possibly live off your art' (2007, 223–4).

## Festival city

Thus, by reaching back beyond Motown to jazz, Detroit Jazz Festival invokes a time of coherence. It invokes a time before the motorways cut the city off from itself, one when it was possible to imagine a different future. However, calling forth a time before the economic decline and social rupture is not the same as calling upon a time before the city's bind with the causes of decline. Visually and discursively, the festival plays heavily on the connection with industry, the basis for the golden years, but which also laid the ground to a disjointed Detroit. The entanglement with Detroit's cultural memory as well as Detroit's socio-economic structures is complex and ongoing.

As noted, the festival takes place on Labor Day weekend, the annual celebration of the American labour movement, and was instigated in 1979 by a collaboration between jazz educator Don Lupp and the Detroit Renaissance Foundation, a group of some of the city's most powerful business leaders. It was to be part of the urban regeneration efforts that the Renaissance Foundation was involved in, most notably with the building of the Renaissance Center and a focus on downtown business development. Establishing the jazz festival was a more esoteric or intangible approach, but was still meant to bring people and business downtown, re-establishing the area as an entertainment spot. For the first two decades, the festival was connected with the Montreux Jazz Festival (until 2000), and the label of 'International' was (until 2010) one that drew on the cultural cachet of a renowned European festival. However, its internationalism was also at odds with the sense of the city (and its industry) as a cultural repository.

Since 2007, the festival has had themes or taglines that touch on the identity of the city and its place in national and jazz history: 'The Rumble by the Great Lakes' (2007), which showcased artists from Detroit and Chicago in friendly battle; 'A Love Supreme: The Philly-Detroit Summit' (2008), a more brotherly invitation to another great industrial city with a rich music history; 'Keeping up with the Joneses' (2009), a reference to three Jones brothers who had made lasting contributions to jazz; 'Flame Keepers – Carrying the Torch for Modern Jazz' (2010), which calls on the centrality of mid-century jazz in Detroit (and the United States). The 2011 was the aberrant 'We Bring You the World', with a strong return to the city in 2012 and 2013 with the Chrysler sponsorship and the tagline 'Imported from Detroit' – an extension of an already existing campaign with Chrysler 'celebrating the spirit and determination of Detroit and its residents'. In a press release from 2012 the festival officially links car industry and jazz, as 'both have rich histories in the city of Detroit', stating that the 'partnership between Chrysler and the Detroit Jazz Festival bridges these great histories and brings key elements of our city together' (Detroit Jazz Festival website 2012).

The festival posters also reference and celebrate Detroit in its glory days. The 2009 poster shows the Guardian Building, nicknamed the 'Cathedral of Finance' (Austin 2014), as a beacon of music, connecting the pinnacle of industry and the city's architecture with the music. The 2008 poster depicted a saxophone with the Renaissance Center in the background and the 2012 poster combined the image of a trumpet with a needle gauge, propellers and a belt drive – all making general industrial references. Finally, the festival mainly exists today by virtue of an endowment from Gretchen Valade, heir to the Carhartt Clothing Company and owner of jazz record label Mack Avenue Records. Both invoke the legacy of Detroit as an industrial city (Carhartt produces work wear, and Mack Avenue was the location of Henry Ford's first workshop).

It is tempting to critique the festival for confirming a mythology of an industry and an economy tied up with segregation, displacement, disenfranchisement and financial barriers for Detroit's largely black population. As Bernadette Quinn points out, the '"just add culture and stir" approach to urban regeneration' can be questioned (2005, 928). A series of ticketed events, or events that do not take as their starting point the local resources and culture, can end up as corralled-off events that mainly attract tourists and (white) middle class. Yet, there are multiple layers to the Detroit Jazz Festival which to a large extent lifts the festival out of the category of well-meaning but culturally divorced regeneration efforts. For one, the fact that the festival since 1987 has been free and takes place in the urban space of downtown Detroit is highly significant. This has the effect of opening up the space and the music to one of the most diverse audiences I have ever encountered in my years as festival-goer. In the United States, jazz attracts mainly the white audience – the national average of non-white audiences is 21 per cent – but at Detroit Jazz Festival it is 55.6 per cent (see Jazz Audience Initiative 2011, 2012 Detroit Jazz Festival Annual Report). The difference is striking and important. It signals that pricing is a significant barrier which once removed allows for a wider participation (the majority of festival-goers (36 per cent) plan on spending less than $60 downtown during the festival).

But it also signals that Detroit Jazz Festival is a celebration of a black art form in a black city. As pointed out previously, the connection between Detroit, bebop (or mid-century modern jazz) and Detroit's history and identity as a black city is rooted in black cultural institutions and practices. Jazz people in Detroit, and a good deal of the discursive material surrounding the festival, continuously refer to the city as 'Bop City'. Thus, when the programming of the festival overwhelmingly falls on the side of bebop/modern jazz, it functions as a direct homage to the musical history and community of black Detroit. This emphasis on community is also carried through in the activities of the festival that reaches beyond Labor Day weekend. The festival is throughout the year engaged in education and musical events.

The other significant factor that anchors the festival in the city is the way urban space is utilized. Walking past empty lots and derelict buildings, arriving on Woodward is a shock and a delight to the senses. There's clearly a party going on. Downtown Detroit becomes pedestrianized and humanized via the closing of traffic and the filling out of the wide swathes of asphalt with vendors and audiences (see Figure 49). In the evening the buildings recede in the dark, the big open spaces suddenly become intimate. The music enters into the fabric of the city – creating a different sense of place – what music anthropologist Steven Feld (2005) would call an acoustemological sense of place – a form of knowledge/experience that is anchored in a dynamic and sonic sense of time-space (2005, 185).

## Down home in downtown detroit

The official festival map depicts Woodward Avenue as the spinal cord that connects the 'head', Campus Martius and Cadillac Square, with the 'heart', Hart Plaza. Along the spinal cord are vital functions such as vendors, membership and information stalls.[1] The first years of the festival it was confined to Hart Plaza, but as it moved up Woodward, Campus Martius initially became the site for the main stage. However, some of the attributes it has as an urban space – ordered, manicured, open, clean and well-lit – are problematic when presenting live music. Acoustically, the sound tends to disappear, there is no obvious orientation for the audience, and it is essentially not really a place to 'get down and party'. In 2009 and 2010, the space featured the 'Meijer Education Stage', showcasing high school and college bands, forming a synchronous connection between the open, orderly space and education. The main stage has subsequently moved to Cadillac Square. On a regular day, this feels less as a square and more as a wide boulevard. It lacks definition: aside from a few tables with outside service for lunching office workers there is little to induce a passer-by to stop. There is nowhere for the eye to rest or fix itself upon. The perspective is oddly featureless. But during the jazz festival, the somewhat unimaginative perspective of the space is broken by the stage, placed half way down and narrowed by tiered seating along the side (Figure 50). This more enclosed space offers better sound and sight lines. Acoustically, the music almost reverberates off the buildings, in a resounding of the urban topos (Connell and Gibson 2003) (Figure 51). But it is the people filling the space who make it all of a sudden come alive. The programming for this stage focuses on music with a popular

**FIGURE 50** *Festival audience on Cadillac Square.*

**FIGURE 51** *Hank Jones in concert, city buildings as backdrop.*

appeal, mainstream jazz mostly, but also blues gospel, Latin jazz and a little R&B. On the opening night in 2009, a double bill with Hank Jones and Chick Corea establishes the festival's jazz credentials and its audiences: When Hank Jones at one point calls a Thelonious Monk-tune, there are shout-outs to Monk and Jones. This is an audience that knows its jazz.

Midway between Campus Martius/Cadillac Square and Hart Plaza sits the Jazz Talk Tent. It forms an enclosed space that makes for intimacy in the midst of all the hustle and bustle – as you enter, an exhibition of old radios speak of an analogue time, a time when there was time, for conversation and community. Here, various constellations of musicians, journalists and researchers meet for conversations on jazz, history, life and artistic practice. The talks centre on the type of narrative that is most ubiquitous in the jazz community – the anecdote. As an oral mode, it ties in with a foregrounding of voice and conversation in the music culture of jazz itself and this in turn opens up the possibility for the dialogic. It is also a deeply performative mode, perpetually repeated and revised as the neatness of punchlines often demonstrates. This alone is enough to make anecdotes suspicious as accurate accounts, as life rarely provides punch lines. But they are what Kenneth Burke called 'equipment for living', that is, strategies for naming and explaining situations and life (Burke 1973, 304).

This is usually something that takes place informally, whenever jazz musicians get together and start telling stories. Here, the formalized setting may lead to some initial restraint, but soon enough, the moderator gives up control or just joins in as musicians try to out-tell one another, following the same rules of talk that govern a jam session: taking turns, riffing on one another, engaging in friendly competition (Figure 52). The stories focus on

**FIGURE 52** *Musicians joking and calling each other out at the Jazz Talk Tent.*

Detroit once again as a Bop City – where, according to one musician, in the 1940s and 1950s it was always 'butt-kickin' time', while others showing the similarities between how people talk and how they play give a special laid-back, but no-nonsense, inflection to Detroit jazz. The festival offers a space and a kind of extra-musical presentation which invokes the jazz community as well as Detroit as something strong and unique.

The rules of talk/play that govern the jazz talks also govern audience behaviour and musicians off stage. The call and response, the dressing up or dressing down. The shout-outs to musicians, the excitement and the umbrella shared with the person sitting next to you. There is a sense of relish in the chance to voice these matters and to celebrate and enjoy community – both the larger (inter)national jazz community and Detroit. As Roger Abrahams points out, 'if anything like community still exists beyond a reflexive nostalgia, it emerges through the agreement to celebrate itself in ceremony or festival. Meeting and moving together, a group articulates its sense of community by sharing an intense physical and emotional moment which generates feelings of togetherness' (Abrahams 2005, 9).

Hart Plaza is the heart of the festival. Again, this mainly hard surface space, which does nothing to induce the passer-by to stop and rest unless one walks down to the river, is transformed by the festival: the smells of food, sense of open space and music from three different stages all meet with the thunder of the Dodge Fountain (see Figure 53). This creates synaesthesia; 'the rich connections inherent in multiple sensation sources, the tingling resonances and bodily reverberation that emerge from simultaneously joint perceptions' (Cytowic quoted in Feld 2005, 181). Such overload of the senses, where one

**FIGURE 53** *Hart Plaza, another 'hard surface place ... transformed by the festival'.*

sensory perception overlay the next, produces a perceptory disintegration of borders – one that also translates to behaviour as Abrahams points to when stating that, at festivals, 'the boundary police have deserted their posts' (2005, 11). When music is played in an outside space it affects a number of performance aspects. Audience behaviour changes. There is more coming and going, more shuffling around to get comfortable. The really hardcore festival-goers bring their own camping chairs, effectively setting up camp and staking a claim to their own little space. Food and drink are being consumed. Dancing may spontaneously take place, as well as shouts of recognition or derision. The audience is as much the producer of the performativity of the event as the musicians.

The music is also affected. Musicians have to contend with wind, sun, occasionally rain, and extra-musical sounds as well as perhaps music from neighbouring stages that seep into their performance. Acoustics may be amplified or lost, depending on the surrounding structures, the number of audiences and 'noise'. I add the quotation marks here, because I do not consider the non-musical sounds of a festival as noise. Noise may be thought of as sound without meaning or direction, but at a festival like this all sounds come together in the production of presence. (Here I draw on Hans Ulrich Gumbrecht's notion of the materialities of communication as producing presence: 2004, 17.) Again there is a blurring of boundaries, between the musical and the extra-musical, between producers and consumers, between place and sound. The acoustic permeates the urban space and the structures reflect, obstruct or reverberate with the sound, creating sonic space.

During the jazz festival, the urban space of downtown Detroit is reconfigured as it resounds with the memory of Detroit as a city worth celebrating. This sonic process is not (only) an echo of times past but a resonance on what is. At the jazz festival things come together and we fall into step. These memories function not as reactionary, backward-looking stoppages in the community. Rather, they are what places are made of – a series of what-used-to-bes that offer the raw material for what can be. As de Certeau (1984) states, 'the memorable is that which can be dreamed about a place' (109). If musicking is a ritual that reflects the ideas of ought-to-be relationships in the world, then in Detroit for four days in late summer, it is all there: the music, the zoot suits, the barbecue ribs, the lemonade, the hoop earrings, the inclusive and generous 'no-cost' entry, African masks and three-dollar sunglasses, the tap dancers, the fall-outs and the shout-outs. The festival.

## Notes

1 The following description and analysis of physical spaces of the festival is based on personal observations made at the Detroit International Jazz Festival in 2009.

## References

Abrahams, Roger D. 2005. *Everyday Life: A Poetics of Vernacular Practices.* Philadelphia: University of Pennsylvania Press.

Austin, Dan. 2014. 'Guardian Building.' *HistoricDetroit.org*. http://www.historicdetroit.org/building/guardian-building/.

Binelli, Mark. 2012. *Detroit City Is the Place to Be: The Afterlife of an American Metropolis*. New York: Henry Holt & Co.

Bjorn, Lars, and Jim Gallert. 2001. *Before Motown: A History of Jazz in Detroit, 1920-60*. Ann Arbor: University of Michigan Press.

Burke, Kenneth. 1973. *The Philosophy of Literary Form: Studies in Symbolic Action*: Berkeley: University of California Press.

de Certeau, Michel. 1984. *The Practice of Everyday Life*. Berkeley: University of California Press.

Connell, John, and Chris Gibson. 2003. *Sound Tracks: Popular Music, Identity and Place*. London: Routledge.

Detroit Jazz Festival. 2012. 'Chrysler named 2012 Detroit Jazz Festival presenting sponsor'. http://www.detroitjazzfest.com/pressrelease42.html. Accessed 16 September 2014.

*Detroit Jazz Festival Annual Report*. 2012. http://www.detroitjazzfest.com/pdf/2012%20Annual%20Report_final.pdf. Accessed 15 September 2014.

Farley, Reynolds, Danziger Sheldon and Holzer Harry J. 2000. *Detroit Divided*. New York: Russell Sage Foundation.

Feld, Steven. 2005. 'Places sensed, senses placed: toward a sensuous epistemology of environments.' In David Howes, ed. *Empire of the Senses: The Sensual Culture Reader.* Oxford: Berg, 179–91.

Foglesong, Richard E. 2003. *Downtown: Its Rise and Fall, 1880-1950*. New Haven, CT: Yale University Press.

Gumbrecht, Hans Ulrich. 2004. *Production of Presence: What Meaning Cannot Convey*. Stanford, CA: Stanford University Press.

Jazz Audience Initiative. 2011. 'Regenerating the jazz audience: results from a multi-site survey of jazz ticket buyers and prospects' report. http://www.jazzartsgroup.org/wp-content/uploads/2011/09/JAI-Ticket-Buyer-Report_FINAL.pdf. Accessed 16 September 2014.

'Juan Atkins interview.' 2011. *Afropop Worldwide*, 14 June. http://www.afropop.org/wp/2434/juan-atkins-interview/.

Levine, Philip. 2007. 'Detroit jazz in the late Forties and early Fifties.' In Sascha Feinstein, ed. *Ask Me Now: Conversations on Jazz and Literature*. Bloomington: Indiana University Press, 213–29.

Macías, Anthony. 2010. '"Detroit was heavy": modern jazz, bebop, and African American expressive culture.' *Journal of African American History* 95(1): 44–70.

Martelle, Scott. 2012. *Detroit: A Biography*. Chicago, IL: Chicago Review Press.

Poses, John W. 2010. 'Detroit's jazz festival turns into labor of love for violinist.' *Columbia Daily Tribune*, 5 September 2010. http://www.columbiatribune.com/arts_life/ovation/detroit-s-jazz-festival-turns-into-labor-of-love-for/article_6c21081e-e0e8-556b-89af-4531ca8dadc7.html.

Quinn, Bernadette. 2005. 'Arts festivals and the city.' *Urban Studies* 42(5–6): 927–43.

Ramsey, Guthrie P. 2003. *Race Music: Black Cultures from Bebop to Hip-Hop*. Berkeley, CA: University of California Press.
Rohter, Larry. 2013. 'For a classic Motown song about money, credit is what he wants.' *The New York Times*, 31 August. http://www.nytimes.com/2013/09/01/arts/music/for-a-classic-motown-song-about-money-credit-is-what-he-wants.html.
Small, Christopher. 1998. *Musicking: The Meanings of Performing and Listening*. Hanover, NH: University Press of New England.
Smith, Suzanne E. 1999. *Dancing in the Street: Motown and the Cultural Politics of Detroit*. Cambridge, MA: Harvard University Press.
Sugrue, Thomas J. 1996. *The Origins of the Urban Crisis: Race and Inequality in Postwar Detroit*. Princeton, NJ.: Princeton University Press.
US Census Bureau. 2013. United States Census Bureau/American FactFinder. 'Detroit City, Michigan - Population Estimate 2013'. 2013 Population Estimates Program U.S. Census Bureau. http://factfinder2.census.gov. Accessed 21 August 2014.

# CHAPTER THIRTEEN

# Branding, sponsorship and the music festival

*Chris Anderton*

This chapter examines the relationship between music festivals and sponsorship/branding in Britain. This is an important area to examine because the remarkable growth of the music festival sector over the past 20 years has been paralleled, and partially driven, by an expansion in commercial sponsorship initiatives. This includes enhanced media coverage on radio, television and the internet, and the emergence of specially created on-site brand activities and brand-centric events. This chapter defines festival-related sponsorships, examines how sponsors and brands (Figure 54) work with festivals and concludes by questioning how broad changes in society may have supported a shift in perceptions and attitudes towards commercial sponsorship.

A report prepared by the copyright collection agency PRSforMusic in conjunction with the brand agency Frukt found that music-related sponsorship activities were worth a total of £104.8 million in the United Kingdom in 2012. Of this, live music sponsorship was worth just over £33 million, which was split between festivals, tours and venue naming (PRSforMusic/Frukt 2013). The importance of such festival support was underlined in 2013 by James Drury (general manager of UK Festival Awards Ltd) who stated that 'For many festivals, sponsorship of some shape or form is a vital income stream' (Drury 2013, 25). Among other things (discussed further below), sponsorship can provide financial security in a risky and volatile market and enable promoters to secure the headline acts needed to help sell tickets to their events. Indeed, the loss of sponsorship support is one of several reasons why festivals may fail to succeed (Getz 2002).

**FIGURE 54** *The pop festival's branding opportunity: Strongbow cider tent, Isle of Wight, 2007.*

The expansion of commercial companies into the promotion, branding and sponsorship of music festivals has not been welcomed by all festival-goers and commentators. For instance, when the commercial music promotion company Mean Fiddler (later renamed Festival Republic) took a stake in the Glastonbury Festival in 2002, the relationship was criticized by, among others, the anti-corporate activist organization Corporate Watch, which claimed that Mean Fiddler was taking a share of the net profits, and that radical groups previously welcomed at the festival had seen their ticket allocations cut or withdrawn (Michaels 2002; see also Osler 2005). More recently, Lena Corner's article for the *Independent* (UK) newspaper provided a useful summary of the position held by those who fear the influence of commercial sponsorships and branding upon music festivals:

> For a while, there has been an increasing feeling that festivals have shifted too far from their original hippie-spirited ethos. The point was to offer an alternative reality. Now, it's a slick industry. The television rights have been sold, and with that have come price rises, mass audiences and corporate domination – the antithesis of everything they stood for. (Corner 2012)

This quotation (and Corner's article as a whole) is suffused with what has been referred to as an ideology of the 'countercultural carnivalesque' (Anderton 2009, 2011, forthcoming) through which outdoor music festivals have come to represent much more than cyclically held events with (or without) camping. Instead, in this ideology they have become central to an alternative or imaginative history of Britain that traces countercultural and youth culture ideals from the 1950s jazz fans of Beaulieu Jazz Festival through to the peace and love politics of the hippies and the 'Woodstock Nation' (see Bennett 2004 for a number of chapters on this topic) and onwards to the post-hippie neo-tribes of the New Age Travellers and the later 'Free Party' ravers (see Sandford and Reid 1974; Clarke 1982; Collin and Godfrey 1997; McKay 2000, 2004; Worthington 2004; St John 2009). In the process, outdoor rock and pop music festivals in particular have been theorized as contemporary flowerings of what Mikhail Bakhtin termed the 'carnivalesque': a temporary period of 'letting loose' in which societal norms are inverted, removed or mocked, authority critiqued and consumptive or transgressive behaviours taken to extremes (Bakhtin 1984; Stallybrass and White 1986). A range of countercultural interests has been added to this, such as pro-environmentalism, anti-materialism, anti-corporatism, social justice, New Age beliefs and a nostalgic desire for a pre-capitalist, mythological or enchanted society (Hetherington 2001; Worthington 2004; Partridge 2006). Above all, perhaps, is the belief that outdoor music festivals offer utopian possibilities, that they are (or should be) times and places that provide 'freedom from' social norms and expectations and 'freedom to' play with, transform, or create new norms (Turner 1982, 36). Hence, contemporary trends in festivals towards commercialization and sponsorship are negatively linked to other trends such as the increasing regulation, standardization and domestication that these bring (St John 2009, 9–13).

Outdoor music festivals have, as shown later, adopted a variety of strategies for dealing with sponsorships, and while there are some promoters and festival-goers who regard sponsorships with suspicion, the majority of festivals make use of sponsorship opportunities in order to provide financial support, additional attractions and assistance in marketing, promotion and media coverage. Several studies (such as Havas 2012; Drury 2013) have also shown that there is increasing acceptance or support for live music sponsorship and branding activities at festivals, though such studies tend to rely on audience surveys at large-scale music festivals where sponsorship is prevalent, rather than a broader sample of all event types.

## Definitions and forms of sponsorship

Two regularly quoted definitions of sponsorship in broad terms are those produced by the International Chamber of Commerce (ICC) and by the International Events Group (IEG):

> any commercial agreement by which a sponsor, for the mutual benefit of the sponsor and sponsored party, contractually provides financing or other support in order to establish an association between the sponsor's image, brands or products and a sponsorship property [such as a festival] in return for rights to promote this association and/or for the granting of certain agreed direct or indirect benefits (ICC 2003, 2); a cash and/or in-kind fee paid to a property [such as a festival] in return for access to the exploitable commercial potential associated with that property. (IEG 2000, 1)

In each case the sponsor enters into a commercial transaction whereby it provides money or services in return for the direct or indirect benefits of exploiting (also known as 'leveraging' or 'activating') the association between the festival and the sponsor (discussed further below). This separates sponsorship from philanthropy, which may be defined as the donation of funds or services without the expectation of receiving a commercial return. However, there is a grey area between these two positions, as many festivals operate with non-commercial sponsors, while smaller events in particular often benefit from various kinds of informal arrangement. Furthermore, the ICC definition suggests that sponsors are seeking to benefit from the semiotic associations of their involvement with music festivals (whether festivals in general or the image of specific events). In effect they are aiming for alignment between their own brands and the brand of the sponsored event. This is as true of non-commercial sponsors and corporate philanthropy as it is of the kinds of commercial sponsorship agreements that are focused on in this chapter. For instance, non-commercial sponsors have imperatives to satisfy regarding the continuance of their own income streams; hence their festival sponsorship decisions may have important implications for their own future funding. As the above definitions refer to events in general, the following typology is suggested with regard to music festivals.

First, there are 'non-commercial' sponsorships in the form of grants or donations provided by regional and local governments, private organizations or individuals and, in the United Kingdom, the Arts Councils and the National Lottery. For instance, the Green Man Festival in Wales receives support from the Welsh Assembly, the National Lottery and the Bevan Foundation, in addition to both the Arts Council of Wales and the Arts Council of England. Here the 'return on investment' for the sponsor may relate to a set of cultural, social, economic or touristic goals that the festival organizer must duly address. There is a politics of such sponsorships which is beyond the terms of this present chapter, yet in need of further research. For instance, how and why are decisions made regarding which music festivals to support, and by implication which organizations, locations, social groups and genres of music will or will not benefit from that support?

Secondly, there are informal arrangements of reciprocity which have similar effects to formal sponsorships in terms of in-kind benefits received by festival organizers, but which are not fully philanthropic in nature. For instance, many small festivals rely on favours from companies and individuals who provide services or equipment for free or at a discount. This support helps to build goodwill within the local music community, and this in turn may translate into future business opportunities, or the return of in-kind favours to the sponsor by those involved in the festival organization. Unlike formal commercial sponsorships, these arrangements are typically organized without a written contract and while such supporters are sometimes acknowledged on event posters or literature, there may be no clear indication of the existence of the relationship to festival-goers. The benefits to the sponsor instead lie in forging or bolstering business-to-business relationships.

Finally, there are formally contracted commercial sponsorships with local, national and international businesses where the aim is to achieve a commercial return of some form on the investment made. Various motivations can be proposed: to build brand awareness and visibility, to increase sales and/or market share, to introduce new products or services and to either differentiate the brand from its competitors or reposition it within the marketplace. Central to all of these aims is the assumption that by aligning a brand with a festival, the sponsor will gain access to a specific target market (or aspirational market) that is receptive to sponsor messages because they are experiencing the 'good times' that festivals offer, and so will come to associate those good times with the sponsor. This is, effectively, a form of corporate image management aimed at forging a credible link between a specific brand and a particular event, audience, lifestyle, genre and/or activity. Additional motivations include internal communications and business-to-business relationships, especially through the use of VIP ticket allocations for selected suppliers, clients and staff.

Typical business sectors at the national and international level include telecommunications, financial services, alcoholic beverages and soft drinks, clothing and footwear and various forms of media. Since the turn of the millennium, the range of sponsorship deals has increased, particularly towards lifestyle-related products and services such as car manufacturers, restaurants, supermarkets, confectionery, fragrances, hair and make-up products and so on. However, two particularly important sub-categories deserve further discussion: 'pouring rights' and 'media rights'.

Pouring rights give a specific company control of a festival's bars and the choice of drinks on offer (though this may be split between alcoholic and soft drinks). A major example is Carlsberg UK, which signed a deal with Live Nation in 2008 (renewed for a further 5 years in 2013) that gives the company pouring rights at all the main festivals related to Live Nation. This includes Download, Wireless and Creamfields, as well as the Reading and Leeds Festivals (since Live Nation is the majority shareholder of the holding company which owns Festival Republic). As a result, all of these festivals offer Tuborg lager and Somersby cider (both brands of Carlsberg) for sale in the arena bars, to the exclusion of other brands: an effective on-site monopoly that is supported by the interdiction against festival-goers bringing their own alcohol into the performance arena (though they can take their own alcohol into the campsites). One effect of such deals and arrangements is that it reinforces the perception that major festivals are becoming too 'alike', too 'corporate' or only interested in making profits from the captive festival audience within the arena.

Media rights are agreements made with radio stations, television channels, magazines (both online and print) and various providers of online media services. The companies involved may provide cash sums to the festival, but are more likely to provide benefits in kind in the form of free advertising in return for access to exclusive content from the festival, such as previews, photography, exclusive artist interviews, film clips, VIP access and permission to produce on-site news sheets or festival-specific Apps for smartphones. Mainstream media coverage of outdoor music festivals has grown considerably since the early 1990s, with the now-defunct *Melody Maker* producing its first pull-out festival guide in 1993, and Glastonbury Festival gaining televised coverage for the first time in 1994. The increased visibility and championing of festivals in the traditional media, together with a broadening of interest online and in fashion, lifestyle and celebrity gossip titles, has helped to drive changes in public perceptions of the sector, making festivals more accessible and desirable for a wider part of the population and contributing both to the sector's growth and to the broadening of corporate sponsorship interest (see also Anderton forthcoming).

## Leveraging and activation

Leveraging (or badging) is a relatively passive form of sponsorship in which the sponsor's logo is placed on festival posters, tickets and wristbands, and on the official website and souvenir programme. The most visible examples are 'title' or 'presenting' sponsorships, where the brand name is incorporated into the name of the festival and naming rights for individual stages, tents or areas within the festival arena. The festival's logo is often used on the sponsor's products or promotions (such as in-store displays and on-product competitions), while online leveraging is conducted through the brand's own website and social media channels. The aim of the latter is to forge ongoing relationships with festival-goers by encouraging Facebook 'likes', Twitter 'followers' and the collection of personal data useful for marketing initiatives. Leveraging also refers to on-site advertising and free product sampling, as well as backstage hospitality and product-gifting provided to journalists and selected suppliers and staff of the sponsor. Press and social media are particularly important to both sponsors and festival organizers as they provide promotion/awareness for the event and sponsors, and because the impact of sponsorship is often measured as column inches in magazines (traditional) or social media hits (known as 'impressions' – including website visits, Twitter 'followers' and Facebook 'likes'). If these figures are good, sponsors will believe that they have achieved a return on their investment and so be attracted to renew their support. Moreover, positive social media impressions can potentially attract both new sponsors and new attendees.

Leveraging has been seen in music festivals for many years, with alcohol sponsorships particularly prevalent. For instance, in 1986, the Guinness

Brewery launched the Harp Beat campaign to promote its Harp Lager brand. It sponsored over a hundred live concerts in that year, including an event at the Milton Keynes Bowl. In 1987, the annual Monsters of Rock festival at Donington Park added 'Harp Beat 87 presents' to its posters and advertisements. However, there was no on-stage branding at the festival, and sponsorship of rock music in the United Kingdom was still in its infancy during the 1980s. This began to change when the Mean Fiddler organization became involved with the long-running Reading Festival. The 1989 event was 'supported by Melody Maker' (which became a stage sponsor in 1991), and during the 1990s the event gained additional sponsorships from the likes of Doc Martens, Carlsberg, Virgin Megastores, MTV, Red Bull, Converse and Loaded. A title sponsorship was then negotiated with Carling lager, which saw the festival renamed The Carling Weekend from 1998 to 2007, and the introduction of a sister event of the same name in Leeds from 1999 (see Figure 55).

The term 'sponsor activation' appears from the early to mid-2000s (Wakefield 2012, 146) and marks a shift towards experiential marketing. The leveraging or 'badging' of events with a logo was seen as an ineffective way to engage consumers; instead, sponsors focus on delivering 'added value' activities, services and settings relevant to a festival context in order to foster active and interactive engagements with their brands. The aim is to create playful, imaginative and memorable multi-sensory experiences that not only become associated with the sponsor but are also regarded as enhancing the festival experience as a whole (Pine and Gilmore 1998; Carù and Cova 2007a). Drengner et al. (2008, 138–9) refer to such activations as 'event marketing': the creation of an event/activity which propagates marketing messages. At larger events, there may be many such activities

**FIGURE 55** *Carling Leeds Festival stage 2006.*

within the boundaries of the festival arena, situated within both the public and the backstage VIP areas depending on the particular aims of the sponsor involved.

Backstage activations target key opinion formers and media who will hopefully disseminate stories about those activations, and so publicize the sponsor relationship. In contrast, arena activations are aimed at festival-goers in general and are intended not only to 'add value' to their experience, but also to stimulate positive word-of-mouth coverage across social media platforms. Carù and Cova (2007a, 41) note that sponsor activations are experiential spaces which need to be 'enclavized' (separated off), 'secured' (under the control of the brand) and 'thematized' (through the use of relevant designs and narratives). The first two elements are important because the festival setting as a whole is one in which there is a high degree of distraction from other people, brands and entertainments, while the final element is crucial for the brand to construct a compelling, distinctive and memorable setting and experience (Pine and Gilmore 1998).

A good example of sponsor activation is the Southern Comfort Juke Joint (Figures 56 and 57), which won the 2012 Best Brand Activation Award at the UK Festival Awards. It was a specially created venue (enclavized and secured), designed (thematized) to look like an authentic run-down New Orleans 'juke joint' (a semi-legal drinking den of the past), with neon signs and a rough-looking corrugated iron and wood façade. Inside and around this hyperreal space there was a house party atmosphere generated by DJs, a New Orleans–style jazz band and a number of people employed to create characters such as 'Reggie Two-Step', who would engage directly with the public. The bar served a variety of cocktails based on Southern Comfort, and the overall aim was to help position the alcohol brand as a fun, creative and youthful drink that could be enjoyed in clubs throughout the year, while generating positive press and social media awareness. In a short video about the Southern Comfort Juke Joint festivals campaign, branding

**FIGURE 56** *The Southern Comfort Juke Joint at UK festivals, 2012.*

**FIGURE 57** *New Orleans–style parade band and second liners in Southern Comfort promotion.*

company Frukt stated that its main aims were to change the perception of Southern Comfort by fusing the brand's Louisiana heritage with a modern house party vibe and to tour the activation around the United Kingdom's top festivals. It reported that in 2012 the Juke Joint received 100,000 attendees across four festivals, with audience surveys finding a 92 per cent positive response to the brand experience and over 45 per cent of respondents stating that they were now more likely to drink Southern Comfort (Frukt 2012).

## Strategies for engaging (or not) with sponsors

I want now to introduce and discuss three key sponsorship engagement strategies for festival organizers: affirmation, acceptance and avoidance. Affirmation refers to festival promoters who actively embrace sponsorship propositions or work with brands to create 'sponsor-owned' events: ones which are created specifically for a brand. The larger commercial events managed by national and international concert promoters are perhaps the most obvious examples of the affirmation strategy, as they accept numerous sponsorships and can negotiate with those sponsors across more than one event. It is interesting to note that Live Nation now refers to its festival sponsors as 'partners' (as does Glastonbury Festival), thus attempting to lessen the negative connotations that some festival attendees see in the term 'sponsorship'.

Acceptance refers to festival promoters who want or need the benefits of sponsor support but who make ideological or ethical decisions about which sponsors to work with. For instance, the Sunrise Celebration website states the following:

> Our partners are carefully selected based on their values and suitability to our core aims as a festival and nation. We believe that innovative partnerships add value to Sunrise and help us in our quest for sustainability on all levels. (Sunrise Celebration 2014)

Festivals which adopt the acceptance strategy typically seek local business sponsors, those with similar ethical or environmental ideals, or those who promise to donate some of their income to charitable causes. A variant of this strategy is that adopted by the Glastonbury Festival, which accepts corporate sponsors but does not promote them on its website and marketing materials. This 'covert' form of sponsorship includes long-term relationships with mobile network operator EE (formerly Orange), which provides on-site recharging facilities and free wi-fi, and the BBC, *Guardian* newspaper and Q music magazine, which provide key media services. Glastonbury Festival has received criticism about its sponsorships, with some arguing that the media side of the event now dominates or overshadows its countercultural heritage (Street 2005).

A common element to the strategies of affirmation and acceptance is the need for 'congruence' or 'fit' between the values and attributes of the sponsor and those of the festival and its audience (Drengner et al. 2011). A poor 'fit', or a poorly imagined and delivered activation, can lead to criticisms of both the brand and the festival. One such example is the 'Show Me Your Sloggis' stage at V Festival in 2007 and 2008, which aimed to promote a unisex range of underwear (Sloggis). In addition to a stage with DJs, dancers, skateboarders and a fashion show, free samples were thrown to the crowd and a special photo booth was set up for festival-goers to enter the brand's search for 'the world's most beautiful bottom' (with a modelling contract and other prizes for the eventual winner).Several hundred festival-goers reportedly entered the competition in 2007, yet a reviewer at Virtualfestivals.com described the stage as 'leery, cringey and unnecessary', while the general opinion of the activation was that it was inappropriate for a festival context (Roberts 2009).

The final strategy is avoidance, where festival promoters consciously choose to manage their event *without* sponsorship support. A high-profile example was Vince Power's Hop Farm Festival (2008–12) which proclaimed a back to basics ideology and sought to survive by booking high-profile artists to drive sell-out attendances. After initial success, the difficulty of this position was finally demonstrated in 2013 when the event was cancelled because of poor pre-event sales and Power's company went into administration. An alternative justification for sponsor avoidance lies in the continued influence of the countercultural carnivalesque (Anderton 2009). Shambala Festival, for example, lists a number of 'guiding principles' on its website that illustrate this:

> Festivals should be an alternative vision of society. They should be utopias, places where interacting with fellow humans isn't a hassle but a pleasure. [The festival is] 100 per cent independent and will always be so. This means being free of any external agendas or demands, excessive advertising and branding and mindless consumerism. (Shambala Festival 2014)

Nevertheless, large corporately run events with a heavy brand presence in the form of sponsor activations have grown in number and popularity over the past 20 years while, as noted earlier, surveys of festival-goers suggest that sponsorship is either accepted as a necessary part of controlling costs and securing headliners, or indeed viewed as an attractive part of a festival's entertainment offering.

## Audience acceptance of sponsorship and branding

Rojek (2013, 14–6) argues that events such as music festivals respond to 'the urge to go beyond narrow, private concerns and the rigmarole of habitual, regimented existence' and that they are capable of establishing or reinforcing both individual and group identities, especially since the media typically portrays them as 'catalysts of life-affirming exhibitionism, festivity and transcendence' (103). He places events firmly within the 'hospitality, leisure and tourism industries' (1); in his view, rather than being heirs to a countercultural heritage, contemporary music festivals may be examined as consumer commodities and spectacles much like the shopping malls, casinos and theme parks discussed by Bryman (2004) and Ritzer (1999). These use simulated settings to create hyperreal experiential products, where hyperreality is defined as an 'inclination or willingness among members of the culture to realize, construct, and live the simulation' (Firat and Venkatesh 1995). From this perspective, contemporary music festivals are simulations or pastiches, which merely play with the imagery and ideas associated with the countercultural carnivalesque. They may not be 'real' but are treated as if they are, hence their experience is legitimized. For instance, the Southern Comfort Juke Joint created an imaginary version of a New Orleans bar that never existed, complete with New Orleans–style parade band and second liners (Figure 4), while many festivals trade upon a loose 'Woodstock Nation' or Glastonbury Fayre–style narrative of peace, love and freedom, or the perceived image of the late 1980s/early 1990s rave culture (Anderton 2009, 2011, forthcoming).

The growth of music festival sponsorship is indicative of changes in the development of the wider consumer society. The 1990s saw the introduction of commercial satellite and cable television, the sponsorship of individual television programmes (for instance, the popular soap opera *Coronation Street* gained its first sponsor in 1996), and the growth of the internet with its now-almost-ubiquitous advertising banners and links. Popular internet sites, music streaming services, email providers, computer games and social media channels all make considerable use of sponsorship and advertising, and contemporary festival-goers in the 16–24 age range in particular have grown up with this world. Furthermore, Miles argues that consumerism has 'become part and parcel of the very fabric of everyday life' (1998, 1), such that people work with commodities to help frame their sense of self, and to communicate to others through the consumption choices they make: that music festivals should be used to further this work, or that contemporary consumers should be willing to accept sponsorship and branding at outdoor events, should come as no surprise.

Nevertheless, Carù and Cova (2007b) warn that festival-based sponsor activations offer shallow and manipulative forms of experience that leave little room for truly participatory activity. Instead, festival-goers are urged to take part in activities and settings that are staged for the benefit of sponsors and are closely controlled by them. In this sense, festival-goers may actually be more passive than active in such situations, while truly creative, self-directed and participatory experience may be restricted to the campsites where the control of sponsors and organizers is generally weaker.

To conclude, I have suggested in this chapter that the countercultural carnivalesque underpins objections to the rise of sponsorship and branding at festivals, while changes in consumer society and the commercialization and growth of the music festival sector as a whole mean that these objections are not shared by all. There are significant financial pressures involved in promoting festivals, hence sponsorship of one form or another has become a useful and sometimes necessary way for festival organizers to mitigate the risks involved. Nevertheless, the growth and diversification of the festival sector over the past 20 years means that space exists for events to follow each of the strategies of brand affirmation, acceptance and avoidance identified above. In the contemporary festival market there may well be something for everyone, though whether these events offer truly participatory experience or hyperreal simulations remains a matter for continued debate.

## References

Anderton, Chris. 2009. 'Commercializing the carnivalesque: the V Festival and image/risk management.' *Event Management* 12(1): 39–51.

Anderton, Chris. 2011. 'Music festival sponsorship: between commerce and carnival.' *Arts Marketing* 1(2): 145–58.

Anderton, Chris. Forthcoming. *Music Festivals in the UK*. Aldershot: Ashgate.
Bakhtin, Mikhail. 1984. *Rabelais and His World*. Trans. Helene Iswolsky. Bloomington, IN: Indiana University Press.
Bennett, Andy, ed. 2004. *Remembering Woodstock*. Aldershot: Ashgate.
Bryman, Alan. 2004. *The Disneyization of Society*. London: Sage.
Carù, Antonella, and Bernard Cova. 2007a. 'Consumer immersion in an experiential context.' In Antonella Carù and Bernard Cova, eds. *Consuming Experience*. London: Routledge, 34–47.
Carù, Antonella, and Bernard Cova. 2007b. 'Consuming experiences: in introduction.' In Antonella Carù and Bernard Cova, eds. *Consuming Experience*. London: Routledge, 3–16.
Clarke, Michael. 1982. *The Politics of Pop Festivals*. London: Junction Books.
Collin, Matthew, and John Godfrey. 1997. *Altered State: The Story of Ecstasy Culture and Acid House*, 2nd edition. London: Serpent's Tail.
Corner, Lena. 2012. 'Music festivals: are our field days over?' *Independent (UK)*, 25 January. http://www.independent.co.uk/travel/news-and-advice/music-festivals-are-our-field-days-over-6293950.html. Accessed 26 July 2014.
Drengner, Jan, Hansjoerg Gaus and Steffen Jahn. 2008. 'Does flow influence the brand image in event marketing?' *Journal of Advertising Research* (March): 138–47.
Drengner, Jan, Steffen Jahn and Cornelia Zanger. 2011. 'Measuring event-brand congruence.' *Event Management* 15(1): 25–36.
Drury, James. 2013. *The Festival Awards Market Report 2013*. The UK Festival Awards/CGA Strategy.
Firat, A. Fuat and Alladi Venkatesh. 1995. 'Liberatory postmodernism and the reenchantment of consumption.' *The Journal of Consumer Research* 22(3): 239–67.
Frukt. 2012. 'Southern Comfort Juke Joint.' http://www.wearefrukt.com/work/southern-comfort-juke-joint. Accessed 1 September 2014.
Getz, Donald. 2002. 'Why festivals fail.' *Event Management* 7(4): 209–19.
Havas. 2012. *Digging the Dirt on European Music Festival Sponsorship*. Report by Havas Sports and Entertainment, *ignition*, and Cake.
Hetherington, Kevin. 2001. *New Age Travellers: Vanloads of Uproarious Humanity*. London: Cassell.
ICC. 2003. *ICC International Code on Sponsorship*. Paris: International Chamber of Commerce. http://www.sponsorship.org/freePapers/fp01.pdf.
IEG. 2000. 'Year one of IRL title builds traffic, awareness for Northern Light.' *IEG Sponsorship Report* 19(23): 1, 3.
McKay, George. 2000. *Glastonbury: A Very English Fair*. London: Victor Gollancz.
McKay, George. 2004. '"Unsafe things like youth and jazz": Beaulieu Jazz Festivals (1956-61), and the origins of pop festival culture in Britain.' In Andy Bennett, ed. *Remembering Woodstock*. Aldershot: Ashgate, 90–110.
Michaels, Lucy. 2002. 'Has Glastonbury sold out?' *Corporate Watch,* 5 June. http://web.archive.org/web/20070805222543/http://archive.corporatewatch.org/news/glastonbury.htm. Accessed 28 July 2014.
Miles, Steven. 1998. *Consumerism: As a Way of Life*. London: Sage.
Osler, Fiona. 2005. 'Know your enemy: the end of Glastonbury?' *Red Pepper* (July). http://web.archive.org/web/20051024234526/http://www.redpepper.org.uk/KYE/x-kye-July2005.htm. Accessed 8 August 2014.

Partridge, Christopher. 2006. 'The spiritual and the revolutionary: alternative spirituality, British free festivals, and the emergence of rave culture.' *Culture and Religion* 7(1): 41–60.

Pine, B. Joseph II and James H. Gilmore. 1998. *The Experience Economy: Work is Theatre and Every Business a Stage*. Boston, MA: Harvard Business School Press.

PRSforMusic/Frukt. 2013. *UK Brand Spend in Music*. Report by PRSforMusic/Frukt.

Ritzer, George. 1999. *Enchanting a Disenchanted World: Revolutionizing the Means of Consumption*. Thousand Oaks, CA: Pine Forge Press.

Roberts, Jo. 2009. 'Music festival sponsorship.' *Marketing Week* (9 July). http://www.marketingweek.co.uk/music-festival-sponsorship/3002146.article. Accessed 31 July 2014.

Rojek, Chris. 2013. *Event Power: How Global Events Manage and Manipulate*. London: Sage.

Sandford, Jeremy, and Ron Reid. 1974. *Tomorrow's People*. London: Jerome Publishing.

Shambala Festival. 2014. 'Our guiding principles.' http://www.shambalafestival.org/essential-info/our-guiding-principles/. Accessed 3 September 2014.

Stallybrass, Peter, and Allon White. 1986. *The Politics and Poetics of Transgression*. Ithaca, NY: Cornell University Press.

St. John, Graham. 2009. *Technomad: Global Raving Countercultures*. London: Equinox.

Street, John. 2005. 'Wellies, check. Bolly, check.' *Times Higher Education Supplement* (July): 8.

Sunrise Celebration. 2014. 'Partners.' https://www.sunrisecelebration.com/about/partners. Accessed 3 September 2014.

Turner, Victor. 1982. *From Ritual to Theatre: The Human Seriousness of Play*. New York: PAJ Publications.

Wakefield, Kirk L. 2012. 'How sponsorships work: the sponsorship engagement model.' *Event Management* 16(2): 143–55.

Worthington, Andy. 2004. *Stonehenge: Celebration and Subversion*. Loughborough: Alternative Albion.

# CHAPTER FOURTEEN

# Everybody talk about pop music: Un-Convention as alternative to festival, from DIY music to social change

*Andrew Dubber*

*... it's not like a traditional type of festival, but yeah – let's say a musical celebration and bringing people together.*

UN-CONVENTION CO-FOUNDER RUTH DANIELS, 2014

*Un-Convention began in 2008 as a small gathering of grassroots and independent music industry professionals over two days in a church hall in Salford, UK. The event featured music performances and seminars about the ways in which artists and small, entrepreneurial music businesses could be sustainable in the digital age. Importantly, the gathering acted as a networking opportunity for a sector of the industry that had previously not had access to professional networks. The event took place against a backdrop of In The City, a major music industry event in Manchester. Delegates from Belfast proposed a follow-up event in their own city, and Un-Convention became a recurring and repeatable platform for the independent sector. The Belfast conference changed the parameters of Un-Convention in line with the needs and suggestions of participants within the local independent music ecology, while keeping with the broad theme of sustainability, innovation and mutual support.*

*From there, Un-Convention events have been held further afield: in Groningen in the Netherlands; Oxford, Swansea; Mumbai, India; Medellín, Colombia; Brisbane, Australia; Sao Paulo, Brazil and beyond. And back to Salford (see Figures 58 and 61). Along the way, there has been a shift in focus to incorporate issues of music as a tool for social change, inspired by participants and threads of the conference that have been introduced by Colombian and Indian delegates – and, most recently, music as a political force has become a significant element of the Un-Convention brief. As the organisation expands, and multiple simultaneous events start to take place in different nations, the original vision and focus of Un-Convention has necessarily shifted, and the scope and parameters of the events have broadened. This chapter examines the phenomenon of Un-Convention as both industry seminar and music festival, and the ways in which it has grown and adapted to accommodate a perceived shortfall in representation and engagement with music enterprise outside of the mainstream.*

At the turn of the twenty-first century, the technological and political-economic context within which the music industries operate changed dramatically. While the process of digitalization had been taking place for some years, it became clear around this time that the impact of that process was something that the institutions and organizations of music business would no longer be able to ignore. After the rapid rise and closure of Napster – and the proliferation of peer-to-peer filesharing networks that followed – people who worked in the music industries found that not only was consumer behaviour altering, the tools, strategies, challenges and opportunities were also shifting dramatically. While the vast majority of the public discourse surrounding that change centred on notions of 'piracy' and its effect on the major recording industry (see, for instance: Mardesich 1999; Alderman 2001; Barnet 2001; Graziano and Rainie 2001; Senate 2001; White and White 2001), the implications caused concern, upheaval and uncertainty across all sectors of the music business.

In the first few years of the new century, a number of social networking platforms (in particular, MySpace) began to achieve widespread popularity – and these were quickly embraced by some in the independent music sector as platforms for promotion at a time when many labels were struggling for marketing budget. By 2005, a number of public forums, blogs and websites (including my own New Music Strategies[1]) emerged that discussed the ways in which the independent music sector could approach and make use of these new technologies and adapt to the online environment. However, the advice and insight was not universally embraced by the industries, and despite the comparative popularity of these blogs, that knowledge was not widely accessed. To a large extent, the independent music practitioners making use of the knowledge available online were something of a self-selecting group: by definition the ones who were already both active internet

**FIGURE 58** *Un-Convention Salford, 2010.*

users and those seeking new, alternative methodologies rather than simply a protectionist stance for older modes of practice.

From this context, Un-Convention arose as a grassroots series of independent music knowledge events that bring together music workers and musicians in a hybrid conference and music festival format. While these sorts of conversations were taking place online, Un-Convention provided a geographically specific site for face-to-face conversations and dialogue about strategies for independent music as well as a celebration of that music and culture. What began as a response to the changing music industries as a way for the independent music sector to share advice, strategies and methodologies has, over time, become an international platform for a series of interventions and projects around music as a tool for social change. As a grassroots organization, there is little in the way of documentation and published material surrounding Un-Convention, and for that reason, much of the information and material for this chapter comes from two primary sources: an internal report document supplied to me by Un-Convention co-ordinator and co-founder, Jeff Thompson, and a personal telephone interview with co-founder and former Un-Convention organizer, Ruth Daniel.[2]

In February 2008, the Association of Independent Music (AIM), in association with a cohort of British universities, organized a 'Northern Edge' seminar in Manchester to discuss the changing music industries and the ways in which those changes were affecting the independent music sector. At that event, a number of local independent music businesses were represented, and it was remarked upon throughout the day that this gathering of small labels was rare – if not unprecedented in the region. The fact that the event had been organized by an external, national institution whose remit is to represent the interests of independent music is significant. It provided the neutral territory for dialogue, which was able to transcend the competitive mistrust that had derailed previous attempts by the owners of Fat Northerner Records to gather other local independents together to share ideas. In that context, the benefits of comparing notes, discussing challenges and working together to attempt solutions became more obvious, and the members of Fat Northerner, Humble Soul, Concrete Recordings, Chocolate Fire Guard and some other labels committed to working together with some of the speakers at the event (the author included) to create an event centred around the idea of collaboration rather than competition.

The meeting was not altogether unique. Other events and networking opportunities existed to discuss music in the digital age. Large industry events such as Midem and South by Southwest (SXSW) bring both major and independent music businesses together to address many of these same issues. These larger festivals have emerged from a different music industry context than the one in which these independent labels are situated, however – both commercially and culturally. South by Southwest was launched in 1987 and has grown from a local music festival to a globalized industry event that includes a film festival, an interactive technology conference, a music festival and music business conference. Midem (Marché International du Disque et de l'Edition Musicale) was established in 1967 and runs as a tradeshow and networking event for the larger recording industry. Both events focus on the music industry as a series of institutionalized practices, offering a forum for business talks, political and legal discussions about the industrialized music industries, as well as showcases of artists and labels who aim to participate in that larger-scale music business. However, these smaller, independent labels were finding that while it was necessary to attend these events where possible, the economics of doing so were prohibitive and the returns appeared to be diminishing. Fat Northerner's Jeff Thompson recalls going 'all the way to Texas and the most important contact I met there was a guy who ran an indie label in Huddersfield' (Thompson 2014b).

In addition to the distances needed to travel and the costs associated, the scale of economics in different music scenes meant that those outside the axis of the global music industries found themselves unable (and some were unwilling) to relate to the advice and discourse available at these industry events. This was not simply a division of major record labels and independent record labels. Howard Mills of Humble Soul recalls attending an indie label seminar in London for a discussion on 'marketing on a shoestring', where the shoestring example they used was a budget of £15,000 to promote a release – a sum entirely out of reach for most independent music organizations and collectives, particularly those outside the globalized music industries situated in the capital. In addition, there was a clear sense that London was the UK home of music business, with opportunities to meet others and discuss, but there was very little available to the local Greater Manchester scene.

At a local level, people working within independent music found themselves in a situation where collaboration rather than competition appeared to be the only possible response to the changing environment. Fat Northerner's Ruth Daniel observed:

> It was either that people had started to change, or the change had filtered out people that weren't prepared to be more open and weren't prepared to do things in a different way. So ... all of a sudden people wanted to talk to each other because basically, everyone was fucked. Anyone who had any sort of music business was struggling to make it sustainable or make any money out of it, and of course things were happening in really different ways. (Daniel 2014)

Manchester was already home to an annual music industry conference and trade fair along the lines of the larger music industry events. Called In The City, this was much more accessible for the local record labels, as airfares and hotels were no longer budgetary items to consider when attending. However, the conference was primarily the domain of the global recording industry and those larger labels able to afford the high entrance fee for their executives to attend. Label partners Thompson and Daniel approached In The City organizers to propose a panel session aimed specifically at the smaller labels, but were unable to convince them to allow a heavily discounted entrance so that the target audience might be able to attend.

In response, Ruth Daniel, Dan Thomas and Jeff Thompson of Fat Northerner, Howard Mills of Humble Soul and Duncan Sime of Red Deer Club met to arrange their own event – perhaps simply a gathering at a local pub. According to Thompson, not only had the AIM seminar provided the impetus, and the difficulties encountered with the major music industry event provided the motivation, but there had also been a shift in attitudes within the independent sector that made such a gathering possible:

> My take is that by 2008 everyone was becoming increasingly unsure of how the industry was going to evolve and as a result people felt more compelled to actually get together and talk to one another. (Thompson 2014b)

The first Un-Convention was held on the same weekend as In The City in October 2008, at Sacred Trinity Church in Salford, near Manchester. Un-Convention was conceived as a mix of conference and label showcase, featuring talks and panel sessions during the day and performances at night. The event featured local and international independent artists including Denis Jones, Sophie's Pigeon (808 State member), Graham Massey's Toolshed, Silverclub, Cynic Guru from Iceland and Pacific from Sweden. As a mix of independent music festival and grassroots industry symposium, Un-Convention connected with a constituency of dedicated music fans. Attendees were not simply consumers of music, but people who had chosen to express their music fandom through involvement in recording, releasing and promoting their favourite local artists. Organizers applied the skills and low-to-no-budget tactics they had developed in the promotion of artists and records to the Un-Convention event. They used free web tools such as Wordpress[3], and University of Salford students contributed logo designs for the festival. Thompson sent 'a few hundred emails/posts to every message board, rehearsal room, recording studio, college, etc. I could find. We also got some flyers and posters printed for free' (Thompson 2014b).

There was some press coverage leading up to the event[4] and between 70 and 80 people attended over the course of the weekend. Ticket prices were low (£18 for the entire event), and representatives of the independent music industry came from around Manchester and Salford as well as from further around the country. There were attendees from Cornwall, Derby, Swansea and Belfast, all of whom had encountered similar difficulties in accessing applicable and relevant knowledge to their own grassroots music businesses. One attendee, Michael Cassidy from I Think Music, remarked that Un-Convention represented 'a shift in focus that is going to allow a new group of people to be able to understand how the music industry works', and suggested that there should be 'more conferences like this in more places' (Thompson 2014b).

For Tony Morley of Leaf Label, Un-Convention was 'a way of focusing people to discuss things with each another, and generate their own groups of people that can facilitate new things happening'. Nick Fitzsimons of Belfast's Penny Distribution was so enthused by the event that he committed to organizing a similar event in Northern Ireland. As he described, 'The main thing about Un-Convention Manchester was the sense of camaraderie, that we were all pushing toward the same goal and most importantly, that we weren't alone in that endeavor' (Thompson 2014b). For Ruth Daniel, this was the start of a 6-year period in which Un-Convention spread across the globe. However, in order for the event to travel to other places, the organizers felt they needed some clarity and control over what it was that made the event work. To that end, they composed a short manifesto[5] that set the parameters for the ethos of the festival and provided a guideline for those regional and international partners in their ambitions to run their own

Un-Convention event. The parameters of that manifesto were very broad (for instance, 'Un-Convention is a forum for ideas, for creativity, for shared experiences and knowledge and for seeing and hearing great artists'), but it provided a simple template that other places could use as a starting point for local Un-Convention events. According to Daniel,

> One of the things that we were sure about was that we wanted it to stay true to those principles we started out with, and that there wasn't suddenly a massive commercial sponsor coming in from the music industry, or Jay-Z's producer turning up and doing a panel. That really wasn't what we ever wanted it to be about. (Daniel 2014)

The events were not identical in format, however. At the Belfast event, new components such as a 'speed networking' meeting were added, and in Groningen – the first international Un-Convention – there was a much greater focus on media creation. Panel sessions were recorded on video and attendees interviewed on camera, while websites were being created and social media discussions were captured and propagated through a 'Twitter Fountain'[6] – a Dutch portal that displays online comments in a dynamic style intended to be projected onto a screen at conference events.

In 2010, to commemorate the thirtieth anniversary of Joy Division singer Ian Curtis's death, Un-Convention was invited to be part of a series of events in his home town of Macclesfield, near Manchester, called 'Unknown Pleasures'. Fat Northerner Records' Dan Thomas suggested that the event could revolve around the making of a record in a single day. Artists would perform live throughout the Un-Convention event – which would also include the conference-style panel sessions – and these music recordings could form the basis of an album to be released online at the day's end. During the event, artists would create visuals, posters and t-shirts to accompany the release, and web developers would build a website for the album. In a further echo of the northern situatedness and awareness of popular music history of Un-Convention practice, this media production workshop became known as the 'Factory' format.

> We clock on, record the bands, mix and master, do the artwork, build a campaign and finish and release the whole thing before clocking off at the end of the day. The thought being that it demystifies the record industry – all the processes are in plain view – and it demonstrates just what is possible on the modern DIY world. (Thompson 2014b)

As a result of the scope of the event's ambition, financial challenges meant that the event was initially in jeopardy and seemed unlikely to progress, but a last-minute partnership arrangement with the Converse footwear company meant that the event became the most well funded in Un-Convention's history. The relationship between a major corporate consumer brand and a grassroots, unconventional independent music movement is a potentially fraught one, and it is perhaps significant that Converse did not sponsor another Un-Convention. However, the desire to make the event happen and the apparent fit of the sponsor's image with that of the festival made the collaboration possible. It is difficult to speculate about the decision that might have been made by organizers if it had been a different brand with the same money. The continuum of business interests from independent to corporate (as well as the continuum of celebrity vs. well-respected artist) can be difficult to navigate; and while opinions have differed throughout Un-Convention's existence as to where the 'sell-out' line may lie, the Converse relationship appeared to cause no particular concerns to the organizers. Converse were already sponsors of the local Macclesfield Town Football Club and had heard about the upcoming event. The brand's interest in association with music events meant that a sponsorship arrangement was a good marketing fit. As a result, a group of invited guests who had either been, or were soon to become, international Un-Convention partners – from Brazil, India, Germany and the Netherlands – were able to attend and speak at Un-Convention Factory Macclesfield. In addition, some bigger names from the world of independent music and the wider music industry were able to participate. New Order's Peter Hook, singer Har Mar Superstar and DJ and filmmaker Don Letts were all invited speakers. The combination of live music, the recording and production of an album in a single day and the range of conference panels and knowledge sessions led to its 'Event of The Year' award in that year's Manchester Music Awards (see Sue 2011).

> The Heritage Centre in Macclesfield was transformed into a factory containing all the elements and processes involved in creating a record. The space was split into different areas – a graphic design studio, a performance and production area, a digital space, a mix studio and an idea/debate area. Participants were free to explore the factory, interact with the invited creatives and ultimately make all the decisions along the way. At the end of the day, the record was available for people to download. (Daniel 2010)

Since Macclesfield, Un-Convention Factory events have been staged in a range of contexts including Buenos Aires, Berlin and Preston. The Factory format has also been adopted and developed by Un-Convention partners around the world and continues to this day. Fabricio Nobre from Goiania, Brazil, runs the format as part of his annual Festival Bananada, where it is known as Fábrica do Som.

While there were differences in format for Un-Convention events, for Ruth Daniel the European events were categorically related (see Figure 59). They represented a 'similar bunch of people with similar conversational topics': independent music business operating in a small-scale economic environment

**FIGURE 59** *A European Un-Convention: Berlin.*

and using digital technologies to promote, distribute, collaborate and reduce costs. However,

> the major change came – and where it got really interesting for me – I think was when it went to India. All of a sudden the conversations weren't the same. They couldn't be the same. And this is where we came up with a methodology about how we put the international events together. (Daniel 2014)

Indian entrepreneur Vijay Nair attended the second Salford Un-Convention. As the winner of the British Council's Young Creative Entrepreneur programme, Nair was in the United Kingdom meeting with members of the music industry. He attended three industry events – The Great Escape in Brighton, Liverpool Sound City and Un-Convention – and decided that the format and content of Un-Convention was the most relevant for the Indian context, where there was little existing infrastructure for independent music at all, despite a proliferation of rock, metal and electronic music that was happening at the time.

Nair arranged for a group of speakers and presenters from Un-Convention to visit India and spend ten days getting to know people within the music sector in Kolkata, Mumbai, New Delhi, as well as Shillong – the 330th most populous city in India, considered to be the country's 'rock music capital' (Sengupta 2008). In doing so, Nair introduced the British visitors to the unique characteristics of the Indian independent music scene, the work that his company Only Much Louder was doing to develop the market, and, importantly, the use of music as a tool for social change. As part of the introduction to the local music industries, Nair included a visit to Delhi's youth development network, the YP Foundation[7] and the associated music charitable organization Music Basti.[8] Music Basti is run by a group of young people who bring professional musicians into homes for children affected by extreme poverty. The musicians perform workshops with the children, encouraging socialization and enhancing literacy and numeracy education through singing, counting and clapping. Music Basti develops programmes, curriculum and projects that enhance the lives of some of the poorest children in the city through the use of music.

By providing this context and immersion, as well as bringing the international Un-Convention delegates to meet with club owners, record label managers, promoters, music press and bands around the country, Nair was able to tailor the Un-Convention event to include information and networking opportunities relevant to local music industry workers, rather than simply replicate the advice and discussions that took place in the comparatively mature popular music industry ecosystem of Great Britain and Europe. As Daniel put it,

> People [in India] could learn from the fuck-ups of the past music industry [in the UK]. A lot of people came from the UK to basically sort of start from scratch with India and build something that worked for India. (Daniel 2014)

The Mumbai edition of Un-Convention took place in the premises of the British Council and featured panel sessions, presentations, debates and live performances that brought together artists and independent music workers from across the country. Significantly, the opening keynote presenter was Bant Singh, a lower-caste Dalit Sikh labourer from Punjab. Singh is an activist and folk singer whose young daughter was raped by powerful, land-owning men in 2000. He took the men to court and secured a conviction, which was reportedly the first time that a Dalit from the region had done so against an upper-caste member. Singh was subsequently attacked in retribution, held at gunpoint and beaten with iron rods and axes, before being left for dead. Singh was taken to hospital and refused treatment for thirty-six hours, before a doctor finally took his case. Both lower arms and one leg had to be amputated. The doctor was later suspended for his actions (Sengupta 2006).

At Un-Convention, Singh spoke about the connection between his music and his political activism and discussed the power of music as a tool for social change. As a result of his presentation at Un-Convention, several of the participants began a project to record and disseminate the music of Singh (Singh 2010). This theme of music as a tool for social change continued as Un-Convention spread to other places outside Europe. Ruth Daniel was contacted by cultural producer Martín Giraldo and invited to visit Medellín in Colombia to establish an Un-Convention event there. As a result of her visit, the organizers of Un-Convention began to establish a methodology for working internationally. Giraldo formed an advisory board of local people who represented different aspects of the music scene, and these stakeholders contributed to the format and the programme of the event.

> I still think Un-Convention in Medellín is the best one we've done in terms of what Un-Convention is really about – which was about going into communities, doing work in communities, all the music that we had was representative of what was going on in Medellín at that point. (Daniel 2014)

While the majority of the Un-Convention event in India had focused on establishing a more traditional, Western-style independent music infrastructure that included touring networks, promotions, record labels and gigs, the addition of social elements such as the Music Basti visit had instigated a shift in focus that became more pronounced as the festival was established in Latin America. Daniel's own recollection of the event in Colombia, and what happened as a result, emphasizes that shift in focus.

> It had to be about the social context more than anything else, because that's what was most important in that place. It was no longer about the elite. The focus changed completely. In terms of my personal involvement and realising this is where I want to be – this is where that really took place. (Daniel 2014)

In Colombia, Un-Convention delegates from the United Kingdom were taken to neighbourhoods that are not normally visited by tourists. In the barrios of Medellín it can be dangerous even for locals to venture outside their own communities. In each of the neighbourhoods visited by the Un-Convention group, they were introduced to hip-hop musicians and producers who work with young people to develop skills in rapping, breakdancing and graffiti art (see Figure 60). The purpose of these hip-hop schools are to give children and teenagers an alternative to an involvement in gangs, drugs and violence. At Un-Convention Medellín, a concert was held in the city centre that brought together many of these artists, who performed in front of a large gathering of people from across a range of communities. People who may have shot at one another if they had been seen in one another's *communa* danced together in the city streets.

> For me, that was the moment when ... you talk about the power of art to bring people together. It was just so evident there. It doesn't matter where we're all from or gripes we've got with each other because of territory. We're just going to be together and that's because of hip hop. For me that was just mind-blowing. As I walked through the square – I still remember now and I still feel emotional now – I just burst into tears because I was like ... wow, that's powerful. (Daniel 2014)

**FIGURE 60** *Un-Convention Medellín, Columbia, 2012.*

The impact that the Un-Convention event had, both on the visitors and on the residents of Medellín, demonstrated a deeper connection with music and greater opportunities for the organization than simply to discuss popular music marketing and distribution. This impact informed the direction and development of future Un-Convention events.

> That was what really excited me. So when we came back to do it in the UK, I was really conscious of that. The next one in Salford was in 2010, and it was in Salford Lads' Club. We took it out into the streets of Salford, and it was more about engaging and being involved in the community. Also, the conversations changed. It was about music and social change: Billy Bragg, Jarvis Cocker, politicization of music – and it did kind of go off in more of that tangent. But for me, the event that nailed that was the Manchester Un-Convention which was of course very much later. The strand of that that we did in Hulme was an absolutely perfect example of doing something in a community. I was as excited about that as I was about being in Colombia because we managed to get all of the artists that had come out of Hulme – that real kind of mixed community. We opened up spaces that hadn't been used for years and years and years, we did stuff outside on the streets, and it just felt like that's the same vibe. And because that came out of Colombia, that really changed what we were trying to do in the UK. (Daniel 2014)

Arguably, with the increased emphasis on music's social and political aspects, in addition to its ongoing focus on the strategies for producing, releasing, marketing and distributing independent music[9], Un-Convention became something other than it had originally set out to be (see Figure 61). And while there may have been some repeat attendees at Un-Convention

**FIGURE 61** *Un-Convention Salford 2010: the politicization of music panel discussion.*

events looking for additional promotional tips, online marketing advice or methodologies for distribution using digital technologies, the urgency for grassroots independent music information lessened in the years since Un-Convention's establishment. A wide range of popular sources of information became available and more widely disseminated. Blogs and newsletters such as New Music Strategies, The DIY Musician Blog, Music Think Tank, Hypebot, Digital Music News, Sound Music Sound Money, Lefsetz Letter, Bob Baker's Indie Music Promotion Blog and others like them provided much of the advisory and independent music industry information role that Un-Convention had originally aimed to perform.[10] Of course, Un-Convention remains as much about networking as about education and knowledge exchange, and the events bring together music industry professionals and aspirants to discuss issues surrounding their practice, and to make connections, do business and attempt to make a sustainable living through music enterprise. With reference to the addition of social justice elements, however, Un-Convention stands apart in kind, not simply in degree, from its major industry analogues (Thompson 2014a).

It is, of course, the case that many pop festivals address themes of social justice. With a range of different strategies, outcomes and interventions, Un-Convention was more methodology than format or theme. While it shares many of the characteristics of a pop festival, a conference or a music industry trade event, it is difficult to categorize in any of these ways. Rather than simply provide a platform for the dissemination of trade information, what Un-Convention had instead established was a series of interconnected networks. Those networks, rather than the events themselves, became the purpose of Un-Convention. For this reason, Un-Convention events were not simply developed to repeat a model that had been established in that first Salford event in 2008. Or rather, the events did follow that model, but in the model so much was about meeting the needs and interests of each localized independent music community, rather than about addressing a particular series of topics and issues that were of interest to that Salford community, as if these were universal to all localized independent music communities.

Un-Convention started as a series of events but has been deliberately evolved in response to the changing environment and needs of its constituents to deliver a much broader range of initiatives. The organization's mission statement is now as follows:

> Un-Convention is a UK based global music network and development agency. Our events and projects bring together artists and practitioners to share knowledge and expertise. Through this we develop new and innovative approaches to building sustainable careers and alternative models for the music industries. (Thompson 2014a)

For instance, Un-Convention Uganda was primarily about setting the foundations for creating a musical identity for East African music (see Figure 62). Un-Convention São Paulo centred around situating the solidarity economics of the independent music sector in a tradition of oppositional and countercultural musical traditions, and in particular, punk music. In Caracas, there was a strong emphasis on using digital tools to capture and archive local musical cultures (Figure 63).

> The things that underpinned everything was that it was unconventional. Whether that's about unconventional spaces like doing it on a barge, or something else – it's not like a traditional type of festival, but yeah – let's say a musical celebration and bringing people together. (Daniel 2014)

However, despite the diversity of events in the different locations around the world, some threads and themes developed as central to Un-Convention

**FIGURE 62** *Un-Convention Uganda, 2013.*

**FIGURE 63** *Un-Convention Caracas 2012.*

as the organization matured and developed in response to the different communities with which it intersected. From the promotion of music as culture rather than as merely a commodity, to the development of sustainable and ethical means of organizing the economics of independent music business; from music as a tool for social change and political activism to the importance of preserving and archiving local popular music culture; Un-Convention developed an ethos and a mission. And in doing so, the organizers discovered that Un-Convention may not itself be the ideal vehicle for delivering that mission in every instance.

> In March 2010 I helped set up the Salford Music Co-op as a means of ensuring regular activity for the local music community (since the Un-Con events were only happening sporadically). It became apparent that conference events in themselves don't necessarily do a great job of that (although certainly some level of community and relationships comes out of them) – hence this was the first of a number of initiatives to make Un-Convention more than just a series of conferences. (Thompson 2014b)

Thompson still runs Un-Convention, but in addition to working as a member of the Salford Music Co-op, it is also the organizer of the Off-Axis network[11] – a touring network based on the solidarity economy principles of the *Fora do Eixo* networks of collectives in Brazil. Through Off-Axis, Thompson is able to enact some of the principles that the Un-Convention events helped uncover, encourage and help disseminate, but was not structured in a way to support. Similarly, for Ruth Daniel, the mission and the Un-Convention vehicle became incompatible, and she has instead left to focus on projects that are ongoing in nature.

> I'm no longer part of Un-Convention. At the end of last year there were two events that we did – one in Russia and one in Puerto Rico. I worked on them for a long time and I was really looking forward to both of them, but then I was massively disappointed when we did them. It wasn't anything to do with the organisation, it was just that I realised – we're going to Puerto Rico, and we're bringing a bunch of international people ... and this was something that was said right at the very beginning by Colombians: We're going in somewhere, we're there for a week, and then we're leaving. What is the actual impact of that? And we went back to Colombia last year and we got some feedback ... and it was like: 'You came – and then you left.' (Daniel 2014)

The critique of Un-Convention as the music industry knowledge event equivalent of parachute journalism is perhaps a little unfair, however. While the international delegates attending Un-Convention may not have started lasting and ongoing projects in Medellín, Caracas, Mumbai or Goiania directly following the Un-Conventions that were held there, the event has, in fact, planted seeds that have already borne fruit, and new projects come out of the networks formed through Un-Convention even several years after those events have taken place.[12] For Thompson, the organization 'very consciously evolved from stand-alone events in the beginning to being about longer-term projects which genuinely aimed at making a difference in the places we worked' (Thompson 2014a). The lasting impact of Un-Convention lies both in the networks of people who now work together on projects outside the events and on the shift in focus that took place within that organization (see the Events Archive of the Un-Convention website for, currently, details of the over sixty #UNCON events around the world). To a large extent, through Un-Convention, the independent music industry in Britain, as well as in a variety of places around the world, has been exposed to and confronted with new ways of organizing music enterprise, different ways of thinking about popular music culture, the creation of a hybrid popular music festival/convention, as well as other reasons for creating and disseminating music, and different possible meanings for that music. Thompson maps the scope:

> This covers everything from gig-swapping and student exchanges with the first events in the Netherlands, to developing the music co-operative in Uganda (and now Kenya), through to the linked events

> in Lancashire…, to a two-year youth engagement project we are running in Wythenshawe (one of the biggest council estates in Europe with some of the highest rates of gang-related activity, drug abuse and gun crime in the UK) inspired by the work in Medellin; and ultimately to Off Axis, that allows us to engage with artists all across the UK on an ongoing basis, and hopefully in the future, further afield. We're also currently working to put together a two-year project in Ethiopia to archive traditional music,… and a project based in Switzerland to work with artists from across eight countries on ongoing cultural exchanges. And we're still planning events in places like Stoke, Hastings and Guatemala for next year, but all with legacy projects built into them to ensure it's not just a one-off happening. (Thompson 2014a)

As Un-Convention continues to evolve, and as other interventions both related to and independent of its organization pick up aspects of its work in other ways, the work that those involved have done using the festival as a vehicle has had a significant impact on the ways in which a large number of independent music organizations operate and think about what they do. That the festival has integrated ideas about popular music culture from academia and industry practice; has involved itself both in public and commercially funded endeavours; has taken lessons from the Anglo-American popular music industries to places outside their influence and vice versa; and has itself been the platform for interventions that use music as a tool for profound social change accord it its importance.

## Notes

1 http://newmusicstrategies.com

2 While central to Un-Convention's global events organisation from its beginnings until 2013, Daniel has now left Un-Convention to focus on music as a tool for social change projects in Africa.

3 http://unconvention.wordpress.com/

4 http://www.bbc.co.uk/manchester/content/articles/2008/10/02/051008_un_convention_feature.shtml

5 http://unconventionhub.org/manifesto

6 http://twitterfountain.nl

7 http://www.theypfoundation.org/

8 http://musicbasti.org

9 Of the 60 Un-Convention events that have taken place, 8 have included a specific and primary focus on the social and political aspects of music.

10 For further information see the following websites: http://newmusicstrategies.com/; http://diymusician.cdbaby.com/; http://diymusician.cdbaby.com/; http://www.musicthinktank.com/; http://www.hypebot.com/;

http://www.digitalmusicnews.com/; http://soundmusicsoundmoney.blogspot.com/; http://www.lefsetzletter.com/wordpress/; http://bob-baker.com/buzz/category/indie-music-promotion/

11 http://offaxisnetwork.com/

12 For instance, as a result of my own involvement in Un-Convention Goiania and São Paulo, I have commenced work on a documentary feature film about the Fora do Eixo networks of independent music collectives in Brazil.

## References

Alderman, John. 2001. *Sonic Boom: Napster, MP3, and the New Pioneers of Music*. Cambridge, MA: Perseus.

Barnet, Richard D. 2001. *Controversies of the Music Industry*. Westport, CT: Greenwood.

Daniel, Ruth. 2010. 'Un-Convention Factory – Macclesfield.' Last modified 2010. https://vimeo.com/12218674. Accessed 10 October 2014.

Daniel, Ruth. 2014. Telephone interview.

Graziano, Mike, and Lee Rainie. 2001. The Music Downloading Deluge. Washington DC.

Mardesich, J. 1999. 'Music & the net - How the Internet hits big music - Mr establishment: Val Azzoli, co-CEO, Atlantic Group - The rebel: Michael Robertson, mp3.com.' *Fortune* 139(9): 96-+.

Senate, United States Congress. 2001. *Committee on the Judiciary: Music on the Internet: is there an upside to downloading?: hearing before the Committee on the Judiciary, United States Senate, One Hundred Sixth Congress, second session, July 11, 2000*. Washington: U.S. G.P.O.: For sale by the Supt. of Docs., U.S. G.P.O., Congressional Sales Office.

Sengupta, Amit. 2006. 'Untouchable India.' *Index on Censorship* 35(4): 82–4.

Sengupta, Somini. 2008. 'Town in India rocks (no use to wonder why, babe).' *New York Times* (23 June). http://www.nytimes.com/2008/06/23/arts/music/23dylan.html. Accessed 7 October 2014.

Singh, Bant. 2010. *Word Sound and Power*. New Delhi Films. http://www.youtube.com/watch?v=Nj38RJcjOkg. Accessed 14 October 2014.

Sue, David. 2011. 'Manchester Music Awards: Event of the Year.' *City Life* (11 January). http://unconventionhub.org/city-life-david-sue-fri-07-january-2011. Accessed 15 October 2014.

Thompson, Jeff. 2014a. 'Re: Un-Convention Chapter (draft).' 14 October 2014.

Thompson, Jeff. 2014b. Un-Convention Overview (internal report). Un-Convention.

Unconvention website. 2014. Events Archive. http://unconventionhub.org/uncon/archived. Accessed 14 October 2014.

White, Ron, and Michael White. 2001. *MP3 Underground*. Indianapolis, IN: Que Corp.

# INDEX